"Excellent! This is one of the best books on the Inklings I've ever read."
Walter Hooper, literary advisor to the C.S. Lewis Estate

"No subject fascinates me as much as the creative interaction of the Inklings, and I am glad to read this new account. It is a brisk and honest retelling of the group and its members, always mindful to connect the Inklings and their ideas to their larger context. It is Duriez's best book to date. I recommend it."
Diana Pavlac Glyer, author of *The Company They Keep: C.S. Lewis and J.R.R. Tolkien as Writers in Community*

"With *The Oxford Inklings*, Colin Duriez takes us deeper into the world of the Inklings than the commonly known facts about the writers to see how their scholarly work shaped their imaginations and their popular writing. Few people know the Inklings as intimately as Duriez who makes us feel as though he has just come from a morning with them at the Eagle and Child."
Harry Lee Poe, author of *The Inklings of Oxford* and *C.S. Lewis Remembered*

"This is a valuable addition to Inklings studies, suitable both for beginners and for more seasoned readers. For those who don't know too much about the Inklings, Duriez provides a readable and well-rounded overview of the lives and works of Lewis, Tolkien, and their friends who comprised this famous literary band of brothers. Duriez is well-known for his thorough and diligent research, so this book also offers surprising and delightful insights even for readers who are familiar with earlier studies of the Inklings. *The Oxford Inklings* is enjoyable and enlightening for readers of all levels!"
David C. Downing, author of *The Most Reluctant Convert* and *Looking for the King*

"Here Colin Duriez extends his early excellent work on the friendship of Lewis and Tolkien to an examination of the mutually supportive relationships of all the Inkings in context. There is a particularly useful chronology of their friendship and creativity. This is a comprehensive exploration of inter-Inklings relationships in which Duriez's research is of its usual depth and quality and written in lucid prose that is a pleasure to read. It has the r e Inklings' 'merriment, pi
Revd Dr Jeanet

"In this book, Colin Duriez offers readers an engaging, thoughtful look at the fascinating group of writers known as the Inklings. Building upon previous studies by Humphrey Carpenter, Diana Glyer, and others, Duriez brings new insights to bear as he contextualizes the thought and work of the Inklings, illuminating what drew them together as well as the profound yet still elusive influence they had upon each other. *The Oxford Inklings* is a worthy addition to the shelves of all who love the writings of C.S. Lewis, J.R.R. Tolkien, and their friends."
Marjorie Lamp Mead, Associate Director, The Marion E. Wade Center, Wheaton College, Illinois, USA

"Just when I thought nothing new could be said about Lewis, Tolkien, Barfield, Williams, and the others, gifted author Colin Duriez presents fresh and fascinating insights that I will remember long after I place *The Oxford Inklings* on a shelf among my treasured favourites."
Carolyn Curtis, author, editor, speaker, whose latest book is *Women and C.S. Lewis – What his life and literature reveal for today's culture*

Some previous books by this author relating to the Inklings:

Tolkien and The Lord of the Rings: A Guide to Middle-earth (2001)

Tolkien and C.S. Lewis: The Gift of Friendship (2003)

A Field Guide to Narnia (2004)

J.R.R. Tolkien: The Making of a Legend (2012)

Amazing and Extraordinary Facts: J.R.R. Tolkien (2012)

C.S. Lewis: A biography of friendship (2013)

The A-Z of C.S. Lewis: An encyclopedia of his life, thought and writings (2013)

THE OXFORD
INKLINGS

LEWIS, TOLKIEN AND
THEIR CIRCLE

COLIN DURIEZ

LION

Published by Lion Books
an imprint of
Lion Hudson plc
Wilkinson House, Jordan Hill Road,
Oxford OX2 8DR, England
www.lionhudson.com/lion

ISBN 978 0 7459 5634 3
e-ISBN 978 0 7459 5792 0

First edition 2015

Acknowledgments
Evert effort has been made to trace the original copyright holders
where required. In some cases this has proved impossible. We shall
be happy to correct any such omissions in future editions. For full
acknowledgments please see p. 288.

A catalogue record for this book is available from the British Library

Printed and bound in the UK, December 2014, LH26

TO LEICESTER WRITERS' CLUB

Contents

It is… easy to see why Authority frowns on Friendship. Every real Friendship is a sort of secession, even a rebellion… Hence if our masters… ever succeed in producing a world where all are Companions and none are Friends, they will have removed certain dangers, and will also have taken from us what is almost our strongest safeguard against complete servitude.

C.S. Lewis, *The Four Loves*

Preface

The Inklings were an influential group of writers, along the lines of the Lake Poets or the Bloomsbury Group, centred most notably on C.S. Lewis, and with J.R.R. Tolkien also at the core. They met regularly in the pubs of St Giles, Oxford to talk, and in the college rooms of Lewis at Magdalen College or Tolkien at Merton College to read and discuss their latest writings, and to talk more widely. My book explores their lives, their writings, their ideas, and most crucially the influence they had on each other. A defining purpose behind the group emerges that celebrates its diversity and lack of formality, based on a profound understanding of friendship. My book seeks to explain the mystery of how this eclectic group of friends, without formal membership, agenda, or minutes, came to have a purpose that shaped the ideas and publications of the leading participants.

Those who have enjoyed the now-famous writings of core members such as Lewis, Tolkien, Owen Barfield, and Charles Williams often find that the existence of the Inklings takes on a great importance for them. Questions then start to emerge: who else was involved with the Inklings, and why do Owen Barfield and Charles Williams matter so much? What

11

difference did the Second World War make to the group, and why did they eventually stop meeting? This book explores the group's complex and fascinating interactions both within and outside the circle. I also consider the Christian faith of the group's members – of various, often surprising strands – which was a defining influence.

Although the Inklings were a literary group of friends, the membership was not made up exclusively of academics but included professional people from varied walks of life, from a doctor to a British army officer. The club existed in times of great change in Oxford, through the 1930s, 1940s, and 1950s, and petered out only with Lewis's death in 1963. Tolkien occasionally referred to it in his letters, once describing the club as an "undetermined and unelected circle of friends who gathered around C.S. L[ewis], and met in his rooms in Magdalen. Our habit was to read aloud compositions of various kinds (and lengths!)".

Almost thirty years earlier, Tolkien had written to his publisher, Stanley Unwin, about Lewis's science-fiction story *Out of the Silent Planet*. He spoke of its "being read aloud to our local club (which goes in for reading things short and long aloud). It proved an exciting serial, and was highly approved. But of course we are all rather like-minded". It is clear from Tolkien's letters that the Inklings provided valuable and much-needed encouragement as he struggled to compose *The Lord of the Rings*.

Another member, Oxford Classics don Colin Hardie, wrote of the Inklings and its literary character in 1983, around fifty years after its inception: "Oxford saw the informal formation of a select circle of friends, mostly writers or 'scribblers' (reminiscent perhaps of the 18th-century Scriblerus Club, whose members were Pope, Swift, Gay, Arbuthnot, author of the Memoirs of Martinus Scriblerus, and others…).''

Most of the men in the circle of the Inklings were select friends of C.S. Lewis. It is inevitable, therefore, that there will be some overlap with the content of my book *C.S. Lewis: A biography of friendship*, which features a number of Lewis's friends. In particular, I refer to certain events that are pivotal both to Lewis's life and to the development of the Inklings as a group. I've done my best to keep any overlapping to the minimum. Where I've taken up material that is also in the biography of C.S. Lewis, it is here in an entirely different frame and setting. Thus the organization of each book is very different. Whereas accounts of Lewis's friends in the biography serve to illuminate Lewis the man, and the development and shaping forces in his life, in my depiction of the Inklings, such accounts of friends are there to throw light on the group and its distinctive life and interactions as a community of friends.

I have been researching and writing on the Inklings for over forty years now, and this book draws on that work. Some contributions to essay collections or reference books are to be found in the bibliography. In 2000, my friend the late David Porter and I put together *The Inklings Handbook*, now long out of print. Even in the years since that book appeared there has been much new research on the group.

My own exposure to the Inklings was a process of gradual discovery. After reading C.S. Lewis's *Mere Christianity* in class during my schooldays, I began reading everything I could find by the same author, little realizing the extent and range of his writings. Through this reading I gradually discovered Tolkien, Charles Williams, Owen Barfield, and the existence of the Inklings. I also added to my reading other writers who had influenced them, such as George MacDonald. Their writings provided me with a key to why I liked so many other writers, many in the fields of science fiction and fantasy, but others where the connection was at first less clear, such as with William Golding and John Fowles. The list, like the road, goes ever on and on.

I mentioned that my interest in the Inklings has been long-standing, and as a result this book has inevitably been influenced by the work of others. Of those who have also written at length on the Inklings, particularly helpful have been Diana Glyer, Humphrey Carpenter, Gareth Knight, and Hal Poe. My visits to The Marion E. Wade Center at Wheaton College, Illinois and the Special Collections Reading Room at the Bodleian Library in Oxford have been invaluable. Though long ago now, conversations I had with David Porter (often by telephone late at night) as we worked on our *Inklings Handbook* opened up the world of this extraordinary group of writers. As well as acknowledging my debt to those who have written on the Inklings, my thanks are also due to those who have been directly involved in the publication of this book, such as my editors, Ali Hull, Margaret Milton, and Helen Birkbeck, and also Jonathan Roberts, Leisa Nugent, Rhoda Hardie, and others at Lion Hudson.

Introduction

C.S. Lewis and the dinosaurs

In 1954, C.S. Lewis was at a turning point in his life. For nearly thirty years he had been a fellow and tutor in English at Magdalen College, Oxford. Though a popular lecturer with an impressive string of groundbreaking academic publications to his name, from *The Allegory of Love*, which came out in 1936, to *English Literature in the Sixteenth Century*, published in 1954, he had been passed over several times for a Chair of English. In his personal life, it was over three years since Mrs Janie Moore, the woman he had looked after as devotedly as if she were his mother, had died, freeing him from a self-imposed burden of care. His brother, Warren, however, was falling into alcoholic blackouts with worrying frequency.

Lewis had also recently taken a change of direction in his writings, from a muscular intellectual defence of Christian beliefs as a high-profile apologist, to putting his creative energies into more overtly imaginative prose and fiction. *The Chronicles of Narnia* had flowed from his pen and also an autobiography, *Surprised by Joy*. This book focused upon an experience he called "Joy", which had led him from atheism to a belief in God, and was soon to be published.

15

Then came an invitation from Cambridge University, offering him a newly created Chair of Medieval and Renaissance literature. Even before he was asked, the distinguished electors, who included two from Oxford (one of whom was his fellow Inkling J.R.R. Tolkien), had unanimously voted for Lewis as their first choice. Despite strong initial reservations, reflecting the swirl of issues he faced in his life at that time, Lewis was eventually persuaded to accept the post. Tolkien played a decisive role in persuading him. He could, Lewis found, remain living in Oxford but spend part of each week during term time living in his Cambridge college, in rooms large enough to house his essential library.

When Lewis presented his inaugural lecture in Cambridge on 29 November 1954 – his fifty-sixth birthday – he decided not to play safe. The public lecture gave him a platform from which to set out a defence of the "Old Western" or "Old European" values that he, along with Tolkien, had championed in their work, in both fiction and non-fiction. Both were central members of the Inklings, and the thrust of Lewis's lecture might perhaps provide an initial insight into the heart of what the Inklings were all about. Were they reactionaries, standing against the flow of a new world that was being built according to a blatant modernist blueprint? Or was there a strategy in their concerns that could point to a different kind of contemporary world, rooted in old virtues and values? Could there conceivably be a modern society that was marked by continuity rather than discontinuity with the past? He donnishly called the lecture *De Descriptione Temporum*: "a description of our time".

One friend of Lewis's who wished to be at the lecture but couldn't attend was Dorothy L. Sayers, of detective-fiction fame. She encouraged her brilliant friend Barbara Reynolds to attend, and Reynolds duly reported on it to her. On reading that report, Miss Sayers concluded that Lewis had been remarkably restrained! She replied to Barbara Reynolds: "It sounds as though he had been on his best behaviour – he can sometimes be very naughty and provocative – but he probably thought that his Inaugural was not quite the moment for such capers."[1]

Another female friend of Lewis's, however, was there lending her support: Joy Davidman Gresham. She was an American poet and novelist who had come to live in England partly at least to further her friendship with him. At first, she had mainly been a very interesting pen pal. Later, she was to become his wife.

In a letter dated 23 December 1954, Joy Davidman described the lecture to a fellow American and friend of C.S. Lewis, Chad Walsh, as:

> … brilliant, intellectually exciting, unexpected, and funny as hell – as you can imagine. The hall was crowded, and there were so many capped and gowned dons in the front rows that they looked like a rookery. Instead of talking in the usual professorial way about the continuity of culture, the value of traditions, etc., he announced that "Old Western Culture", as he called it, was practically dead, leaving only a few scattered survivors like himself …

C.S. Lewis dramatically challenged the big division commonly made between the medieval period, which, as he saw it, had been discarded as having no relevance for life and culture today, and a forward-looking Renaissance. Privately he joked about whether he should have taken on the Chair of Medieval and Renaissance literature at the English School in Cambridge, as he believed that the Renaissance as it is commonly understood never happened! (In fact, the university had deliberately brought the two periods together in the newly created post, with C.S. Lewis in mind for it.) As an alternative, Lewis put forward what he considered to be the real break in Western culture, in the light of which the differences between the Middle Ages and the Renaissance are overwhelmingly outweighed by the affinities between the two periods:

Roughly speaking we may say that whereas all history was for our ancestors divided into two periods, the pre-Christian and the Christian, and two only, for us it falls into three – the pre-Christian, the Christian, and what may reasonably be called the post-Christian... I am considering them simply as cultural changes. When I do that, it appears to me that the second change is even more radical than the first.

Between Jane Austen and us, but not between her and Shakespeare, Chaucer, Alfred, Virgil, Homer, or the Pharaohs, comes the birth of the machines... this is parallel to the great changes by which we divide epochs of pre-history. This is on a level with the change from stone to bronze, or from a pastoral to an agricultural economy. It alters Man's place in nature.[2]

In the light of such a perspective, we can see that the fiction of his fellow Inkling, Tolkien, very much embodies the themes of Lewis's lecture, even though Lewis offered generalizations of a scale Tolkien would rarely attempt, at least in public. Tolkien's "Old Western" themes can be seen clearly, for instance, in the way he explored the related topics of possession and power. Possession is a unifying theme in his stories, from the craving of Morgoth – a high-ranking angelic being – to have God's power of creation, to the temptation of wielding the One Ring that faced many protagonists in *The Lord of the Rings*. The wrong use of power is characteristically expressed by Tolkien in magic, embodied in the misuse of mechanism and technology. Morgoth, Sauron, and Saruman, all of whom embraced the dark side, experiment with genetic engineering – the creation of robot-like orcs – and use or encourage the use of machines created with the aim of extending their powers. The Ring itself is a machine, the result of Sauron's technological skills. It is in fact a super-machine, which goes beyond incorporating an artificial intelligence to carrying and containing in some way much of its maker's powers (or part of his soul, to use a different language).

Tolkien contrasts this evil magic with art, typified in the Elves, who have no desire for domination of others. Similarly, Lewis saw a machine-centred attitude, or technocracy, as the modern form of magic, seeking to control and possess nature for ends that turn out to be destructive of our very humanity, and he expressed this theme in his final science-fiction novel, *That Hideous Strength*.

In his inaugural lecture, Lewis defined the "Old West" by placing it in sharp contrast to our modern world. The Great Divide lay, he believed, somewhere in the early nineteenth century. It was as much a social and cultural divide as a shift in ideas and beliefs. On the other hand, Lewis saw positive values in pre-Christian paganism that prefigured the Christian values he so championed. That paganism belonged to a vast period of continuity that predated the Middle Ages and included the classical antiquity of Greece and Rome. He declared in his lecture that "Christians and Pagans had much more in common with each other than either has with a post-Christian. The gap between those who worship different gods is not so wide as that between those who worship and those who do not". The post-Christian in our modern age of the machine, by being severed from the "Christian past", is in consequence doubly cut off from the "Pagan past".

Lewis brought his lecture to an end with a stunning piece of rhetoric that drove home his convictions about the past and the modern West, and his status as an "Old Western Man" within the new milieu:

> It is my settled conviction that in order to read Old Western literature aright you must suspend most of the responses and unlearn most of the habits you have acquired in reading modern Literature. And because this is the judgment of a native, I claim that, even if the defence of my conviction is weak, the fact of my conviction is a historical *datum* to which you should give full weight. That way where I fail as a critic, I may yet be useful as a specimen. I would even dare to go further. Speaking not only for myself but for all other Old Western men whom you may meet, I would say, use your specimens while you can. There are not going to be many more dinosaurs.[3]

Joy Davidman observed, in her letter to Chad Walsh, that Lewis claimed "the change to the Age of Science was more profound than that from Medieval to Renaissance or even Classical to Dark Ages, and that learning about literature from him would be rather like having a Neanderthal man to lecture on the Neanderthal or studying paleontology from a live dinosaur!".[4]

As a woman, Dorothy L. Sayers could never be part of the Inklings – even in the 1950s, when it was only a pub-based conversation group. However, she had an obvious affinity with Lewis's mindset, as is clear from her letters. A few months after the inaugural Cambridge lecture, she concluded a letter to "Jack" with: "All good greetings from your obliged and appreciative fellow-dinosaur." The warmth of her friendship is also revealed in the previous sentence, which playfully refers to Lewis's Cambridge college, Magdalene: "I hope the Lady who sits upon the Waters is gracious to you."[5] The Lady is Mary Magdalene, and the "Waters" is a reference to the River Cam, beside the college.[6]

Lewis must have known that there would be a reaction to his lecture. As he no doubt expected, it did not go down well with an influential element at the university. They effectively saw the new professor (and perhaps even the new Chair) as a strategy from the murky depth of a stagnant backwater to revive the corpse of a lost Christendom. Ruffled, their response was lightning quick. *Twentieth Century,* in February 1955, devoted its entire issue to the unfolding disaster in Cambridge. Its twelve contributors, from a range of disciplines, were at one over "the importance of free liberal, humane inquiry, which they conceive to be proper not only to a university community but to any group that claims to be civilized". Novelist E.M. Forster was one of them. He was indignant that religion was attacking humanism. By "humanism", the contributors actually meant "Orthodox Atheism", as Lewis saw it. E.M. Forster declared that humanism's "stronghold in history, the Renaissance, is alleged not to have existed".[7] Lewis had blown the trumpet. The walls of humanism might be weakened.

The BBC did not share such an alarmist view. It took the unusual step of broadcasting an inaugural lecture from a new professor. In April 1955, C.S. Lewis redelivered his Cambridge lecture as a two-part series in front of a BBC microphone, under the title "The Great Divide".

To obtain another glimpse of what might be a group affinity among members of the Inklings, it is necessary to take a backward glance to nearly twenty years before the lecture in which Lewis declared himself a dinosaur and valuable relic of the Old West. If a kind of group mind or shared worldview existed, we could presume that important members of the Inklings were fellow dinosaurs or valuable specimens of a lost, Old Western culture, given Lewis's weight in the circle. The event that might cast light on the more ultimate concerns of the Inklings only included two members, the close friends Lewis and Tolkien, but nevertheless represents a key moment in the group's literary output. That point, two decades before Lewis's introduction to Cambridge, represented a crisis period in their lives. Both had published little scholarship for a substantial period, though Lewis's *The Allegory of Love,* many years in preparation, would soon appear, as would Tolkien's milestone essay on *Beowulf.*

The event was a conversation that took place sometime in the spring of 1936. As well as their regular Thursday-night Inklings gatherings, Lewis and Tolkien were in the habit of meeting in Lewis's college rooms of a Monday morning, then decamping to the Eastgate Hotel, conveniently nearby. According to Tom Shippey, both must have felt anxious and under-published, with only each other to keep them writing. Both frustrated writers felt that their ambitions to be significant poets had been thwarted, even though both had devoted "immense time and energy to writing poetry".[8]

On the particular spring Monday in question, on which Lewis and Tolkien met as usual, the former presented a challenge. In doing this, he might well have been inspired by a novel by Charles Williams that he had recently read, called *The*

Place of the Lion. This was a rare work of modern-day Christian fantasy, which in turn owed something to the fiction of G.K. Chesterton, a favourite writer of Lewis's. In a letter written later in the year to a friend, Leo Baker, Lewis clearly had by then also read Charles Williams's novel *Many Dimensions*, and commented: "In the rare genre of 'theological shocker' which Chesterton (I think) invented, these are superb."[9]

Certainly, even with Chesterton and this new discovery of Williams's fiction, Lewis was deeply dissatisfied. It is quite probable that after the two had settled into the chesterfield in Lewis's white-panelled rooms, and were comfortably drinking in the smoky haze from their pipes or cigarettes, Lewis said something like: "You know, Tollers, there's far too little nowadays of what we like in stories. There's nothing for it but we write something ourselves." He knew Tolkien would agree. Perhaps one or the other mentioned Williams's *The Place of the Lion.*

The Place of the Lion gives us a good idea of what both Lewis and Tolkien liked in contemporary fiction. It had been lent to Lewis earlier in the year by fellow Inkling Nevill Coghill. In fact, the book had made such a deep impression on Lewis that he had written to its author, who worked at the London branch of the Oxford University Press. He had been bowled over by its heady mix of Plato and the biblical book of Genesis, and the days of creation played an important part in the plot. He also felt that it had an unsettling relevance to the foibles of his profession as a university academic.

In a letter to a close friend, Arthur Greeves, he had shared his discovery. The story, he explained, was based on Plato's theory of the other world (a theory that had shaped much of Western thought over the ages). Here the archetypes or originals of all earthly qualities exist, such as beauty, love, and the "hedgehogness" of the hedgehog. In Williams's novel these primeval archetypes were absorbing their real copies in our world back into themselves – at the beginning of the story, all butterflies on earth flew back into the original butterfly. The processes of creation began to flow back to the state they were in at the beginning of time, and consequently the world itself was threatened by non-existence. In that same letter Lewis remarked, "It isn't often now-a-days you get a Christian fantasy."[10]

Early in the story, two friends get caught up in a search that is under way for an escaped lioness. Shortly afterwards, the two see another lion. It soon becomes evident that this is no ordinary lion. It had

> the shape of a full-grown and tremendous lion, its head flung back, its mouth open, its body quivering. It ceased to roar, and gathered itself back into itself. It was a lion such as the young men had never seen in any zoo or menagerie; it was gigantic and seemed to their dazed senses to be growing larger every moment... Awful and solitary it stood... Then, majestically, it moved... and while they still stared it entered into the dark shadow of the trees and was hidden from sight.

There is something perhaps of the future Aslan in that description, even though there is no evidence that it is a source of elements of Narnia. It is perhaps more feasible that Williams, and Lewis, more than a decade later, were drawing on an ancient form of human imagining. But whereas Aslan is the glad and good creator, the lion archetype in Williams's story has become a destructive power through human tampering with the forces of creation.

By coincidence, Charles Williams had been reading the proofs of Lewis's *The Allegory of Love*, a learned and elegantly written study of courtly love in the Middle Ages. Rarely had he been so excited by one of his firm's publications. Rather overwhelmed, he decided to write to Lewis, but received a letter from Lewis before he could. This praised *The Place of the Lion*, and invited Williams to attend an Inklings meeting in Oxford. That letter is the first documented use of the term "the Inklings", by Lewis or other members. It throws important light on the nature of the club, from its early years. Lewis enthused:

> A book sometimes crosses one's path which is… like the sound of one's native language in a strange country… It is to me one of the major literary events of my life – comparable to my first discovery of George MacDonald, G. K. Chesterton, or Wm. Morris. … Coghill of Exeter put me on to the book: I have put on Tolkien (the Professor of Anglo–Saxon and a papist) and my brother. So there are three dons and one soldier all buzzing with excited admiration. We have a sort of informal club called the Inklings: the qualifications (as they have informally evolved) are a tendency to write, and Christianity.[11]

The letter included an invitation for Williams to meet the group one evening in the summer term, and to be Lewis's guest at his college. Williams frequently visited Oxford in his capacity as an editor at the London branch of the Oxford University Press, to liaise with the Oxford branch. In July that year, for instance, he met the youthful poet W.H. Auden in Oxford. An important part of his responsibility was to build the poetry list.

Charles Williams replied to C.S. Lewis by return of post, his affinity with Lewis's way of thinking clear. Williams wrote: "I regard your book as practically the only one that I have ever come across, since Dante, that shows the slightest understanding of what this very peculiar identity of love and religion means."

Nevill Coghill remembered that first meeting: "[Lewis] introduced him to the Inklings... to our great delight."[12] It was Coghill who had come across *The Place of the Lion* and introduced the story to Lewis by vividly retelling the plot and relaying the cosmic scope of the story. After Lewis, his brother, Warren, Tolkien, and perhaps also Barfield read the novel, creating the buzz of excitement in the group.

Tolkien described what happened when Lewis presented the challenge, on the spring morning when the two met as usual, that he and Tolkien needed to write a story that would be the sort of thing they both liked. In letters written in later years, he refers to the event on five separate occasions, which underlines its importance to him. In one letter, he even identified it as the origin of his follow-up to *The Hobbit – The Lord of the Rings*. At some point, Lewis had suggested that one of them should write an excursionary tale about space, and the other one on time. He pulled out a coin and they tossed for who wrote which. The result was that Tolkien was assigned to write a time story and Lewis a space one.

To both men it was a challenge, as up to this point they had published only poetry (with little success) and scholarly publications relating mainly to medieval language and literature. Now they were pledging to write fiction that would appeal to a wide readership. True, there was one exception. Lewis had published a story called *The Pilgrim's Regress,* in the manner of the seventeenth-century *The Pilgrim's Progress,* but it had garnered a modest readership. In Tolkien's case, he had privately written extensive stories and other matter concerning his invented world of Middle-earth, particularly its First Age. This would not be published until after his death, in *The Silmarillion*, the twelve volumes of *The History of Middle-earth*, and other books. Popular fiction was another matter, though. Tolkien's *The Hobbit* was soon to go to his publisher.

The first fruit of C.S. Lewis's excursion into space was *Out of the Silent Planet*, published in 1938 after being read aloud to the Inklings. Tolkien's initial attempt at a time-travel book, *The Lost Road*, which might also have been aired to the Inklings, was abandoned. In its place, he took up writing a sequel to the popular *The Hobbit* (1937), but aimed at an adult readership. In a letter to a reader of the recently published first two volumes of *The Lord of the Rings*, Tolkien once again recorded his memory of the conversation in which Lewis had presented the challenge, and wrote of the long labour, and the reward and encouragement he had received from its publication. It was a conversation that changed both their lives.

CHAPTER 1

Through love and beyond
Charles Williams, the enigmatic Inkling

It is more than likely that Charles Williams met C.S. Lewis and then the other Inklings quite soon after their enthusiastic exchange of letters, sometime in the spring or early summer of 1936. Williams would then have been close to fifty, with around nine years of his life left and fifteen books to bring out. He had already developed the distinctive ideas that were so to appeal to Lewis in particular. His two volumes of poems relating to King Arthur were yet to appear, as were his novels *Descent into Hell* and *All Hallows' Eve*. Also still to come was his celebrated history of the Holy Spirit in the church, *The Descent of the Dove*, which played a part in the conversion to Christianity of the poet W.H. Auden. It was not until the war years that he met regularly with C.S. Lewis, Tolkien, and the Inklings, in the last five and a half years or so of his life.

Charles Williams was one of a number of writers admired by Lewis, Tolkien, and other dominant figures in the group. This admiration may well have been a tacit recognition by one or several of the Inklings of affinities with their group spirit or even their worldview, however vaguely they saw it. These were writers such as George MacDonald, G.K. Chesterton, and even, for Owen Barfield, the highly unorthodox Rudolf Steiner, the founder of a religious movement called anthroposophy, which has an esoteric interpretation of Christianity (including a belief in reincarnation), science, and culture. There were also more recent authors who were or would be recognized by Inklings members as being the kind of thinker or writer that they liked, such as Dorothy L. Sayers and E.R. Eddison. For medievalists like Lewis and Tolkien, there were poets and thinkers over the vast period of the Middle Ages and the Renaissance who gave them nourishment and inspiration, such as Edmund Spenser, Dante, and the author of the great Old English poem *Beowulf*, as well as the Church Fathers Athanasius and Augustine and others who influenced the period, such as Boethius. Classicists such as Colin Hardie or the classically erudite among the group, such as the polymath Lewis, would have easily recognized affinities with their concerns even further back, in pre-Christian, pagan Greece and Rome.

An affinity, a shared outlook, and even an almost unconsciously accepted worldview are hard to present in the abstract. The life and impact of Charles Williams does, however, shed an admittedly rather complex light on whatever held the Inklings together, if they were more than simply a group of Lewis's friends. Williams is an enigma who perhaps mirrors the mystery at the heart of the Inklings. An obscure group of professional people and Oxford dons were brought together by a desire to write and by a traditional Christianity considered outmoded by many in the mainstream. They nevertheless encouraged and helped to bring about writings by C.S. Lewis and Tolkien in particular that are now popular throughout the world and which have been transposed into modern media, such as films using CGI (computer-generated imagery), thereby gaining a global appeal. What would have seemed a premodern eccentricity to many of their contemporaries at Oxford turned out to have an astounding postmodernist appeal, beginning after Lewis's death in the 1960s.

Who was Charles Williams? John Wain, an undergraduate when Williams was in Oxford during the Second World War, remarked: "How many people have tried to describe this extraordinary man, and how his essence escapes them!"[1]

Williams's birthplace was London, and it was to this city that he was to give his allegiance. His London accent indicated his origin, contrasting as it did with the cut-glass tones of many he was to encounter among the Inklings and Oxford dons.

He was born in one of a row of three-storey Victorian houses in Spencer Road (later renamed Caedmon Road), near the Holloway Road between Highbury and Holloway, on 20 September 1886, and was christened Charles Walter Stansby Williams. His sister, Edith, was born in 1889. His father, Walter, who had also been born in London, was a foreign correspondence clerk in French and German for a company involved in importing goods. Charles's early memories included the clop-clopping of horses, the rumbling metal-clad wheels of city traffic, and the distinctive sound of steam trains on the nearby viaduct over Hornsey Road. Walter and his wife, Mary, had a devout Christian faith and it was the family custom to attend the nearby St Anne's Church, sometimes twice on a Sunday. Mary remembered that Charles invariably marched "into church as if he owned the place" and joined in the singing with gusto.

The family lived in London until Charles was eight and Edith was five. By that time his father's eyesight was failing, and the firm that employed him was in terminal decline. Walter had been told that the only hope for saving his vision was to live nearer the countryside. This was a blow to him, as he was as attached to the metropolis as Charles was later to be. However, the family moved to St Albans, less than twenty miles to the north of the capital. The city is named after the first known Christian martyr, and was originally a major Roman settlement, located on the old Roman road of Watling Street.

Walter and Mary set up a shop in St Albans called The Art Depot, selling artists' materials and stationery. The shop had two substantial windows and Mary, ever inventive, curtained them simply. Years later, Charles's wife, Florence, was to write of it: "I loved that shop and residence and its garden." She found the residential part of the building attractive, with "Victorian furniture polished and plain in design with no Victorian hotch-potch". Florence described Charles's mother as a woman of strong vitality: she outlived her son by nearly three years, dying at ninety-two. Mary Williams was excellent company and full of enjoyment of life, in spite of her hard struggle against poverty.

Her husband read widely until his sight became too bad, and had poetry and short stories published in a range of periodicals. He was very interested in his gifted son, guiding and encouraging him. This affectionate and helpful relationship between father and son can be paralleled with that between the writer George MacDonald (one of the "literary household gods" of the Inklings, according to a young member)[2] and his father in the Scottish Highlands, far earlier in the nineteenth century. It contrasts sharply with the often fraught and far less happy relationship that C.S. Lewis had with his widowed father. Charles and Walter took long walks together in the Hertfordshire countryside, and he was to dedicate his third book of poems to "my father and my other teachers".

When he was about eight, just after moving from London, Charles Williams began his schooling at St Albans Abbey School and four years later he gained a County Council scholarship, which enabled him to go to St Albans School. Unlike most of his later Inklings friends, but like J.R.R. Tolkien, he thus had a grammar-school education rather than boarding at an elite public school. Grammar schools originally emphasized classical languages (initially Latin), but later developed an increasingly broad curriculum, always with an academic emphasis.

At this school Charles made a lasting friendship with a boy named George Robinson, who saw things as he did, sharing his tastes, favourite books, and attempts at writing. With Charles and his sister, Edith, Robinson sometimes acted in plays performed for the family circle. The opening lines of one of these plays – Henry Wadsworth Longfellow's *The Golden Legend* – show that Charles's interests then were similar to those in later life: the conflict between the powers of good and evil. The opening reads: "The spire of Strasbourg Cathedral. Night and Storm. LUCIFER, with the powers of the Air, trying to tear down the Cross."

Some of Charles's fantasy-building, recalled by his friend Robinson, was very comic. But there was a deeper side to the rather serious, shy youth. Charles imagined himself and his friends participating in myths and rituals. This habit of seeing daily life in terms of ceremony, fantasy, and myth was lifelong. The masques he later wrote in the 1920s for fellow staff of the OUP were an extension of this proclivity; the parts were written for and acted by Charles's colleagues. Even his employer, the head of the London branch, was connected in Williams's mind with his imaginative creation, the Emperor in Byzantium, who was part of the world of his Arthurian poetry.

Charles and George Robinson both gained places at University College, London, and began study in Gower Street, near the British Museum, in the autumn of 1901. They were both fifteen. The Latin professor at the time was the poet A.E. Housman, but Charles was to make no reference to any influence of his teaching in his future writing. Charles took courses in mathematics, literature, history, and languages.

Unfortunately, with Walter now blind enough to be disabled, Charles's parents could not afford to keep their brilliant son on until the end of his three-year course at University College. He was forced to leave after two years. Seeking alternatives, Charles failed the Civil Service exam for a Second Division Clerkship. Prospects looked gloomy for him. His kindly Aunt Alice, however, discovered an advertisement for a minor job at the Methodist Bookroom[3] in London and posted it to Charles, who subsequently began working at the bookshop in 1904. Edith remembered, years later: "The work there was mostly packing, but at the same time he attended classes at the Working Men's College [in London], where he met Fred Page, who introduced him to the Oxford University Press."[4]

In those early days, Williams and George Robinson belonged to a discussion group in St Albans who called themselves the "Theological Smokers". Robinson recalls that "over pipes, cigarettes, coffee and cakes" they "explored the universe, regretted non-conformity, had a sneaking regard for but kept a wary eye on His Holiness – all… enlivened by the fondness which Charles and I had for changing our positions halfway through the discussion, so that we could see what was on the other side!" Charles Williams enjoyed such lively, opinion-changing discussions throughout his life, culminating in the give and take of the Inklings' gatherings.

He made two acquaintances at the evening classes at the Working Men's College, Crowndale Road, in Camden Town, who became close friends: Harold Eyers and Ernest Nottingham. Charles lost both companions in the First World War, Eyers in May 1915 and Nottingham in 1917. For his part, he was rejected for military service because of a noticeable neurological disorder that caused his hands to tremble and shake, a condition that he put down to a severe bout of measles when young.

It had been through the camaraderie of the Working Men's College that Charles had got to know Fred Page of Oxford University Press. Page had needed help with the proofreading of a complete edition of William Thackeray that was going through the press. On Page's recommendation Charles was employed by the publishing house, and he was to remain on their staff until his death. Though Williams was destined never to leave the London office of the OUP, the office itself was to move to temporary accommodation in Oxford thirty or so years later for the duration of the Second World War. While there, it remained the "London office".

During the early years of his employment, Charles added a unique quality to life in the OUP building near St Paul's, in the City of London (the business centre). The atmosphere was recalled affectionately by his biographer, Alice Hadfield, who later worked there. It was characteristic that metaphysical debates would occur halfway up staircases, and the library became the setting for the masques written by Charles. One of these featured the lamentable theme of a lack of readers for an OUP book on Syrian nouns!

Around this time Charles married his sweetheart, Florence Conway of St Albans, whom he was to call Michal, after King David's wife who mocked her royal husband when he danced before the Lord. She was tall, confident, and lively, with expressive dark eyes. They had met while helping at a parish children's Christmas party. This was the twenty-one-year-old Charles's first experience of romantic love, and it shook him to the core. It was not long before he had written a sequence of sonnets based on falling in love, which became his first book of poems *The Silver Stair*. The collection's technique was derivative of a number of established poets.

The publication of the book in 1912 was paid for by the husband of the poet Alice Meynell. This couple had befriended and encouraged Williams, whose abilities they recognized. It was his first contact with other authors simply on the strength of his own writing. Previously, Wilfrid and Alice Meynell had nurtured Francis Thompson, and published his poems.

Charles and Florence did not marry until April 1917, when he was thirty and she almost that age. It is perhaps significant that they decided to set up home in London, well away from their families in St Albans. Their first flat was at 18 Parkhill Road, NW3, near Hampstead. In 1922, Michael Williams, their only child, entered their lives. Charles held the view that children were distinguished strangers with whom communication was difficult, if not impossible. Nevertheless, he participated in the inevitable disruption of normal routine created by baby Michael's arrival.

In the autumn of that year of change, Charles started what was to become a regular engagement – giving adult evening classes on literature for the London County Council at the City Literary Institute and other venues, to supplement the modest family income. His usual commitment was a weekly two-hour session. Then he would come home and settle down to writing. Florence recalled: "When Charles was writing his life of Sir Francis Bacon I was aroused at one a.m. to hear details of that great man's passing. I heard the last two chapters of The Greater Trumps at three a.m...."

The rule of the LCC evening lectures was one hour of lecturing and one hour of questions. The then undiscovered Dylan Thomas came in later years to hear his lectures. Charles was concerned about Thomas's penniless state, which was far worse than that of most poets.[5] Dylan Thomas commented on the quality of the lectures to Williams: "Why, you come into the room and talk about Keats and Blake as if they were *alive*!"[6]

Charles carried over his style of teaching into his Oxford lectures during the Second World War. The response of an undergraduate at that time is therefore likely to have captured the flavour of the previous long years of lecturing. John Wain, who later became a member of the Inklings, remembered: "He ranted and threw back his head... and stamped up and down on the platform, but there was always the feeling that he was not doing it to impress us with his own importance, but rather with the importance of the material he was dealing with. His mood never seemed to fall below the level of blazing enthusiasm. Great poetry was something to be revelled in, to be rejoiced over, and Williams revelled and rejoiced up there before our eyes. When he quoted, which he did continually and from memory, he shouted the lines at the top of his voice like an operatic tenor tearing into an aria... it was magnificent."[7]

Charles's unique style, revealing his eccentricities, was in evidence in the 1930s when he gave popular talks at a girls' school, the head teacher of which, Miss Olive Willis, was a friend of his. One pupil acted out her impression of Charles (whom they affectionately nicknamed "Chas. Bill") speaking on poetic drama to her cousin, Lois Lang-Sims. Later in life, Lois was to get to know Charles closely.

No professional clown, it would seem, could have beaten his performances. In graphic imitation of his antics, my cousin would stride up and down an imaginary stage, grimacing like a maniacal monkey, clasping her arms about her as she mimicked his habit of seizing one of the stage curtains in a wild embrace while the school held its breath. "We always think it's going to come down on his head when he does that, but it hasn't – yet."[8]

One of the deep strands in Charles Williams's life was an interest in magic and the occult. He became connected with a branch of the Rosicrucians, of whose far-flung variations Aleister Crowley and W.B. Yeats were members. All such societies were secretive, and thus information about their inner workings is vague. Charles belonged to a splinter group called the Fellowship of the Rosy Cross, founded by A.E. Waite, which was marked by esoteric secret rituals that did not involve magic. Charles's active membership lasted between four and ten years.[9] Some esoteric elements of this movement, which Charles left in the 1920s, can be found in his fiction. The Tarot cards, for instance, are at the centre of his novel *The Greater Trumps*. They were used merely as apparatus in the stories, though, not as beliefs – the novels express an orthodox Christianity, as captured in church creeds.

C.S. Lewis met W.B. Yeats in 1921 when the Irish poet lived in Oxford and was full of his form of Rosicrucianism. Lewis perhaps based the wizard Merlin on him in his novel *That Hideous Strength*. Charles also met Yeats on occasions, and there is a photo of the two men posing for a photograph, both in suits and wearing homburg hats, with Yeats looking the more relaxed.

Interest in spiritual, mystical, and occult groups was a trend among writers in the early twentieth century, and those who were exploring included Christians of various shades and hues, including Evelyn Underhill and Owen Barfield. Barfield became convinced, in the 1920s, that the arcane teaching of anthroposophy was not only Christian, but a highly important expression of Christianity in the twentieth century. Its esoteric and very unorthodox interpretation was, he believed, the right one, leading the way in the evolution of human consciousness. Evelyn Underhill wrote on mysticism and Christian spirituality, and composed three novels, including *The Grey World*.[10]

Charles lifted the symbolism of alchemy and the Jewish Kabbalah from his involvement with the Fellowship of the Rosy Cross and built them into his Christian writings. They formed a pattern of imagery rather than a replacement for the central teachings of Christianity, and in these writings he increasingly distanced himself from the misuse of power characteristic of the darker side of such secret movements. He was deeply aware of the dangers of such misuse, and struggled with them in his personal life.

Charles Williams had a charismatic personality, and his teaching in evening classes, like some of his books, had a strong hold over people, He gained a popular following, and there were some who wished him to lead them in some kind of group or religious order. His popular theology was becoming indirectly enshrined in his novels, in theological books such as *He Came Down From Heaven* (1938), *The Descent of the Dove* (1939), and *The Forgiveness of Sins* (1942), and in his Arthurian poetry. Even his literary studies would examine the theological implications of romantic love, as in *The Figure of Beatrice* (1943), on Dante's poetry. As someone whose commitment to the Anglican Church was lifelong, Williams at first resisted the pressure to form a religious group. Eventually something like a religious order was formed, which worked within Anglican worship and practice. David Porter, who wrote on the Inklings, explains Williams's concept of "Co-inherence", which lay at the centre of the companionship he created:

All life depends on mutual giving and receiving, ultimately derived from the Trinity and most powerfully displayed on the cross [of Christ]. This idea runs through all his writing... Charles Williams portrays the experience of being "in love" as a kind of naïve apprehension of Co-inherence, a heightened awareness of the interdependence and interconnectedness of all. In 1938 Charles Williams proposed the formation of an Order, a proposal which is set out in the Appendix to *The Descent of the Dove*, which is dedicated to "The Companions of the Co-inherence". The seven statements of the Order declared Co-inherence to be a natural and supernatural matter, by nature Christian; cited such precepts as "Am I my brother's keeper?" and "Bear ye one another's burdens"; and invoked the atonement as "the root of all".[11]

The strong charismatic hold he had over many people, including women followers, could too easily be misused, as seems to have been the case in his imposition of disciplines on his tolerant and uncomplaining adult followers. This included Charles's own variety of inflicted penance, such as writing out lines, standing in corners, having ankles tied with string, being smacked with a ruler, and even bizarre rituals with a ceremonial wooden sword from his days with the Fellowship of the Rosy Cross. His final novel, *All Hallows' Eve* (1945), which he would later read in instalments to the Inklings, clearly repudiates the practice of magic and the self-centredness of its power. A central malevolent character, Simon the Clerk, is perhaps modelled on Aleister Crowley, who had a certain notoriety.

For all his strangeness, the abiding impression Williams left with both his most devoted followers and those fellow authors who admired him (such as T.S. Eliot. W.H. Auden, and C.S. Lewis) was of a saintly man, who was at home in both ordinary and mystical realms. Alice Mary Hadfield, Williams's biographer and one of his followers who openly described the disciplines he imposed, concluded:

> C. W. might talk to you for an hour, he might take you out for tea, write letters to you, ring you up, make you read verse, learn collects, keep your temper once a week, write essays for him, but after a month your attention was more directed to the Holy Ghost and to Milton than to C. W.[12]

By 1936, as we have seen, when C.S. Lewis and Charles Williams first made contact, Charles had published five novels and a sixth was in preparation. Much of his poetry is quite difficult to understand, and so is some of his prose, when writing on literary subjects or popular theology. The novels, however, by necessity, are accessible, and introduce the main themes of Charles's highly imaginative thinking. Getting to know his themes through the novels helps us to understand his most important poems, the sequence based upon legends of King Arthur, which started to appear in 1938.

Charles's first and least accomplished novel was *Shadows of Ecstasy,* which did not appear for perhaps seven years after its writing, as he was at first unable to get it published. It finally came out in 1933, and centres on a university professor, Roger Ingram, "carried away" by poetry. He is attracted by a mysterious figure of great charisma, Nigel Considine, who seems to have conquered death itself. Considine leads a mass uprising from Africa against the white races of Europe.

War in Heaven (1930) was Charles's first published novel. It shows that he felt that the movement of every human being towards heaven or hell, and the nature of good and evil, were the most fascinating themes for a story. The novel opens like a conventional detective story with a mystery body lying in a publisher's office. An important theme (running through many of the novels) is the misuse of power. By the discovery of the legendary Holy Graal (Charles's preferred spelling), a retired senior publisher seeks control over others and over death itself.

His next novel, *Many Dimensions* (1931), reveals many people trying to use an ancient, precious stone of King Solomon for their own ends: political, economic, plain selfish, or even health ones. Those in whom good holds sway see that the temptation to misuse the stone must be resisted and renounced. There are parallels with the Ring of Power in Tolkien's later work *The Lord of the Rings.*

The Place of the Lion (1931) was the novel that led to C.S. Lewis's friendship with Charles Williams: he was deeply impressed by its remarkable blend of "Genesis and Platonism", as noted earlier. In Charles's hands, Platonic ideas – spiritual powers – become terribly real. At the centre of the story is a vision of hell that provides the background to the ordinary decisions and actions of people; evil turns some of them literally into beasts, as dominant powers within transform them. Salvation lies in becoming like the new Adam, the divine human, who has the ultimate power over creation.

In *The Greater Trumps* (1932), Henry Lee and his grandfather, by possession of the original Tarot cards, desire union by magic with the power of destiny, which creates and controls the matter of life. At one point, a giant snowstorm is conjured up by using the cards and becomes out of control, with terrifying results. Henry is saved from destruction by the selfless love of his fiancée, Nancy Coningsby.

Descent into Hell (1937) was in preparation when it is likely that Lewis and Charles Williams first met. It concerns Pauline Anstruther's discovery of the doctrine of substituted love – that is, taking literally Christ's command to bear one another's burdens. This basic theme of Charles's writings was to deeply influence C.S. Lewis, and later in life he came to believe that he had actually taken on some of his dying wife's pain. The novel is one of Charles Williams's best.

It would take a whole book to set out the themes explored in the novels, the secret to understanding Williams's later, important Arthurian poems. But this brief overview can at least point to his affinity with the Inklings prior to his knowledge of and introduction to the group.

In 1933, C.S. Lewis had published his first work of fiction, *The Pilgrim's Regress*, the purpose of which was explained rather cryptically in its subtitle, "An Allegorical Apology for Christianity, Reason and Romanticism". Charles Williams's thought and writings centre on those three themes highlighted by Lewis: Christianity, reason, and romanticism.

Like Lewis, at the time of their first acquaintance Charles Williams was a member of the Anglican Church, though distinctly High Anglican (unlike Lewis, who claimed to be neither especially High nor Low Church, and had a strong Puritan streak).[13] Theologically, Charles was somewhere between Lewis and the staunch Roman Catholic J.R.R. Tolkien. His allegiance remained to Anglicanism from childhood to death. His beliefs, like those of his friend Dorothy L. Sayers, were based on the historic creeds of the church. And, also like her, he was a writer of lay theology, beginning with *He Came Down From Heaven* in 1938. He emerged as one of a movement of influential lay theologians, which would also include Dorothy L. Sayers and C.S. Lewis, and already was represented by writers such as G.K. Chesterton and T.S. Eliot. Charles Williams probably first met Eliot in 1931 at one of Lady Ottoline Morrell's famous literary gatherings, which she hosted at that time in the Bloomsbury area of London. Both appeared regularly on her guest list.[14]

John Heath-Stubbs, poet and critic, pointed out: "Charles Williams' thought is based not on abstract premises but on the experience of human relationships – man's relationship to a personal God and to his fellow creatures, whether as individuals or in society."[15] Though Williams firmly placed lived experience before abstractions, he still held to a high view of reason. Anne Ridler, another poet, felt that in "Charles Williams' universe there is a clear logic, a sense of terrible justice which is not our justice and yet is not divorced from love".

Williams felt passionately that the whole human person must be ordered by reason to have integrity and spiritual health. At the same time, he rejected the idea that what is real should be equated with the abstractions of theoretical thought. This is why, when he discovered the writings of the nineteenth-century Danish Christian thinker Søren Kierkegaard, he was deeply attracted to them. Kierkegaard put actual human existence before concepts about mankind that come from vast philosophical or scientific systems, and felt that individuals disappeared in such accounts of reality. Kierkegaard's views had had a huge impact on the continent, but Charles Williams was to introduce him to the English-speaking world through his influence as a senior editor at OUP. *The Present Age* (1940) would be the first of a number of published translations of Kierkegaard's writings, and carried an introduction by Williams.

Charles's feeling for the importance of human lived experience was expressed most of all, however, by his fervent commitment to romanticism. His attachment to it is expressed in the central place he gives to what he called "images" (or symbols). His concern was particularly with the experience of romantic love, and the theological implications of human love as an image pointing far beyond itself, as C.S. Lewis pointed out in his Introduction to *Essays Presented to Charles Williams*.

When, later in his marriage, Charles developed a second love, for a librarian working for OUP called Phyllis Jones, he took that experience seriously. As is to be expected, this caused strain in his marriage and could have ruined it, though in its final years there appears to have been something of a mature return to his first happiness with Florence, captured in his huge body of wartime letters to her. This was despite his master–acolyte relationship with another young female follower, the writer Lois Lang-Sims (who felt more for him than he did for her).

He never abandoned his commitment to Florence, but he used the experience of loving Phyllis Jones to explore romantic love in literature, and to energize his creativity.[16] He found romantic love, in all its theological implications, given voice in the poetry of Dante, such as *La Vita Nova* (*The New Life*, published about 1292) and in *The Divine Comedy*, which the Italian began composing around 1307. Charles wrote much about the love of Dante for Beatrice, whom the Italian poet momentousely encountered in a street in Florence in the thirteenth century. Charles also explored romantic love through his later poetry and in his novels. It is not surprising that he was so delighted with C.S. Lewis's exploration of medieval courtly love in *The Allegory of Love*, which was going through the press at OUP, leading to his "fan" letter to Lewis in 1936.

This was the fallible man and Christian mystic with a rapturous imagination who appears to hold at least part of the secret of what might have kept the Inklings together as a group, if they were indeed more than simply a circle of Lewis's friends. In their shared interest in human experiences that symbolically pointed beyond the world, were they in fact some kind of contemporary manifestation of the historic Romantic Movement? Were the likes of William Wordsworth, Samuel Taylor Coleridge, Keats, and Shelley their forerunners? Certainly, Charles Williams was to have an enormous impact upon both C.S. Lewis's thinking and his writing. How Charles affected the group of friends when he joined them in Oxford at the outbreak of war must await a later chapter.

CHAPTER 2

Roots and shoots

Friends who will become Inklings

Survivors of the First World War trickled back to Oxford after demobilization, joining students too young to have served. The veterans had often gained scholarships to Oxford colleges some time before being commissioned for war. These included C.S. Lewis, Owen Barfield, and Nevill Coghill, all of whom would belong to the Inklings in future years. Lewis and Barfield sat the Oxford scholarship examination in December 1916, gaining places at University College and Wadham College respectively.

Most of the Inklings who would meet on Thursday evenings in the early days of the group's existence in the 1930s were born in the 1890s or very early in the twentieth century. They were the wartime generation. Several of the future Inklings became friends as undergraduates. Tolkien already had his Oxford degree – gained in 1915 – but returned to Oxford after the war and tutored and worked for the *Oxford English Dictionary* (then called the *New English Dictionary*) for a time. He was therefore older than most of the future Inklings.

Oxford had been severely deprived of students during the war, and many of those who did remain in those years were doing officer training, preparing to go to France or Belgium. C.S. Lewis, for instance, was a student undergoing military training from April to September 1917. By his nineteenth birthday that year, 29 November, Lewis was on the Western front, about to experience trench warfare as an infantryman. At the time Lewis was training in Oxford, there were merely 315 students in residence, around 120 of whom were members of the Officer Training Corps. He returned to Oxford to study in 1919.

By 1919 and into the early 1920s, the mood of Oxford had been transformed. New friendships were valued amid memories of friends lost. Out of a group of half-dozen students Lewis had trained with, four officers died in battle, while Lewis and another officer were wounded, Lewis severely. Nevill Coghill remembered, in the context of his new friendship with Lewis, that:

> [w]e were uninhibitedly happy in our work and felt supported by an endless energy.
>
> There was no reason why we should not have been happy; we had both just emerged safely from a war which (we then believed) had ended war for ever. We had survived the trenches, the nightmare was over, we were at Oxford, we were in our early twenties. The old order seemed not only restored but renewed; life and art lay before us for exploration and the interchange of ideas, and we seemed to be experiencing what happened to Odin and his fellow-gods when they returned after their long twilight; finding their golden chessmen where they had left them in the grass, they sat down and went on with the game.[1]

Coghill and Lewis had met at a high-powered discussion class run by Professor George Gordon while each was doing the English honours degree course in a mere year. Coghill's college was Exeter. Like Lewis, Coghill was Irish, but, unlike him, he came from the south of the island. As was his wont with people who interested him, Lewis described Coghill in the diary he was keeping at the time. His first impression was that Coghill "seems an enthusiastic sensible man, without nonsense, and a gentleman…". Though Coghill's courtesy appealed to Lewis, as a hard-edged atheist at that time Lewis was ruffled to discover that this intelligent and "best-informed" member of the discussion class was a Christian.

Literary critic John Carey points out in the *Oxford Dictionary of National Biography* that Nevill Coghill had been brought up in the

old-world atmosphere of the south of Ireland, where
sailing, fishing, hunting, shooting, and the painting
of pictures provided gentlemanly pleasures… A tall,
handsome figure with rather leonine features, he was
known in Oxford for the charm and vivacity of his
conversation and the fineness of his taste.

In the second term of their year in the English School, Coghill and Lewis took the first of many long walks together. Walking was one of Lewis's great loves, and a number of his friends over the years would join him in walking holidays. Because of Lewis's fondness for tramping the chalk South Downs, one friend called a group of his walking friends "The Cretaceous Perambulators".

On the walks Coghill and Lewis shared at that time in

the Oxford countryside, the conversations would anticipate what became typical among the Inklings group of the future. Coghill remembered the two fervently talking about literature and life as they energetically walked along the skirts of the Hinksey hills outside the city. They would share what they thought of the reading they had been assigned by their tutor. Both were delighted by their discoveries of early English poetry. Lewis, he recalled, "would suddenly roar out a passage of [Old English] poetry ... his big voice boomed it out with all the pleasure of tasting a noble wine".

Another undergraduate friend of Nevill Coghill was, like him, a student at Exeter. This was the exuberant and ready-witted H.V.D. Dyson, who would become known to the future Inklings as "Hugo". (Nicknames and the use of last names were common in Oxford, perhaps reflecting the enduring influence of the private schools that most students and teaching staff of that time had experienced.)[2] After training at the Royal Military Academy at Sandhurst, Dyson had been thrust into the war, fighting in the Battles of the Somme and Passchendaele (where he was so badly wounded that he had an out-of-body experience).

Dyson and Coghill were members of the college's exclusive Essay Club, where they encountered another future Inkling, J.R.R. Tolkien. Tolkien had studied at Exeter College some years before, when he had been a club member. Now that he was back in Oxford working on the *New English Dictionary* and doing some tutoring for the university, his connections with the college and the club were renewed. On 10 March 1920, Tolkien read an abridged version of a story from his then private mythology, "The Fall of Gondolin". The piece was received enthusiastically. The club minutes capture the afterglow of the meeting:

As a discovery of a new mythological background Mr Tolkien's matter was exceedingly illuminating and marked him out as a staunch follower of tradition, a treatment indeed in the manner of such typical Romantics as William Morris, George MacDonald, de la Motte Fouqué etc.... The battle of the contending forces of good and evil as represented by the Gondothlim and the followers of Melko was very graphically and astonishingly told, combined with a wealth of attendance to detail interesting in extreme....

"The Fall of Gondolin" came from the burgeoning creation of his Middle-earth, which was quickened into life by Tolkien's experience of fighting in the Battle of the Somme, and losing two of his closest friends. It marked the first public (but very tentative) exposure of the fiction he was to work on for the rest of his life. Through this Essay Club meeting, Dyson and Coghill became acquainted with the older man whom they would one day befriend and join with in the hurly-burly of the Inklings.

It was not until several years later, after C.S. Lewis had started working permanently in Oxford as a fellow and tutor in English at Magdalen College in 1925, that he got to know and eventually became friends with Tolkien and Hugo Dyson.

Owen Barfield

Besides Nevill Coghill, other friends of C.S. Lewis from that time just after the war can be singled out, one of whom was to become very much a central figure in the Inklings: Owen Barfield.

Like Charles Williams (but without the accent), Barfield was a Londoner. He was born in Muswell Hill, north London, on 9 November 1898, just weeks before C.S. Lewis, and lived at 6 Grosvenor Gardens until he was six or seven. The family then moved further out to Whetstone in the borough of Barnet, a wealthy area on the northern fringes of greater London. Owen had two sisters and a brother, and was the youngest of the siblings.

The household was comfortably secular and full of books and music. They were frequently visited by aunts, uncles, and many cousins (both parents being from large families). Barfield described himself as the offspring of "more or less agnostic" parents. Mr and Mrs Barfield had been brought up as non-conformists, perhaps Congregationalists, but later on church had no place in their lives. Barfield remembered them respecting Jesus as a person, but the natural air they breathed in their household was one of scepticism about religion.

Owen's mother, Lizzie, was musical, a gifted pianist. His father, Arthur, had been deprived of a proper school education, but achieved the status of a City of London solicitor. Lizzie Barfield, a suffragette, was active in feminist politics at the grass roots, which included taking part in open-air meetings in London's Hyde Park. There she found the barracking of drunken men an ordeal. Though her husband was in sympathy with her views, they eventually felt that her activism might jeopardize his reputation as a City solicitor. Later in his life, Barfield was to show active concern for social issues such as caring for the environment and protecting the unborn child.

Just before he was eight, Owen was sent to an all-boys junior school in Highgate. The independent school had been nearby when he lived in Muswell Hill, but now, dressed in a red blazer and red cap, he had to travel by train with a season ticket from Whetstone. Along with rote learning of the multiplication tables, he began Latin and French from the onset. At around the age of twelve, Barfield remembered, he crossed the road to join the upper school. At that time, the poet Samuel Taylor Coleridge was buried in a neglected vault beside the school chapel (his remains were moved in 1961 to a nearby parish church). Perhaps Barfield's schooldays mark the beginning of Coleridge's great influence on his thought. At school he shone in gymnastics, which correlated with his love of dancing.

As he moved up the school, he began to suffer from a stammer, a condition not helped by the fact that one of his Classics masters was visibly irritated by it. It was made even more difficult because not only did he stutter when speaking Greek or Latin, but sometimes he was unable to speak at all. At one point it reached the stage at which he felt, as he went to bed one night, that he would prefer not to wake up. Though the stammering didn't burden him all the time, he sensed it as a shadow over his life. When he was singing, reciting poetry, or acting it wasn't a difficulty at all, but although the condition did not affect his academic work it did get in the way of his social life.

At school, Owen valued the friendship of Cecil Harwood, who would remain a lifelong friend. Harwood shared his love of English literature. They both relished the fact that another Classics master, Mr Doughton, would regularly make a point of devoting an hour to freely discussing works of literature.

The shadow of the war in which vast armies clashed in France meant that the activities of the school's Officer Training Corps were much more intense. The extensive route marches and exercises in khaki uniform delayed his long journey home to Whetstone. Barfield recalls: "After a full day at school on either one or two days a week I had to go on a route march....

By the time you'd had… all this military exercise afterwards and the train journey home you were pretty well worn out. A bit of a strain all that time."[3] He also had to attend a church parade: "I was very embarrassed because we never went to church and I didn't know when to stand up and when to sit down."[4] The whole involvement with the Officer Training Corps rankled rather with a boy who was influenced by his family's attitude that patriotism was somewhat phoney and jingoistic. It was a dark time, and grew darker. Frequently, news reached the school that boys who had left to fight had been killed.

In the spring of 1917 Barfield was called up; he was then eighteen. He was anxious to avoid becoming an infantryman (because, he thought, "the average expectancy of life of a young infantry officer by the time we'd got to 1916 or 1917 was about three weeks after he had got out there").[5] As an alternative, he served with the Royal Engineers.

Like Tolkien before him, he joined the signal service. This involved learning about wireless communication and studying the theory of electricity. The fact that his elder brother had already taught him Morse code was a great help. By now it was late 1918, and the armistice was signed while he was still undergoing army training. He was fortunate therefore to have had no experience of fighting at the front line. He was posted to Belgium and post-war activity. He found there that not only was there little to do, but that wireless communication was not widely in use. He was not particularly acquainted with pigeons, who were still employed to carry messages.

The army did give him the chance, however, to get involved in education while awaiting demobilization, which helped him to make discoveries in English poetry, and encouraged him to write more of his own. As he had already been awarded a scholarship to study at Oxford, all he could do was wait.

It was October 1919 before he got off the train at Oxford station. His college was Wadham, near Blackwell's bookshop and the Bodleian Library. Here he initially read Classics, but then thought better of it and switched to English. (His schoolfriend Cecil Harwood had already started his studies – his college was Christ Church.) It was as an undergraduate that Barfield formed his lifelong and enormously influential friendship with C.S. Lewis, after being introduced by a mutual friend, Leo Baker. This relationship led to his becoming one of the most important members of the Inklings.

Barfield experienced what *The New York Times*, in its obituary of him nearly eighty years later, insightfully called an "intellectual epiphany".[6] It happened as he was reading the works of Romantic poets such as William Wordsworth, Samuel Taylor Coleridge, and John Keats for his university studies, and his affinity with the Romantic Movement endured for the rest of his life. Barfield remembered that reading experience clearly:

> What impressed me particularly was the power
> with which not so much whole poems as particular
> combinations of words worked on my mind. It seemed
> like there was some magic in it; and a magic which not
> only gave me pleasure but also reacted on and expanded
> the meanings of the individual words concerned'.[7]

Language, Barfield discovered, had a unique power to transform human consciousness. It also captured changes that took place in this consciousness over time. A sort of archeology could be practised on language, as he undertook when he wrote his book *History in English Words* (1926).

The importance of poetry to the very way that we see the world was a strong element in the friendship of Barfield and C.S. Lewis. When the two met, Lewis was far more widely read in poetry than Barfield. Though, like Lewis, Barfield grew up in a household full of books, Lewis was by far the more bookish. While Lewis thought about everything, Barfield tended throughout his life to stay focused on a number of outstanding insights into the nature of language, particularly poetic language, and upon the historic context of human language. His insights fed into conversations and the writings of those who would be particularly associated with the Inklings, especially C.S. Lewis and Tolkien. It would be some years after Barfield's graduation, however, that he would meet Tolkien and stir up the older man's thinking.

C.S. Lewis

C.S. Lewis's life began in a house bursting with books of all types and hues, in a city that hummed with vibrant, industrial life, in a turbulent country divided by nationalistic politics that would soon take violent expression. He would grow up to be an opinion-shaping man to whom nobody could easily be indifferent. Reactions to him were often polarized – amiable or hostile. As a man, he would look like a jolly, beefy farmer but speak like a philosopher. Sometimes he would seem like a bully in argument but his eyes would easily fill with tears, as when he heard Tolkien read a particularly poignant extract from the "new Hobbit" (later known as *The Lord of the Rings*).

Lewis was born on 29 November 1898 in the wealthier eastern part of Belfast in the north of Ireland. Like Owen Barfield, he was the son of a solicitor, Albert. His brilliant mother was from a church family. His paternal grandfather,

Richard Lewis, was an evangelical Welsh engineer who had made his home in Ireland. The docks near where the child lived were in their heyday, and there could be found the shipbuilders McIlwaine, Lewis and Co., where his grandfather had been a partner. His mother Florence (Flora) was considered to be of more cultured stock, and came from County Cork in the south of the country. Lewis had an older brother, Warren, whom the family called "Warnie". Clive Staples Lewis in his turn soon declared that his name was "Jacksie", which became "Jacks" and then "Jack". The family was forced to accept this choice because of his resolve to answer only to it. He was known as Jack by those close to him for the rest of his life. Jack and Warnie were as close as twins throughout their lives, friends as well as brothers. Warnie became one of the first members of the Inklings.

Belfast in 1898 and into the twentieth century was intensely alive as an expanding industrial city. Its shipyards launched the world's then largest ship, the *Oceanic*, and later the even larger but more short-lived *Titanic* (the *Oceanic* was wrecked in 1914). Belfast's economy led Ireland as it prospered. By 1905 the Lewis family were able to move to a larger, badly planned house, Little Lea, "almost a major character in my story", Lewis later wrote. This house full of books reflected the voracious reading and book-collecting habits of Albert and Flora. The young Lewis explored unhindered, discovering books that were both suitable and unsuitable.

He soon started to find a pattern in those that he particularly loved. These were books that touched upon other worlds, however tentatively. In them, what G.K. Chesterton called "the horns of elfland" could be heard – stories and poetry of what Lewis and his Inklings friends were to call "romance". This interest in stories of distant or other worlds was heightened by the folk tales told him by his nurse, Lizzie Endicott. They were part of the lore of County Down, his native county, which would help to inspire the land of Narnia. The young boy was lost in wonder as he heard stories of the Fair Folk and far-off immortal lands. Throughout their lives, Lewis and his brother spoke of the Little People who seemed to be behind sudden changes in weather, the missing of trains, and similar acts of fate.

Albert and Flora had selected Little Lea because of its view, a view that haunted Jack Lewis's memories throughout his life. It included what he and Warnie called "the Green Hills":

the low line of the Castlereagh Hills which we saw from the nursery windows. They were not very far off but they were, to children, quite unattainable. They taught me longing – *sehnsucht*...[8]

Lewis's technical name for this longing (the *Sehnsucht* of German Romanticism) was Joy, a "sweet desire" that no human experience of love, beauty, art, or literature could satisfy. It was to become a major theme in his writings.

As they grew older, the brothers were able to explore those green hills on their bicycles. From them, one can look south over the woods and pastures of County Down, with the blue mountains of Mourne in the far distance, and Strangford Lough to one's left. It is as if one is looking south over Narnia, with the Eastern Ocean to the left, and the mountains of Archenland on the horizon.

In these happy and secure years, Lewis began composing illustrated stories about "chivalrous mice and rabbits who rode out in complete mail to kill not giants but cats".[9] In creating them, he combined his favourite elements from the books he was reading at the time: knights in armour and animals dressed in clothes. These led to more advanced stories, in partnership with Warnie. They created an "Animal-land" called Boxen, which had a full geography and history. In many ways, these stories bear the mark of Belfast's social history at that time. As a child, Lewis in fact once proclaimed himself a "Home-Ruler" – a supporter of the independence of Ireland from the United Kingdom.

These idyllic times with Warnie were sadly limited, as soon after the move to Little Lea, Warnie was sent off to England to a boarding school. Despite extensive research into the best school for his sons (the plan was that Jack should follow when of age), Albert chose a school in decline, ruled by a head teacher falling slowly into insanity. The boys therefore had to make the most of the holidays between school terms. Warnie revealed nothing of the school's harsh regime to his parents. He learned to endure and survive.

One day, when he was nine, the precocious young author listed his literary works to date:

Building of the Promenade (a tale)
Man Against Man (a novel)
Town (an essay)
Relief of Murry (a history)
Bunny (a paper)
Home Rule (an essay)
My Life (a journal)

The Irish weather played a part in Lewis's development. It seemed to rain often and parents tended to keep their children out of the damp conditions. Tuberculosis was a frequent killer of the young. The resourceful brothers would find books to read, or pull out their pencils or paint brushes. A cousin, Claire Clapperton, was three years older than Lewis and a visitor to Little Lea. Long afterwards she recalled a significant activity on rainy days. In the house there stood a large oak wardrobe; it had been built and hand-carved by their grandfather, Richard Lewis. The wardrobe made a den into which the children climbed. In the dark they would listen silently "while Jacks told us his tales of adventure". Coloured by Lewis's later discovery of wardrobes as portals to other worlds in George MacDonald and E. Nesbit, this became the inspiration for Professor Kirke's wardrobe, which provided a gateway into Narnia.

The Lewis family was Church of Ireland (Anglican) and worshipped at nearby St Mark's, Dundela, where Lewis had been baptized as an infant. Flora Lewis's father, Thomas Hamilton, was rector of the church, and tears came easily to his eyes as he preached. He and his clever, aristocratic wife lived in a shambolic rectory, which stank of cats. In contrast to her husband's views, Mary Hamilton happily employed Roman Catholic servants and supported Home Rule for Ireland.

Through the services, the young Lewis became familiar with the liturgy of *The Book of Common Prayer* and *Hymns Ancient and Modern*. When his mother became seriously ill with cancer, Jack found it natural to pray for her recovery. Even after she died, in 1908, he fervently hoped for a miracle, but the corpse he was forced to view removed this hope. The process of his mother's decline had filled him with inescapable fear.

Albert Lewis is rather a tragic figure. He found the decline and death of his wife almost intolerable. As his deep emotions gripped him, he failed to notice that he was steadily losing his sons as well. Lewis wrote in *Surprised by Joy*, "We were coming, my brother and I, to rely more and more exclusively on each other for all that made life bearable; to have confidence only in each other. . . Everything that had made the house a home had failed us; everything except one another. We drew daily closer together (that was the good result) – two frightened urchins huddled for warmth in a bleak world."[10]

One September evening, a matter of weeks after their mother's death, a four-wheeled cab carrying the brothers rumbled its way to the Belfast quay. Together on the ferry the two "urchins" in uncomfortable school clothes watched the lights of Holywood and Bangor on the banks of Belfast Lough slip away astern. They travelled by train from Fleetwood in Lancashire to Euston station in London, and then took a connection to Watford. Together they endured the regime in a school Lewis later dubbed "Belsen", after the infamous Nazi prison camp. The experience haunted him throughout his life, more than his wartime exposure to the trenches of the First World War. Warren had long ago developed extensive survival skills. Each morning the pupils had to declare how many sums they had done, with fearful consequences for lies. Warren announced with complete honesty that he had done five – the fact that they were the same five every day was never noticed.

In 1910, when the school was closed down, Lewis moved first to Belfast, to Campbell College near Little Lea, for half a term, and then to Cherbourg House, a preparatory school in Malvern, Worcestershire. While a pupil at Cherbourg House he abandoned his childhood Christian faith in favour of a philosophical materialism – a view that ultimately was to empty reality for him of distinctive qualities such as colour, the appeal of a melody, and the particularity and moods of places. For many years thereafter he sought solace in his imaginative life instead. His memories, experiences, and literary discoveries became a surrogate religion. It was just as if his materialism brought a spell of winter to his powerful intellectual life. Warren was close by his brother, studying at Malvern College. In one extreme winter they were able to skate together on a frozen stream.

In September 1913 Lewis won a classical scholarship and entered the "Col". All this time he was writing avidly, composing, among other pieces, a poetic tragedy about his favourite Norse gods, entitled "Loki Bound". His ambition to be a great poet was in its infancy. While at home for the Easter holidays in April 1914, he came to know a near neighbour who would become a soulmate. This was Arthur Greeves, with whom he carried on an extensive correspondence for the rest of his life. These letters to Arthur give rich insight into Lewis's life and into the development of his thought and imagination. In a sense they make up a more complete autobiography than anything else, even *Surprised by Joy: The Shape of My Early Life*. The foundation of the friendship was a common insight into the Joy, with its longing, that was the main and constant theme of Lewis's life and writings.

Lewis was not content until Albert entrusted his son to a private tutor named William T. Kirkpatrick, based in Bookham in Surrey. Lewis called him "The Great Knock" because of the sheer force of his intellectual rigour. Kirkpatrick had successfully tutored Warnie for entrance to the Royal Military Academy at Sandhurst, after he was expelled from Malvern for smoking and various "pranks" that seem mild in retrospect, especially coming from a boy who had lost his mother. Warren observed of his brother, "The fact is he should never have been sent to a public school at all. Already, at 14, his intelligence was such that he would have fitted in better among undergraduates than schoolboys; and by his temperament he was bound to be a misfit, a heretic, an object of suspicion within the collective-minded and standardising Public School system."

Jack's private schooling began in September 1914 and lasted until March 1917. This was one of the happiest periods of his life, and he later named Professor Digory Kirke of the Narnia stories after his mentor. There is something of the tutor's fierce logic in the professor.

Lewis quickly excelled, and soon made up for the lost years, thanks to the keen reasoning of his teacher. Always a walker, Lewis found himself enjoying the beauty of rural England. Bookham was surrounded by wooded landscapes that had given pleasure to Jane Austen around a hundred years before. Hitherto, when he had made a judgment, England had always suffered in comparison with County Down. He also became acquainted with more fantasy writers, such as William Morris. When he found a copy of George MacDonald's dream story *Phantastes* on nearby Leatherhead station, Lewis shared his discovery with Arthur Greeves. In *Surprised by Joy*, Lewis talks of that great work of Christian fantasy as "baptising his imagination" over fifteen years before he came to believe that Jesus Christ was the Son of God. It was around the time that he read *Phantastes* that he had a mental picture of a faun in a snowy wood, carrying parcels, perhaps after he had found a pine wood near Bookham on a heavily snowy day. That mental picture, Lewis tells us, began the Narnian story *The Lion, the Witch and the Wardrobe*, which was written over thirty years later.

Though Lewis was immensely happy in Bookham, the war being fought in France cast its shadow as he thought of the future. He saw Warnie very occasionally on leave. Lewis himself was not old enough to enlist until 1917. He spent his nineteenth birthday, 29 November 1917, on the front lines. By spring 1918, he had been wounded in action by so-called friendly fire, and invalided back to England. During all this time he had been writing poems and preparing a book of them, *Spirits in Bondage*, in the hope of publication.

Warnie had a relatively safe war. He had enrolled in the Royal Army Service Corps after finishing his training at the Royal Military Academy. This meant that his responsibilities were in the infrastructure of the British army, involved in the supply of men, horses, and equipment, and he was never involved directly in the fighting at the front. On occasions they were, however, strafed by enemy fighter planes or had bombs dropped near them. It also meant that when he heard from his father that Jack had been wounded on 15 April 1918, Warnie was able to get permission to visit him. He borrowed a motorcycle and rode the fifty miles from his base to the field hospital at Etaples (known to the British troops as "Eat-apples"), where Jack was being treated. To his relief, he found that his brother's wounds were not as serious as his panicking father had imagined, though they were bad.

C.S. Lewis's convalescence was extensive, marking the end of his active service in the trenches. After some time in hospital near central London, where he started to get out and about, he was moved to a succession of army camps in England, before finally being demobilized in December 1918, the month after the armistice was signed. After a brief holiday at Little Lea in Belfast with Warnie and his father, he returned to Oxford for the Hilary (Spring) term to start his studies at University College.

Warnie, in his turn, took up peacetime army duties. He was posted first to Belgium and then to England, to the Aldershot

Military Garrison. This meant he could travel from time to time to Oxford, about fifty miles away, to see his brother in his college. Then, in 1921, Warnie was posted to Sierra Leone, in West Africa, for a year. After earning a six-month period of leave, which he enjoyed in England, he then served in military bases in Colchester and Woolwich. While on leave in 1922 he visited Lewis's home in Headington, Oxford, meeting Mrs Moore and Maureen for the first time. It was the first of many visits.

Chapter 3

The 1920s

Oxford, wistful dreams, and a war with Owen Barfield

On the Western Front C.S. Lewis had lost an army friend named "Paddy" Moore, who was almost exactly his age. Before Paddy's death, Lewis had promised that should anything happen to his friend, he would take care of his mother and younger sister. This brought life-changing complications into Lewis's undergraduate days, and in fact into his entire life right up to the early 1950s. Lewis was to help to support Mrs Janie "Minto" Moore until her death in 1951, and her daughter, Maureen, for many years. Janie Moore was the first woman whom he self-sacrificially helped. Much later in life, he was to do the same for the woman he married, who at first needed British citizenship and then succumbed rapidly to terminal cancer – Joy Davidman. The early loss of his mother, whom he had been unable to help, even with his fervent prayers, meant that ever afterwards he reached out when he could to women in great need.[1] Particularly after he had become well known for his writings, this was evident from his conscientious and careful responses to frequent letters from women undergoing many kinds of difficulty and wanting advice.

Throughout Lewis's student years and until he was employed by Magdalen College in 1925, the subsistence allowance his father gave him helped the three who made up this new family to survive. As soon as possible after beginning his studies, he moved in with Mrs Moore and Maureen, unknown to his father and his college authorities. Only a few of his friends, including Owen Barfield, were party to the arrangement. One of the many trials involved was the large number of moves from one form of rented accommodation to another made by "the family" in the early years.

One particularly demanding move, requiring a great deal of interior decorating, happened during the run-up to the finals of the last of his three degrees, which was in English. That very same pre-examination period saw the rapid decline and death of Mrs Moore's brother, Dr John Askins, who was staying with the family as he fell into insanity, requiring round-the-clock care. Throughout the Moore years, Lewis cheerfully washed the dishes, solved domestic crises, and ran errands, even when he had many pressing concerns of his own, such as his studies, writing, and wider reading. For about five years from 1922 he also kept an extensive diary, much of which he read (selectively, in all likelihood) to Mrs Moore as it was composed.

Despite these considerable demands on his time and energy, Lewis maintained many friendships in this period. One of the most significant throughout most of the 1920s was undoubtedly that with Owen Barfield, especially after Barfield graduated from the English School in 1921 and began working for the distinctive Oxford postgraduate B.Litt. It was to form the foundation of his influential book *Poetic Diction*. His desire to pursue the relationship between poetry, imagination, and knowledge challenged the teaching resources of the English

School at the time. Failing to find him a supervisor, the university finally agreed to let him pursue the B.Litt without one! C.S. Lewis, however, had no difficulty in engaging with his friend on the subject.

Both friends had aspirations to be poets, and both were prepared to go as deep as the issues led them. They had a remarkable facility in philosophical thinking, and an extraordinary knowledge of English and classical poetry. Their discussions were to lay the foundations for their important respective contributions to understanding literature, the imagination, and the nature of human language. For both, this resulted as much in the writing of poetry and fiction as in works that presented arguments – essays, literary criticism, and the history of ideas. Some of their prose writing was philosophical or touched on important philosophical matters. Barfield was to have a shaping influence on both Tolkien and Lewis, among the future Inklings group.

To get an idea of Barfield's impact on C.S. Lewis, even before Tolkien came on the scene, it is necessary to have a look at some of the dominant ideas flowing around Oxford at the time the two friends were students.

The Freud factor

Perhaps the most radical current crossing 1920s Oxford was what Lewis and his friends called "the new psychology", owing much to the insights of Sigmund Freud in particular. Years later, Lewis commented: "In those days the new psychology was just beginning to make itself felt in the circles I most frequented at Oxford. This joined forces with the fact that we felt ourselves (as young men always do) to be escaping from the illusions of adolescence, and as a result we were much

exercised about the problem of fantasy or wishful thinking."[2]
Fantasy was increasingly seen as unreal and escapist.

A new type of literary criticism, stemming from I.A.
Richards at Cambridge University, was heavily dependent
on recent psychological approaches. Richards reformed
the ways of assessing literature, particularly in *Principles
of Literary Criticism* (1924) and *Practical Criticism: A Study of
Literary Judgment* (1929). He was not impressed with traditional
approaches to the study of literature: "A few conjectures, a
supply of admonitions, many acute isolated observations,
some brilliant guesses, much oratory and applied poetry,
inexhaustible confusion, a sufficiency of dogma, no small
stock of prejudices, whimsies and crotchets, a perfusion
of mysticism, a little genuine speculation, sundry stray
inspirations, pregnant hints and random *aperçus*; of such as
these, it may be said without exaggeration, is extant critical
theory composed."[3]

Richards was influenced by a materialist approach to the
human mind. He in effect adapted new trends in philosophy
to literary criticism, which saw goodness, beauty, and love as
being projected onto the material world of nature (that is, the
"real" world) from human inner states. Values in literature, he
believed, are actually a capacity to satisfy, shape, and improve
the feelings and desires of readers. Literature helps readers
find balance in their conflicting emotions, leading to wholeness
and inner harmony. In this view of literature, literary meaning
was more evident and heightened in poetry than in prose. The
meaning of a poem would become clear from a close reading
of the text itself that was practical and rigorous, rather than
by relying on outside factors such as knowledge of the poem's
social context or of its author.[4] The meaning of literature is
subjective and a matter of the emotions and the psychology

of the reader, rather than about a knowledge of the world. His emphasis was on the reader's response to the literary work. Richards did, however, stimulate a more precise debate about how a work of literature creates meaning than had been common. The study of literature under the influence of this new criticism tended to be confined to poetry and fiction, excluding non-fiction such as biography, diaries, letters, and well-crafted works of philosophy, theology, history, and other disciplines.

In his autobiography, *Surprised by Joy*, Lewis cited the influence of Freudian psychology, particularly, as one of the important reasons for his adopting what he called the intellectual "New Look". This was a view that liberated him, so he thought, and affirmed his secular views:

> There was to be no more pessimism, no more self-pity, no flirtations with any idea of the supernatural, no romantic delusions.... [G]ood sense meant, for me at that moment, a retreat, almost a panic-stricken flight, from all that sort of romanticism which had hitherto been the chief concern of my life.[5]

The "New Look", the Old Look, and Barfield's Anthroposophy

To his astonishment and dismay, Lewis found his great friend Owen Barfield taking exactly the opposite direction from him. Barfield, the secular child of a secular home, was now espousing the Old Look. As far back as 1922 a "Great War" had begun (to give it Lewis's name, borrowed from the recent conflict) between Barfield and him. It didn't in any way threaten their friendship. Indeed, later Barfield was to dedicate his book *Poetic Diction* to Lewis, followed by the aphorism "Opposition is true friendship". The "war" was carried on by letter and sometimes when Barfield and Lewis were together, and often operated on a highly philosophical level. Both drew widely upon their formidable knowledge.

The friendly but sometimes fierce dispute began soon after Barfield's acceptance in the early 1920s of anthroposophy, a "spiritual science" based on a synthesis of theosophy and Christian thought, pioneered by Rudolf Steiner (1861–1925). Steiner applied "spiritual" research based on his background in mathematics and science to his own experiences, which transcended usual perception. Their mutual friend Cecil Harwood also became enraptured of Steiner's views, and soon became an important figure in the anthroposophical movement. According to John Carey, Steiner's "ideas have had a lasting impact on many areas of life, including education, alternative medicine, organic agriculture, art and architecture".[6]

Not long after Barfield abandoned his secular views, he married a professional dancer called Maud Douie, who was some years older. This was soon after his graduation. They had met through their mutual interest in dance, in which Barfield was also accomplished. Barfield was for a large part of the twenties a freelance writer, and he and Maud lived for a time in the Buckinghamshire village of Long Crendon, not far from Oxford. They would sometimes visit Lewis and Mrs Moore, whom they liked very much.

Maud was a devout Christian, and became increasingly unhappy with some strange and esoteric elements she discovered in Steiner's teaching, such as a belief in reincarnation. This was despite its claim to be Christian and its stress upon Jesus Christ's historical incarnation in first-century Palestine. In fact, the atheist Lewis and she became allies against anthroposophy, which was an element of conflict in the "Great War" between Lewis and Barfield. On one occasion, in the diary he kept at that time, Lewis reported a "heart to hearter" that Maud had with Mrs Moore during a visit to "Hillsboro" in Western Road, Headington, the house Lewis shared with "the family". Mrs Moore at this time had not given up her Christian faith.

Lewis noted that, according to Janie Moore, Maud Barfield "'hates, hates, hates' Barfield's anthroposophy, and says he ought to have told her before they were married: [which] sounds ominous. She once burnt a 'blasphemous' anthroposophical pamphlet of his, [which] seems to me an unpardonable thing to do. But I think (and so does [Mrs Moore]) that they really get on [very] well, better than the majority of married people. Mrs Barfield is always glad when Barfield comes to see me because I have 'none of those views'." In fact, Barfield's anthroposophical beliefs created a good deal of tension in the marriage, much to his sorrow.

"Chronological snobbery"

Barfield's arguments in their incessant "Great War" began to erode Lewis's espousal of the "New Look". Under his influence, Lewis saw that a dominant myth of his time was that of progress. Change in itself had a supreme value in the modern world. Until meeting Barfield he had been seduced by this myth, intellectually at least. This is at the heart of why he had adopted the "New Look". He came to see, however, that the "New Look" had the effect of blinding us to the past. One important consequence is that we lose any perspective upon what is good and what is bad in our own time. He explained in *Surprised by Joy*, "Barfield… made short work of what I have called my 'chronological snobbery,' the uncritical acceptance of the intellectual climate common to our age and the assumption that whatever has gone out of date is on that account discredited."[7]

Going out of date, Lewis was forced by Barfield's arguments to concede, might well have nothing to do with something's truth or falsity. From this insight Lewis came to see that his own times, and the "New Look", belonged as much to a period that might itself pass as any previous age. More importantly, like any period it was beset with illusions and assumptions that carried the flavour of its time. Whichever period one lived in, its particular illusions were so familiar and so much part of the age that they were almost hidden in the broadly held assumptions of the time. It was hence considered unthinkable to attack them and unnecessary to defend them.

The "war" with Barfield not only refuted his chronological snobbery; it also convinced him that his materialism, if true, in fact made knowledge impossible! It was self-refuting – a view strengthened by his reading of Arthur Balfour's *Theism and Humanism* in 1924, though he resisted Balfour's Christian conclusions at the time. Barfield light-heartedly said, after their "war" was over, that Lewis had taught him *how* to think. But he had taught Lewis *what* to think. Lewis, it is clear, passed on to him skills in logical reasoning that he had learned in the school of hard knocks from the "Great Knock", W.T. Kirkpatrick. In hindsight, we can see that one of Barfield's biggest contributions to their mutual learning was to help Lewis to become the Christian apologist of the future, lucidly combining imagination and reason. Thinking back over the long years of their "Great War", Barfield said that this had been a "slow business".

In one central area of his thinking, Barfield failed in his battle to change the attitude of his materialist friend. Barfield believed that there has been an evolution of human consciousness, in which the imagination has played an integral role. Lewis never was to accept such "evolution", seeing it as imposing a pattern on history that no human being, or even the human race as a whole, was big enough to see. (He called such an attempt "historicism".) This development of human consciousness is captured in changes in both language and perception. There was originally a unity of consciousness, which over the ages has become fragmented; Barfield believed, however, that in future humans would achieve a greater and richer consciousness, in which spirit and nature will be reconciled.

Barfield's concept of an original unity to human consciousness greatly appealed to Lewis, despite his scepticism about any evolutionary history of language. It also had a great impact on Tolkien's thinking and fiction.[8] Barfield's genius lay in transforming his remarkable insights about the origins of language into an understanding of poetic language itself. Lewis also grew to accept that there are changes to human consciousness at different times, though, for him, it couldn't be said to be an evolution. Barfield's groundbreaking insights were embodied in his *Poetic Diction*, which concerns the nature of poetic language and a theory of how words originally embodied an ancient, unified perception. *Poetic Diction* offers a view of how human knowledge is attained, in which poetry plays a central role. Barfield's belief is perhaps summarized in his claim that "the individual imagination is the medium of all knowledge from perception upward". For him, the making of poetry is an expression of individual human freedom. It is a grave mistake, he believed, to reduce knowledge to power, which leads to an insatiable human desire to control. Rather than controlling, knowledge is meant to participate "in what is".

One of Barfield's most interesting ideas in *Poetic Diction* is that properly employed, imagination is concrete rather than abstract thinking. Following Samuel Taylor Coleridge, Barfield sees imagination as "the perception of resemblance, the demand for unity". His conclusion – which became one of Lewis's central beliefs – is that all meaningful language is at least partly poetic.[9] With this statement, Barfield was refuting the increasingly popular view that scientific discourse is the only means of true knowledge. He would take this further and say that scientific discourse has an imaginative element, employing metaphors and models. Without this element, it would become meaningless.

Original participation

Barfield's idea of "original participation" was one of his most important insights, and it came into increasing focus over the years of the "Great War" with his friend. Both Lewis and later Tolkien became deeply attracted by the idea. In his thinking, as we have seen, Barfield had a vision of an ancient unity, by definition embodied in both perception and language, a unity we have lost. The key to this vision was a sense of what he called "original participation", a sense we can glimpse at times through dreams, poetry, and myth. He believed that this primitive awareness was "pre-logical" and "pre-mythical".[10]

He explained that human beings, in their primitive state, feel themselves to be "a functioning member of the natural world, as a finger is a member of the physical body".[11] Barfield believed that in ancient times, thinking was not detached from participation in the world. In his carefully argued view, the way people experienced reality as a seamless whole was embodied at that time in their language. In a way, their thought was completely poetic in the sense of being non-abstract and figurative. It was, Barfield notes in *Poetic Diction*, "a kind of thinking which is at the same time perceiving – a picture-thinking, a figurative, or imaginative, consciousness, which we can only grasp today by true analogy with the imagery of our poets, and, to some extent, with our own dreams".[12]

In his science-fiction story *That Hideous Strength*, Lewis was to show how animal consciousness might present just a hint of this original human participation. He does this in his affectionate portrayal of Mr Bultitude, the bear in the story. The bear was based on an animal that was a favourite of his and of his brother, Warnie, at Whipsnade Zoo:

Mr. Bultitude's mind was as furry and as unhuman in shape as his body.… Indeed he did not know that he existed at all: everything that is represented by the words *I* and *Me* and *Thou* was absent from his mind. When Mrs. Maggs gave him a tin of golden syrup, as she did every Sunday morning, he did not recognize either a giver or a recipient. Goodness occurred and he tasted it. And that was all.… There was no prose in his life. The appetencies which a human mind might disdain as cupboard loves were *for* him quivering and ecstatic aspirations which absorbed his whole being, infinite yearnings, stabbed with the threat of tragedy and shot through with the colours of Paradise.… Sometimes there returns to us from infancy the memory of a nameless delight or terror, unattached to any delightful or dreadful thing, a potent adjective floating in a nounless void, a pure quality.

A somewhat similar, but higher, type of consciousness is brilliantly captured in Neanderthal prehumans in William Golding's novel *The Inheritors*. Though not as advanced as the unitary consciousness of early humans, as understood by Barfield, prehuman consciousness, as portrayed by Golding, gives an inkling of it. The Neanderthals in the story imagine, rather than use abstract thought, in their musings. Lok reaches a stretch of water, but is confused because the old tree trunk he had expected to use for a bridge wasn't there:

He shut his eyes and frowned at the picture of the log. It had lain in the water from this side to that, grey and rotting. When you trod the centre you could feel the water that washed beneath you, horrible water, as deep in places as a man's shoulder. The water was not awake like the river or the fall but asleep, spreading there to the river and waking up… So sure was he of this log the people always used that he opened his eyes again, beginning to smile as if he were waking out of a dream; but the log was gone.[13]

Is it a coincidence that Golding taught for a while at a Steiner School, Michael Hall in Streatham, London, along with Cecil Harwood, the mutual friend of Lewis and Barfield, where he would have become more familiar with anthroposophy, which was the foundation of many of Barfield's ideas? As an undergraduate, Golding had been introduced to Steiner's thinking by Adam Bittleston, a fellow student who became a lifelong friend. In a review of an essay collection by Rudolf Steiner, Golding appreciated Steiner's quest to find a bridge between the world of the spirit and the physical sciences, writing: "Most of us have an unexpressed faith that the bridge exists." According to his biographer, John Carey, although Golding rejected Steiner's views, the ideas of his friend Bittleston "left a permanent trace on Golding's beliefs".[14]

Though C.S. Lewis remained opposed to Rudolf Steiner's anthroposophy after he called off the "Great War" between himself and Barfield around the time of his conversion to Christianity in 1931, the influence of his friend is clear in his ideas and writings. Lewis was to make no secret of his debt to his friend. Tolkien was also deeply influenced by Barfield after he and Lewis met and became friends later in the 1920s, which led to Tolkien getting to know Barfield and his work.

J.R.R. Tolkien

Tolkien's acquaintanceship with Nevill Coghill and Hugo Dyson may have been only slight at the time when he read his story "The Fall of Gondolin" to the Exeter College Essay Club in 1920. There's a chance that they might have seen him around central Oxford, as he walked to and from his place of work – the former site of the Ashmolean Museum, next to the landmark Sheldonian Theatre. Here he spent his time, as we have seen, working on the *New English Dictionary* and doing some tutoring for the university.

All this changed when he took up the challenging post of Reader in English Literature at Leeds University, about 170 miles north of Oxford. It would be some years before he returned to Oxford and eventually joined C.S. Lewis's circle of friends that became the Inklings.

John Ronald Reuel Tolkien was born on 3 January 1892 in Bloemfontein, South Africa, where his father was establishing a career in banking. His parents were Arthur Reuel and Mabel Tolkien (née Suffield) from Birmingham, England. At the time of his father's unexpected death in 1896, Ronald Tolkien and his brother, Hilary, were in England with their mother, staying with relations while trying to improve Ronald's health in a more suitable climate. They remained there and occupied a rented house in Sarehole, Warwickshire, outside Birmingham. In Sarehole there was an old mill with a stark, towering chimney. It had been at the cutting edge of the industrial revolution, powered by a steam engine, and a stream still ran under its giant wheel. The mill was an iconic memory of childhood for both boys, and lived on in their imaginations. In *The Lord of the Rings*, Hobbiton has a mill, by deep water, which was replaced by a new brick building, which despoiled the countryside.

In his letters Tolkien fondly remembered his mother as "a gifted lady of great beauty and wit, greatly stricken by God with grief and suffering, who died in youth (at thirty-four) of a disease hastened by persecution of her faith". It was true that her Free-Church family was opposed to her conversion to Roman Catholicism, which took place in 1900. Tolkien wrote that it was to his mother, who taught him in the years before his formal education, "that I owe my tastes for philology, especially of Germanic languages, and for romance". The boys' education eventually required that the family move into the nearby city.

Father Francis Xavier Morgan was a Roman Catholic priest serving in the Birmingham Oratory, founded by John Henry Newman. He gave friendship and counsel to the single-parent family. Half Spanish, Father Morgan was an extrovert whose enthusiasm helped them. When Mabel Tolkien fell victim to then incurable diabetes, Father Morgan helped to move them to Rednal, in the countryside near the Oratory retreat, and for the boys to stay with relatives for part of the summer of 1904.

It was for the family a little like being back in Sarehole. Mabel Tolkien died there later that year, and Father Morgan was left with the guardianship of the boys. He helped them financially, found them lodgings in Edgbaston, Birmingham, close to the Oratory, and took them on seaside holidays.

In 1908 Father Morgan found better lodgings for the orphaned brothers on Duchess Road in Birmingham. Here Tolkien fell in love with another lodger, Edith Bratt. Although older than he was, she was attractive, small, and trim, her grey eyes bewitching. Father Morgan (like King Thingol in Tolkien's tale of Beren and Lúthien) disapproved of their love. He was fearful that Tolkien would be distracted from his studies, and ordered the boy not to see Edith until he was twenty-one. It meant a long separation, but Tolkien was loyal to his benefactor, the only father he had really known. When Tolkien nervously wrote of their eventual engagement, Father Morgan accepted it without a fuss. The two were formally engaged when Tolkien was twenty-two, after Edith was received into the Roman Catholic Church.

While Tolkien was a schoolboy at King Edward's School, he had formed a club with several friends, the core members along with him being G.B. Smith, R.Q. "Rob" Gilson, and Christopher Wiseman. Only Wiseman and Tolkien survived the First World War. The group was called the Tea Club (TC) at first, and then later the Barrovian Society (BS), the last because the tea room in Barrow's Stores on Corporation Street in Birmingham became a favourite place to meet. A combination of Tea Club and Barrovian Society gave rise to the final name of the club – the T.C.B.S.

Gilson was the son of the head teacher at King Edward's School, and G.B. Smith, a gifted poet, was another close friend, who commented on some of Tolkien's early poems, including

his original verses about Eärendil (then written "Earendel").
Rob Gilson was killed on the first day of the Battle of the
Somme on 1 July 1916, while Smith received wounds that
proved fatal late that autumn, just after the battle ended. He
wrote to Tolkien some months before his death, speaking of
how the T.C.B.S. – the "immortal four", as he called them –
would live on, even if he died that night. His letter concluded:
"May God bless you, my dear John Ronald, and may you say
the things I have tried to say long after I am not there to say
them, if such be my lot." Shortly before Smith's death, Tolkien
was sent back to England to recover from trench fever. His
experiences at the Somme had a deep and lasting impact on
him, sharpened by the grief of losing two of his closest friends.
Constant recurrences of his condition meant that Tolkien was
never deemed fit enough to return to the battlefield.

Wiseman discovered that he had much in common with
the Roman Catholic Tolkien (although he was a staunch
Methodist). They shared an interest in Latin and Greek,
and rugby football, and loved their frequent conversations.
Wiseman found a ready listener to his discoveries about
Egyptian hieroglyphics, and, in his turn, Tolkien could
naturally share his experiments in inventing languages.
Tolkien and Wiseman continued to meet after the latter
entered Cambridge University. Wiseman served in the Royal
Navy during the First World War and later became head of
Queen's College, a private school in Taunton. Although the
two men did not meet frequently, their friendship was never
entirely forgotten.

Tolkien's friends enjoyed his interest in Norse sagas and
medieval English literature. After leaving school, the four
continued to meet occasionally, and to write to each other,
until the war destroyed their association. Tolkien never forgot

the T.C.B.S. He immortalized them in his idea of "fellowship", as in the fellowship enjoyed by the Company of the Ring. His later friendship with C.S. Lewis and then the Inklings was to help to satisfy this important side of his nature.

After graduating from Exeter College, Oxford in 1915, Tolkien married Edith in 1916. It was during his convalescence from trench fever, while he was still on limited military service, that he began working on what became the body of work collectively called *The Silmarillion*, writing "The Fall of Gondolin" in 1917.[15] Most of the compendium of legends comprising *The Silmarillion* was already written, in its earliest form, by around 1930. This was long before the publication of *The Hobbit*, which almost accidentally grew out of the developing body of legends, which in turn led to the far later publication of the *The Lord of the Rings*.

In a letter written many years later, Tolkien outlined to an interested publisher the relationship between his life and his imaginary world. He emphasized that the origin of his fiction was in language. Like many children he made up languages, he explained, but he never stopped doing so: "As a professional philologist (especially interested in linguistic aesthetics), I have changed in taste, improved in theory, and probably in craft. Behind my stories is now a nexus of languages (mostly only structurally sketched)." Most of the names in his stories, he pointed out, come from these invented languages. "This gives them a certain character (a cohesion, a consistency of linguistic style, and an illusion of historicity) to the nomenclature."

Thus Tolkien's lifelong interest in, and study and teaching of, languages was the source of his imaginative creations, and the roots of his profession were in his early imagination. Just as science-fiction writers generally make use of plausible technological inventions and possibilities, Tolkien used his deep and expert knowledge of language in his fiction. He created in his youth two forms of the Elvish tongue, inspired by his discovery of Welsh and Finnish, starting a process that led to the creation of a history and a geography to surround these languages, and peoples to speak them (and other tongues). He explains: "I had to posit a basic and phonetic structure of Primitive Elvish, and then modify this by a series of changes (such as actually do occur in known languages) so that the two end results would have a consistent structure and character, but be quite different." In a letter to W.H. Auden, Tolkien said that for as long as he could remember he had had a "sensibility to linguistic pattern which affects me emotionally like colour or music".

Equally important as language in Tolkien's complicated make-up was a love for myth and for fairy story, particularly, he says in his letters, for "heroic legend on the brink of fairy-tale and history". He revealed that he was an undergraduate before "thought and experience" made it clear to him that story and language were "integrally related". His imaginative and scientific interests were not at opposite poles. Myth and fairy story, he saw, must contain moral and religious truth, but implicitly, not explicitly or allegorically.

Both in his linguistic and in his imaginative interests, he was constantly seeking "material, things of a certain tone and air". Myths, fairy stories, and ancient words constantly inspired and sustained the unfolding creations of his mind and imagination – his Elven languages and the early seeds of *The Silmarillion*. The tone and quality that he sought he identified with northern and western Europe, particularly England. He tried to capture this elusive quality in his fiction and invented languages.

The stories he invented in his youth – such as "The Fall of Gondolin" – came to him as discoveries, rather than as something that he had created. The unfinished nature of the material is most apparent in several independent tales in *The Silmarillion*, such as "Beren and Lúthien the Elfmaiden", "Túrin Turambar", and "Of Tuor and the Fall of Gondolin". These in the published "Silmarillion" are in fact summaries of tales intended to be on a larger, more detailed scale, but which were never completed. The condensed, summary nature of much of the published "Silmarillion" would present difficulties for many readers.

The ideas and structure of *The Silmarillion* evolved throughout Tolkien's adulthood. The story chronicles the ancient days of the First Age of Middle-earth and before. It begins with the creation of the Two Lamps and concludes with the great battle in which Morgoth is overthrown. The unifying thread of the annals and tales of *The Silmarillion* is, as its name suggests, the fate of the Silmarils, the precious gems that contained light from the earliest days.

The seeds of *The Silmarillion* and Tolkien's other fantasies lay therefore in his childhood, his schooldays, and his undergraduate fascination with language. As a schoolboy, he was delighted to acquire a second-hand copy of Joseph Wright's *A Primer of the Gothic Language* (1892). As a student at Oxford, he chose Comparative Philology as his special subject, so he had Wright as a lecturer and tutor. Wright had compiled a massive English dialect dictionary. He communicated to Tolkien his love for philology and was a demanding teacher and a formative influence on his life.

It was at Leeds University, however, not Oxford, that Tolkien began his distinguished career as a university teacher in 1921. His *A Middle English Vocabulary* was published the following year. E.V. Gordon, a Canadian who had been a Rhodes Scholar at Oxford, was appointed soon after Tolkien to teach in the English Department at Leeds. The two men became firm friends and were soon working together on a new edition of *Sir Gawain and the Green Knight* (1925). For Tolkien, this poem was the high point of medieval romance in the medieval English he loved. Their edition also included a substantial glossary.

During the intensely productive Leeds period, Tolkien composed his own translations of Middle English and Old English texts. These translations were done at various periods: he was working on putting *Sir Gawain and the Green Knight* into modern English in 1923. He then began translating *Beowulf* around 1924 in verse, completing a prose version, it seems, by the spring of 1926, and he may have translated *Pearl* in 1925 or 1926. Both *Sir Gawain and the Green Knight* and *Pearl* are thought to be by the same unknown author from the West Midlands, an area of England with which Tolkien identified and upon which he based the Shire.

These translations were not published for many years. In 1975, two years after his death, *Sir Gawain and the Green Knight*, *Pearl*, and *Sir Orfeo* were published. In 2014, over forty years after his death, his complete prose translation of the great Old English poem *Beowulf* appeared – a poem that had helped to inspire much of his fiction.

While the Tolkien family were living in Leeds, Tolkien started to tell them stories. John had been born in 1917, Michael in 1920, and Christopher in 1924.[16] His first children's book, *Roverandom* (not published until 1998), came from a story he told, inspired by Michael's loss of a toy dog on a seaside family holiday at Filey, Yorkshire.

When Tolkien moved back to Oxford in October 1925

to become Rawlinson and Bosworth Professor of Anglo-Saxon, he had established the direction of the remainder of his life as a scholar and storyteller, though his fiction, with its underpinning mythology, was then only a private "hobby", as he called it. He had, however, published some poetry, and still carried the ambition from the T.C.B.S. days to be a great poet.

Aspiring poets

Owen Barfield had started writing poetry while at Highgate School, but his reading of poetry intensified during the final part of his military service. As we saw, his growing awareness of the effect on him of poetry, even a phrase or word, led to his exploration of human consciousness. He shared his poems with C.S. Lewis, and continued to write poetry, including poetic drama, for the rest of his life. He also wrote short stories (some of which were published at the time), as well as novellas and novels. A major, and ambitious, novel, *English People*, was begun late in the 1920s but never published. According to Barfield's biographer, it has a strong personal thread, imaginatively depicting his spiritual formation. An influential Austrian seer in the novel is transparently based on Rudolf Steiner. C.S. Lewis was an enthusiastic but critical reader of *English People*.[17]

His ambition to write as a profession led Barfield to undertake various freelance tasks. At one time, he wrote regularly for the weekly periodical *Truth*. He also contributed to the *New Statesman* and *The London Mercury*. In 1926, his study *History in English Words* appeared. The dazzling array of his writings at that time boded well for a future as a successful writer, but he felt isolated from the fashionable literary coteries of the period, such as the Bloomsbury Group. Also, times were getting increasingly harder financially.

Barfield's first love was undoubtedly poetry, yet he was the first of the future Inklings to publish fiction. This was an accomplished children's story called *The Silver Trumpet*, brought out by Faber and Gwyer in 1925. It tells the tale of Violetta and Gambetta, twin princesses who have a spell cast over them that makes them love each other even though they constantly disagree about almost everything. A visiting prince, who has a silver trumpet, seeks the hand of a princess, and falls in love with the sweet-tempered Violetta. A servant of the king, a dwarf called the Little Fat Podger, has an emphatic presence in the story. The sound of the trumpet affects all that hear it, and Princess Violetta dreams that she is afloat near the bottom of the sea. In an interview, Barfield described the silver trumpet as a "symbol of the feeling element in life".[18] Some years after its publication C.S. Lewis lent his copy of the story to Tolkien, and it was a great hit in his household.

At this time, Barfield was working on his B.Litt thesis and its subsequent development into what would become *Poetic Diction*.[19] C.S. Lewis, meanwhile, was composing a long narrative poem called *Dymer*, which reflected the impact of the "New Look", and Freudian psychology in particular. Barfield very much liked the work in progress and encouraged his friend to persevere. Lewis also received encouragement and constructive criticism from Nevill Coghill, who was appointed as a fellow in English at his alma mater, Exeter College, after a brief spell away teaching at the Royal Naval College in Dartmouth. Lewis was determined to become established as a poet. Warnie, probably more than anyone else, was later to consider the overall course of his brother's life. With his usual insight, he pointed out:

The remarkable thing about his literary career is that it never occurred to him until a relatively late date that his great achievement would be in prose. *Spirits in Bondage* appeared in 1919, a collection of poems, some of them written in his Bookham days: *Dymer*, a narrative poem, would be published in 1926, the fruit of much pain and effort during a peculiarly difficult period. During all these early years, he thought of himself (though with no great confidence) as essentially a poet.[20]

Dymer gives a sharp insight into the intellectual wasteland in which Lewis lived before he slowly, almost imperceptibly, crept back to Christian belief. The New Look, spawned in the post-war twenties, created an aversion to the climate of romanticism that had been prevalent before the First World War. This wariness was reinforced by memories of the war. Lewis and his friends never adopted such fashionable disillusionment, but this 1920s distrust did, however, lead him to scrutinize and write about the whole basis of romanticism and literary fantasy. Lewis's intellectual searching takes on great significance in the light of the fact that fantasy and the elements of romance in literature were at the heart of both the conversations and the distinctive writings of the Inklings.

A leading commentator on Lewis's poetry, Don W. King, is quite right, I think, in considering *Dymer* Lewis's most important poem. It is a neglected achievement of Lewis's. He put enormous time and effort into its writing, in his desire to be a significant poet. In deliberately writing a narrative poem, he was following the example of poets that he loved, such as Edmund Spenser, John Milton, Shelley, and Wordsworth. When studying under Kirkpatrick, he had tried writing prose versions of the story. The poetic version was begun while

Lewis was an undergraduate, and took him three years to write. Lewis's biographer and friend, George Sayer, wrote that "the main subject of *Dymer* ... is without doubt the temptation of fantasies – fantasies of love, lust, and power".[21]

The tenor of Lewis's poem is avowedly anti-totalitarian. In it, a man, Dymer, abandons himself to a mysterious and passionate girl and brings a monster into the world. In a Freudian twist, the monster murders its father, who transforms into a god. Owen Barfield points out: "It is a myth in which the hero is slain by an unnatural monster of his own begetting and rises again in purity after the fateful encounter."[22] Dymer is the flawed hero of the poem, who escapes from a "perfect city", where he was fed on rations and "on scientific food". This regimented city was modelled, Lewis tells us, on Plato's *Republic*. "I put into it my hatred of my public school and my recent hatred of the army," said Lewis, describing himself as being "by temperament, an extreme anarchist".[23]

Dymer escapes what he thinks is illusion into the wilds of the countryside and then the forest, where he encounters a magical castle and, in a dark boudoir, the woman he makes love with but whose face he does not see. Later, he finds a mortally wounded man from the "perfect city", who recounts scenes of battle and horror clearly reminiscent of what Lewis had experienced in the war. It turns out that anarchy had come to the city. To Dymer's increasing horror, he learns from the man that the rebellion was carried out in his name. In his Preface to a new edition of the poem in 1950, Lewis tells us that in his mind at that time were the turmoils of the Russian Revolution, the Easter Rising, and other conflicts in his divided home country of Ireland.

As well as being anti-totalitarian, the poem implicitly includes Christianity among the desirable illusions that must be ruthlessly overthrown in one's life. The rottenness at the heart of Christianity, it implies, is its erroneous supernaturalism:

Old Theomagia, Demonology,
Cabbala, Chemic Magic, Book of the Dead,
Damning Hermetic rolls that none may see
Save the already damned – such grubs are bred
From minds that lose the Spirit and seek instead
For spirits in the dust of dead men's error,
Buying the joys of dream with dreamland terror.

When Lewis showed drafts of *Dymer* to Barfield and Nevill Coghill (a precursor of the future Inklings), they had both admired it. Coghill later helped Lewis to find a publisher, according to Lewis's biographer, A.N. Wilson. In contrast, even though there were good reviews the poem failed to make much impact on the public, to the disappointment of its author. Narrative poetry was out of fashion, despite Lewis's efforts on behalf of the genre. After Lewis had become well known, the poem was reissued (as we have seen, in 1950, with an explanatory Preface by its author). In 1969 it was republished in a collection of Lewis's narrative poems, and has been in print ever since, awaiting recognition as one of his important works.

Well before Lewis had finished the long task of writing *Dymer*, his simple materialism had finally been abandoned, just as Dymer, in an entirely opposite direction, had rejected illusions of romantic fantasy. Lewis knew, in the mid-1920s, that he had entered difficult waters. His intellectual development at this time was highly complex, but, nevertheless, he had embraced a popular form of idealism as completely as Dymer accepted the fervent embraces of his shadow bride. He had come to see prime reality as an Absolute Spirit. Previously, he had very reluctantly viewed the material world – the world of measurable quantities rather than tantalizing and illusive qualities – as the source of all that is real. We get a hint of this acceptance of a universe of Absolute Spirit in the stanza quoted above. Lewis refers to losing "the Spirit" in a fruitless quest for "spirits in the dust of dead men's error". He was still a long way from believing in theism (believing in a rational, personal being behind, and responsible for, a physical universe). Looking back to that period long afterwards, he however concluded: "Idealism turned out, when you took it seriously, to be disguised Theism."[24]

Lewis's frequent and lengthy discussions with Owen Barfield were behind his abandonment of materialism and, some years later, his renunciation of atheism. When Lewis later got to know Tolkien, he became influenced in the same direction by him, taking him a further step towards Christian belief.

As for Barfield, he eventually came to the decision to move to London and help in his father's law firm. It seems to be after this move that the "Great War" between him and Lewis largely took the form of exchanges of letters. Barfield would continue to visit Lewis in Oxford, however, and Lewis Barfield in London. It was an easily matter to travel between the cities by train, a distance of only sixty miles.

CHAPTER 4

J.R.R. Tolkien returns to Oxford and C.S. Lewis meets God

A thick-set young man of medium height, in his late twenties but wearing older-fashion flannels and a tweed jacket, walked briskly from the Magdalen quad across the large lawns to the New Building. He quickly found Staircase 3 and ascended the old stairs to midway up the three-floor building. There he entered Room 3. It was early October 1925, just before the beginning of the Michaelmas term.

The rooms that he had been given pleased C.S. Lewis enormously. He could see immediately that some furniture and decoration were needed. The views from the windows made him stop and stare. His larger sitting room faced north. Its windows looked out over parkland; no obvious clue revealed that he was, in fact, in a small city. He looked down on restful lawns, but his eyes were drawn to woodland a short walk away, where the trees still wore autumn red. Over the manicured turf a herd of deer grazed slowly and erratically. As he turned his head he could make out the start of a path he had grown to love, a path around the water meadow, known as Addison's Walk. A few quick steps took him to his smaller sitting room and bedroom at the front of the building, which provided a view southwards, across to the older buildings of the college he had just left, with Magdalen's tower looming beyond it.

Lewis anticipated with pleasure staying overnight on weekdays in term time, rather than with Mrs Moore and Maureen in Headington. He also knew that tutorials would be held here for his pupils, usually one to one. His friends could also be entertained here, preferably after dining in the college's Senior Common Room. What he could not then anticipate was that his room would within a few years become a frequent meeting place for a particular group of his friends: the Inklings. We can imagine him sitting down on the comfortable chesterfield, his eyes moving over the simple furnishings, including the white-panelled walls. Near the chesterfield was a very welcome fire grate.

After much anxiety over the future, and several failed attempts at finding a permanent teaching post, Lewis had been offered employment as a fellow and tutor in English at Magdalen College earlier that year. The position ended years of financial uncertainty, during which he had helped to support Mrs Moore and Maureen in their rented accommodation. It also vindicated his decision as an undergraduate to take three degree courses, all of which he passed with first-class honours, and which formed an outstanding base for a career in the teaching of English.

At this time, J.R.R. Tolkien was the newly appointed Rawlinson and Bosworth Professor of Anglo-Saxon at Oxford University and a fellow of Pembroke College, on St Aldate's near the centre of the city. For a time, he had to juggle professorial duties at both Leeds University and Oxford until his successor at the former could begin work. He was still therefore spending much of his time in Leeds. It would not be until January 1926 that Tolkien was able to move his family to Oxford, where they took up residence in Northmoor Road, near Summertown. This was an easy cycle ride from Pembroke College. As a professor, Tolkien held the Chair of Anglo-Saxon – that is, Old English – and his more senior duties were quite different from Lewis's. Whereas both would lecture in the English School, Tolkien had fewer pupils, who were graduates rather than undergraduates, and they came to his home for tutorials and supervision rather than to his college. He was also required, in an informal way, to advance his specialist subject by his own research and publications.

The meeting of the two men would have huge implications for both of them, both personally and in their scholarship, but particularly in their storytelling. Up to this point both had published poetry, Lewis much more so than Tolkien. Neither had published prose fiction. Tolkien already had built up a small but impressive offering of specialist publications in his subject. Lewis was working on a study of allegory and medieval courtly love, which would one day be published as *The Allegory of Love*, the work that would enrapture Charles Williams and lead to his friendship with Lewis. Williams had already written *Outlines of Romantic Theology* in 1924, which revealed how human romantic love helps us to grasp the divine nature. It was not published until 1990, but its ideas were already inherent in Williams's writing and would shape future books such as the novel *The Place of the Lion*.

C.S. Lewis's long narrative poem *Dymer* was mentioned in the last chapter. It was complete as he started his teaching duties, and would be published in September 1926. For Tolkien's part, in his last summer in Leeds he began writing a version of the tale of Beren and Lúthien in accomplished verse, which he was never to complete.[1] He had already written an early prose version.[2] This tale is one of the defining and most significant stories of *The Silmarillion*. The Inklings, if they had been formed then, would have thought of it perhaps as a heroic romance, like the future *The Lord of the Rings*, but on a much smaller scale. A.N. Wilson commented: "Though at times the verse is technically imperfect, it is full of passages of quite stunning beauty; and the overall conception must make it, though unfinished, one of the most remarkable poems written in English in the twentieth century."[3]

The story of Beren and Lúthien is set in an early age of Middle-earth, thousands of years before the events that take place in *The Lord of the Rings*. It embodies many of Tolkien's great themes, such as romantic love, sacrifice, and the workings of providence. It has larger metaphysical themes too – the eventual union between Beren and Lúthien introduces a higher spiritual quality into human life, which has recurring beneficial consequences through Middle-earth's future history (Beren is a human, while Lúthien is Elven and, moreover, the daughter of an angelic being, Queen Melian). The theme of the marriage of an Elf with a human is continued with Aragorn and Arwen in *The Lord of the Rings*.

Through the darkest periods of Middle-earth's history, the story of Beren and Lúthien helped to preserve hope among all those resisting the powers of evil. The story celebrates the triumph of Beren and Lúthien, against all odds, over the formidable power of the Satanic Morgoth. This victory of the weak over the strong anticipates the destruction of the Ring of Power by the vulnerable and peace-loving Hobbits (or "halflings") Frodo and Sam in *The Lord of the Rings*.

At Oxford, Tolkien mostly taught Old English, Middle

English, and the history of the English language. In his first year of teaching, W.H. Auden arrived as a student, one of many distinguished poets and writers who would pass through the English School over the years. Through Tolkien, Auden became deeply interested in Old English literature and its northern European context. When *The Lord of the Rings* was published, Auden wrote encouraging reviews, but many critics failed to understand what kind of literature it was. Auden also greatly enjoyed *The Hobbit*.

Long afterwards, a lecturer at the Graduate School of the University of Toronto who had studied under Tolkien vividly remembered his lectures in those early days: "He came in lightly and gracefully, I always remember that, his gown flowing, his fair hair shining, and he read *Beowulf* aloud.... The terrors and the dangers that he recounted – how I do not know – made our hair stand on end. He read like no one else I have ever heard."[4]

Tolkien had a great power to perform poetry, but the main body of his lectures were to become notorious because of his sometimes mumbled and at times incoherent presentation. Occasionally, chalk in hand, he would turn to write something on the blackboard – perhaps a key word in Anglo-Saxon that he was explaining. Unfortunately he blocked the students' view as he wrote, and then rapidly wiped the board before it became visible again as he faced the class. The poet Philip Larkin was particularly outraged by Tolkien's lecturing style in later years.

At first, Tolkien's lectures were much more accessible than they sometimes later became. He had had a dramatic impact on the English School at Leeds University, swelling the numbers of students of the English language. J.I.M. Stewart, a lecturer, novelist, and famous crime writer (under the pseudonym

Michael Innes), was also a student of Tolkien's at Oxford, and his memory was: "He could turn a lecture room into a mead hall in which he was the bard and we were the feasting listening guests." Stewart was to immortalize Tolkien as a fictional Oxford Professor of Anglo-Saxon called Professor Timbermill, who annoyed his colleagues by writing a "long mad book – a kind of apocalyptic romance" called *The Magic Quest*.[5]

In contrast to Tolkien's sometimes poor lecturing, C.S. Lewis quickly gained a reputation that was to grow and grow as a lucid and excellent presenter who imparted knowledge in an inspiring way.[6] On 23 January 1926, he gave his first lecture in the Oxford English School on a series rather carefully called "Some Eighteenth-Century Precursors of the Romantic Movement". No one listening would have realized for a moment that he had had to prepare very much at the last minute. Lewis had expected to lecture on poetry from that period, which he knew very well. Shortly before the series was due to start, he found out that a senior colleague was going to lecture on the poets. He therefore had to select much less familiar prose writings that would illuminate his theme of anticipations of romanticism.

Lewis's lecturing style was developed very early on. He decided his students would be more engaged if he did not lecture from a script, but ad-libbed from outlines. As a result, he would often work from skeleton notes throughout his teaching in Oxford and later Cambridge, writing out only his chosen quotations. In fact, his remarkable, almost photographic memory meant that he could have recited the quotations without notes; the written quotes, it seems, served only to remind him of the flow of the lecture.

Much of his time was spent in morning tutorials. One of his earliest pupils was the future Poet Laureate John

Betjeman, who only occasionally came up with essays his tutor considered good. Lewis felt that he had a laid-back, lazy approach, and it irritated him. Near the end of that first year, Betjeman turned up at Lewis's rooms for his tutorial one morning wearing slippers. He explained that he had a blister, and hoped Lewis wouldn't mind his footwear. Seeing his evident self-satisfaction, Lewis couldn't help responding that he would very much mind wearing them himself, but didn't mind Betjeman wearing them. Later, Betjeman couldn't forgive Lewis for his own failure to obtain his degree, and aired his dislike in his poetry.[7]

Tolkien and Lewis meet

It was not until the Trinity (Summer) term of that first academic year of Oxford teaching that C.S. Lewis met Tolkien. They both attended an English Faculty "tea" on 11 May 1936. One of those present had taught Lewis as an undergraduate; this was Professor George Gordon, in whose discussion class he had first met Nevill Coghill. Others present were Revd Ronald Fletcher and Margaret Lee, both tutors, and Tolkien. He was, according to Lewis's first impression, "a smooth, pale, fluent little chap".

Lewis wanted to hear about his approach to English. Tolkien appeared to want to bring language and literature studies in the School together more. Afterwards Lewis sounded the professor out on some important issues. He wanted to know what Tolkien thought of Edmund Spenser, one of Lewis's favourite authors. Tolkien seemed to find him unreadable, because of the "forms" used in his poetry. Lewis found that his views on language and literature in the English School leaned towards the language side – that was "the real thing". "All literature," he felt, "is written for the amusement of *men* between thirty and forty." Lewis famously concluded his diary record of the meeting with Tolkien thus: "No harm in him: only needs a smack or so."

Lewis held no antipathy towards the opinionated new professor, who he would discover had a great love of literature, especially if it was more than five hundred years old. It was not long before they became friends, which was after Lewis responded in 1926 or 1927 to an invitation to attend a small society that Tolkien had set up. The Coalbiters (from the Old Norse *kolbitar*) were an informal reading club he initiated soon after beginning to lecture at Oxford. Their purpose was to learn to read and translate Old Norse or Icelandic literature such as the *Poetic Edda*. The name vividly pictured those who draw so close around the hot coals in the bitter winter that they seem to bite them. Attending meetings with Lewis was Nevill Coghill, now a research fellow at Exeter College. The society met in pubs, or in the house of one of the English dons, John Bryson.

Tolkien was the most skilled of the members in these ancient languages. Their variety was for him like the distinctive tastes of vintage wines. He could immediately render the northern texts into modern English, though in a carefully stylized form, to capture some of the tone of the originals. An example of his facility in translation can be found in his modern version of the Old Norse *The Legend of Sigurd and Gudrún*, derived from the poetry of Iceland and Norway.[8] Even though the others made much slower progress, they revelled in the northern stories.

The character of the group itself was different from that of the Inklings. Its members were all university academics, and the meetings were much less frequent – just fortnightly or three times a term, with a very narrow focus. The members were keen to improve their knowledge of old languages belonging to the family of ancient English. Lewis records on one occasion a meeting of the "Icelandics" going on until midnight. The seeds of the Inklings lay more in the fact that two of Lewis's circle of friends were Coalbiters, and it would be out of his larger, more diverse group of friends that the Inklings would distil. For many in the larger group, however, northern myths and legends were par for the course, even without an acquaintance with the old northern languages.

An important consequence of the Coalbiter meetings was that they deepened the friendship of Tolkien and Lewis. Before long they were meeting on their own. Sometimes, after a gathering of the Coalbiters or another of the numerous societies they attended, they convened in Lewis's college rooms to talk far into the night. In a letter to Arthur Greeves in October 1929, Lewis recorded that after an evening meeting at an unnamed society (not the Coalbiters), Tolkien came back with him to his college rooms and his bright fire and "sat discoursing of the gods & giants & Asgard for three hours, then departing in the wind & rain".[9]

The two fell into a regular pattern of meeting at Magdalen College on Monday mornings, when Lewis had no pupils to tutor. The increasingly frequent meetings between Tolkien and Lewis were one of the most important factors in the eventual formation of the Inklings. As their conversations ranged far and wide, and sometimes went beyond "the walls of the world", they gave an indication of what the heart of the Inklings would be. At its centre would be, at the very least, the narrative art of stories of romance – stories that had at least a hint of other worlds, and, behind that art, the essentially human, which transcended mere living.

Lord David Cecil, who would become an Inklings member during the Second World War, pointed to such a quality of transcendence as lacking in much poetry of the eighteenth century: "The descriptions of Nature... are exact, but *they are untouched by the light that never was on land or sea*, but which illuminates all great poetry.... Only when the heart of the poet is touched does his poem glow into real beauty, the sentiment gaining an added ring of pathos from the formal language in which it is expressed."[10]

Soon after they became friends, Lewis started to go to Tolkien's home. There Tolkien would read to him from his work in progress on *The Silmarillion*, including the verse version of the story of Beren and Lúthien. Lewis was given the unfinished poem to take away to read and was delighted by it, offering Tolkien detailed suggestions for improvement.

The conversations between the two friends were of great importance not only for the beginning of the Inklings, but also for their writings, and for Lewis's eventual conversion to the Christian faith, as we shall see.[11] They also had a huge impact on the way English was taught to undergraduates at Oxford.

Among other things, the two dons schemed to bring in a syllabus for the Oxford Honours English School that emphasized continuity with older English literature. Such a syllabus would be in opposition to the strong modernist lobby (see below). After Lewis's death, Dame Helen Gardner (soon to become Merton Professor of English Lanuage and Literature) wrote:

> Perhaps one of the most significant of [Lewis's]
> contributions to the study of English literature at Oxford
> was the part he played with his friend Professor J.R.R.

Tolkien in establishing a syllabus for the Final Honour School which embodied his belief in the value of medieval (especially Old English) literature, his conviction that a proper study of modern literature required the linguistic training that the study of earlier literature gave, and his sense of the continuity of English literature… the syllabus, which remained in force for over twenty years, was in many ways an admirable one.[12]

The Oxford English School was then in its infancy as a separate faculty. There were fundamental differences with its rival and also relatively new Cambridge English School, which was under the influence of the "new psychology" and I.A. Richards (see chapter 3). Cambridge's focus became practical criticism, rather than the broader approach that Lewis and, as he found, Tolkien favoured. They were drawing upon an older view of learning that went back to the earlier ages that he and Lewis loved. Lewis was attracted by the fact that Tolkien was much more than a linguist; he saw language in a broad context. All languages, Tolkien believed, embodied mythologies. With ancient languages, even a single word could yield its secrets to the diligent and attentive philologist.

For Tolkien, "[p]hilology is the foundation of humane letters". In his essay "The Oxford English School" (1930), he points out that in themselves, both literary and linguistic approaches are not adequate to respond properly to the artistry of written works. This was especially so when it came to early works. Philology should straddle language and literature studies, allowing a deeper response than either on its own. Tom Shippey points out that Tolkien saw works of literary art in a philological way, and his own fiction came out of such a vision. In this regard he was like the nineteenth-century German philologists Jacob and Wilhelm Grimm, who produced collections of fairy tales as well as learned scholarship, just as Tolkien's imaginative work sprang out of his philological study.

Tolkien, it appears, hoped to strengthen an attitude that seemed distinctive to Oxford that would make it seemly to be a writer of imaginative literature as well as a properly functioning don or professor. He wanted to restore at least something of Owen Barfield's view of a lost human consciousness that was whole rather than fragmented, a view that both he and Lewis had accepted by 1930 as a profoundly important insight. Whatever Tolkien's private and more public reasons, by three years or so after their first meeting Lewis would be thoroughly behind the changes Tolkien wanted to make to the Oxford Honours English School. These would bring language and literature more closely together, and, even more controversially, end the syllabus in effect with the Romantic Movement at around 1830.[13]

It appears to be much more than coincidence that 1830 was about the point that in C.S. Lewis's inaugural Cambridge lecture a quarter of a century into the future he said marked the "Great Divide". In Lewis's view this was when, as we saw, the age of the machine was ushered in, and Western civilization up to 1830 or so started to pass into being the "Old West". This was a cultural and social divide; the ideas that led to it, Lewis supposed, came from earlier years, perhaps around the time of the Renaissance or the Enlightenment.[14] Certainly, in the view of Lewis and Tolkien, this was the watershed after which the reader essentially belonged to the same world of assumptions and beliefs as the book's author. Therefore, they should not require the sort of help with understanding the text that teachers in the English School were best able to give. This was help with obscurities, guidance with shifts in word meanings, and aid in savouring the imaginative worlds of previous ages. The reformed syllabus essentially represents the "Old West" that both Tolkien and Lewis would champion more widely in their writings (Lewis in both non-fiction and fiction). The culture and worldview of this vast pre-1830 period would be a shared love within the generally premodern and "Old Western" Inklings – that is, most of the group as it existed in the 1930s and 1940s, at least. They would be dinosaurs together, to take up Lewis's later image. Furthermore, those among the Inklings who were Oxford English dons would have their views enshrined in the new syllabus, and knew that they had a fight on to retain their victory.

Tolkien's reformed syllabus was accepted by 1931, and was in place for many years, as Dame Helen Gardner pointed out. It still sets the tone of the English Honours syllabus at Oxford, even though that now encompasses all periods of English literature, just as Cambridge's still has an emphasis on practical criticism, albeit greatly modified from Richards's heavy psychological emphasis. Having in mind Tolkien's success in manoeuvring the change, Lewis at this time dubbed his friend "Lord of the strings".[15]

"The Cave"

There were a number in the Oxford English School who, not surprisingly, were unhappy with the new syllabus. To help to counteract their influence Tolkien and Lewis, with a number of their colleagues, formed a counter "junto" (or junta) – what they called "The Cave", an allusion to the Cave of Adullam in the biblical story of David and King Saul. This cave was the focus of David's resistance to the king.[16] The

Cave, which was formed in 1931 when the new syllabus came in, consisted of several of the larger group of Lewis's friends who would become members of the Inklings. These were, as well as Tolkien and Lewis, H.V.D. Dyson and Nevill Coghill. These four made up over half of the original Inklings group when it first formed, a couple of years or so later. Unlike the Inklings club, the Cave was made up entirely of Oxford academics, and only from the English School at that, and was focused on a narrow aim – the preservation of the new, hard-won syllabus, though they made a point of simply enjoying each other's company.

Probably the most reluctant convert in all England

Lewis's friendship with Tolkien proved crucial to his abandonment of atheism and conversion to Christianity. The conversations between the two reinforced Barfield's attacks on Lewis's materialism and the inadequacies and inconsistencies of his view of the imagination in making sense of reality. They also made him see the importance of Tolkien's approach, as a philologist on the language side of the English School, to literary studies. As Lewis remarked in *Surprised by Joy*: "Friendship with Tolkien… marked the breakdown of two old prejudices. At my first coming into the world I had been (implicitly) warned never to trust a Papist, and at my first coming into the English Faculty (explicitly) never to trust a philologist. Tolkien was both." Another who played an important part in Lewis's conversion was Hugo Dyson. Lewis said that he and Tolkien were the main human means of his acceptance of Christian belief.

After graduating in English in 1922, and completing a postgraduate B.Litt in 1924, Hugo Dyson became a lecturer and tutor at the Reading University, which at that time had an association with Oxford through Christ Church, one of the Oxford colleges. Dyson retained close links with his former university, including being an Oxford Extension Lecturer until 1945, when he became a fellow of Merton College. Reading is only twenty-six miles from Oxford, with a good railway connection that allowed Dyson to visit frequently. When Dyson was introduced to Lewis by his friend Nevill Coghill in 1930, this meant that Lewis had become acquainted with all those who would become the earliest members of the Inklings.

The previous year he had met another future member, the clergyman Adam Fox, with whom he shared many breakfast conversations at Magdalen College. Born in 1883, Fox was older even than Tolkien, and had graduated from Lewis's alma mater, University College, in 1906. Following a number of years as a schoolteacher, he was ordained into the Anglican Church. For health reasons, he was for a while a teacher at a diocesan college in Rondebosch, South Africa. When Lewis met him, he had returned to Oxford to take on the post of fellow and Dean of Divinity at Magdalen. This was at the point when Lewis had either abandoned his atheism or was close to doing so. One of his responsibilities as Dean was to hold "Dean's Prayers" at 8 a.m. in the beautiful college chapel. The self-effacing Fox was also a minor poet, a fact that was to involve the Inklings in controversy at a future date when they threw their weight behind a campaign to obtain for him the post of Oxford Professor of Poetry.

It would take a whole book to trace the twisting path of Lewis's route from a materialist view, through pantheism, to accepting a divine creator behind the universe, and then finally Christian belief – a conversion in which Barfield, Dyson, and Tolkien were all involved, either directly or indirectly.[17] A brief account can point at least to one of the key components of the Inklings – Christianity (the other main element, according to Lewis, being "a tendency to write"). Without the Christian conversions of Lewis and his brother, Warnie (shortly before Lewis's), the make-up and tone of the Inklings would have been very different, if the group as such had even come into being at all.

Lewis described becoming a theist in his autobiography; he acknowledged at last that Nature was not "the whole show": "In the Trinity Term of 1929 I gave in, and admitted that God was God, and knelt and prayed…" He later confessed that he didn't look for God. Rather, God was like the Hound of Heaven in Francis Thompson's famous poem. He pursued Lewis – and it was that intentional pursuit that bothered Lewis. It may have been before his acceptance of God, or at a critical stage later in his move towards Christianity, that Lewis wrote in mock alarm to Barfield (Alister McGrath argues the former, redating Lewis's move to theism as 1930 rather than 1929). Lewis's brother, Warnie, on the other hand, interprets the letter of alarm to Barfield as "one of the first clear indications of Jack's impending re-conversion to Christianity".[18] Whatever the stage in Lewis's transformation, alarming things were happening to him. He said, in the language of his philosophical concerns, that the "Spirit" or "Real I" was tending to become much more personal and, to his dismay, was taking the offensive. In fact, it was behaving just like God. He concluded: "You'd better come on Monday at the latest or I may have entered a monastery."

In *Surprised by Joy*, he widens Thompson's metaphor of the Divine Hound to a pack of hounds that were in close pursuit, hunting him down. He had been driven out of the tangled wood of pantheism and "Absolute Idealism" (the popular philosophy of the time he had espoused)[19] and was almost exhausted in open fields. Among the pack behind him, in company with figures from the past such as Plato, Dante, and George MacDonald, were his friends Barfield, Tolkien, and Dyson!

When Lewis describes his conversion to believing in some kind of God, he joins a cloud of religious mystics: "In the region of awe... in the deepest solitude there is a road right out of the self, a commerce with something which, by refusing to identify itself with any object of the senses, or anything whereof we might have biological or social need, or anything imagined, or any state of our own minds, proclaims itself sheerly objective.... the naked Other, imageless (though our imagination salutes it with a hundred images)."

Lewis claimed to have come to God through experience, rather than by reasoning alone.[20] That knowledge of God was tied up with a lived experience to which he gave the technical name of "Joy". This was an inconsolable longing or "Sweet Desire" that nothing in human experience, whether of nature or art or human love, could satisfy. He slowly discovered that its fulfilment lay beyond the world, in God himself. By centring on Joy, Lewis found an affinity with the "Romantic" tradition of Wordsworth, Coleridge, George MacDonald, and many others who wrote long before the Romantic Movement, such as the poets Henry Vaughan and Thomas Traherne. This was not to say that he owed no debt to very many others, including philosophers and thinkers, such as Plato, Boethius, G.K. Chesterton, and Bishop Berkeley, and Church Fathers such as St Augustine and Athanasius, as his vision of a hunting pack pursuing him makes clear.

Lewis's acceptance of some kind of God behind the universe started to change his feelings. A different note starts to enter his letters to friends and to Warnie, even though he had not yet embraced the vision that would be so evident in his writings after his later Christian conversion. He was still uncertain, and easily alarmed at the idea of a God who, as he then saw it, could interfere personally in people's lives. He abandoned two versions of an autobiography setting out his journey to God, one in verse, and one in prose. There was as yet no ending, no complete resolution. It would be a quarter of a century before he was ready to publish *Surprised by Joy: The Shape of My Early Life,* which traced his pilgrimage to Christianity. Meanwhile, his long conversations with Tolkien continued.

CHAPTER 5

The birth of the Inklings

One of the most important members of the as-yet unformed Inklings is easily overlooked. He would not obviously shape the concerns of the informal group, as would C.S. Lewis, J.R.R. Tolkien, Owen Barfield, and Charles Williams in particular. Yet, throughout the years of the group, with brief exceptions, he would be in daily contact with Lewis. None of the other Inklings would have such a constant and consistent association with a fellow member. His beautifully written diaries, though at times intermittent, give some of the best of the scarce glimpses recorded of the life of the circle. Lewis's letters to him in the first few months of the Second World War include priceless insights into meetings. One of the dominant memories of those attending the gatherings in Lewis's college rooms would be his welcoming presence, his attentive serving of abundant cups of tea and other drinks, and his unfailing courtesy. He was W.H. "Warnie" Lewis, later Major Lewis as he rose in rank in the British army.

During the 1920s, Warnie had been out of the country for lengthy periods as part of his service as a professional soldier. His work overseeing military supplies took him away from England to Sierra Leone on the west coast of Africa for a year, and then to China for three years. His postings at that time were to Kowloon, South China, and then to Shanghai. He arranged with the War Office to make his return sea journey from China on a commercial freighter, so that he could visit other countries en route. After setting out from Shanghai in February 1930, he had a memorable stop in Japan and two landings in the USA. In Japan he visited Kyoto and later Kamakura, where he made a point of seeing the giant Dibutsu Buddha:

> A broad tree lined avenue led up to the Buddha which we had come to see, and there it was, huge and aloof even at two hundred yards distance.… Though it is enormous – about 50 to 60 feet in height – mere size is not its attraction – or rather that it should be possible to cast and carve a master piece of such a size is what gives it its fascination: there is something uncanny in staring up into that huge face which looks down under half closed eyelids with an expression that seems to say "I have always known everything and have always been here, and anything you may do or say in your little life is mere futility." I would like to stop in this place for a few days and come back and look at this statue at various times – early morning and evening – but not on a moonlit night. I must have looked up, into his face, for nearly ten minutes.[1]

The figure had a remarkable effect on him, over a year before his eventual return to Christian faith, and he kept a "fairly good" small model of it for the rest of his life. Ten years later his brother was to write of the human sensation of the uncanny, as a "fringe" of the "numinous", a more fundamental experience that typically gives rise to a feeling of awe. The uncanny is a tell-tale indicator of a larger world beyond the senses, which, in Lewis's view, helped to give rise to religions.[2] Such experiences were of characteristic interest to those who would make up the Inklings.

Pausing in America on his slow journey home, Warnie visited San Francisco (where he was delighted to discover cheap tobacco and the imposing skyscrapers) and Los Angeles. After sailing through the Panama Canal, the freighter stopped at New York. His first view of Manhattan, caught by the sun, struck Warnie as "like some fantastic faery city", or an artist's portrayal of Avalon. His adventures overseas contrasted sharply with his brother's contentment merely to explore limited parts of the British Isles, as much as possible on foot (his only foreign travels were twice to France, first for a childhood holiday and then to fight there, and once for a holiday late in life to Greece with his wife, Joy Davidman, and close friends).

Warnie's thoughts turned more and more to early retirement, although he was still in his thirties. In 1930, before his brother, Mrs Moore, and Maureen moved to a permanent home after years of renting, they invited him to live with them when he retired. Upon his return from China, Warnie had been posted to Bulford in Wiltshire, which was a manageable distance by motorcycle for his frequent visits to Oxford. In October that year, he was able to help his brother and household move into The Kilns, a low-set, semi-rural house in eight acres of grounds.

By December 1930, while on leave and staying at The Kilns, Warnie had come up with a scheme that suited his expectation of a more settled and homely life, and which could occupy his extensive leisure time. It would also feed his enjoyment of writing and chronicling, which had already long found expression in his diary-keeping. The scheme, of which his brother heartily approved, was to compile many volumes based on a vast number of papers acquired after the recent death of their father, Albert, an inveterate hoarder. The project became *The Lewis Family Papers*.[3]

Warnie made as much of a start as he could on the enormous task of sorting out the papers (letters, diaries, photographs, and various documents), typing and arranging the material chronologically. It would eventually absorb the first years of his retirement, during which he would type the material up with two fingers. The pages were then bound into volumes. He added numerous explanatory notes, based on his and his brother's combined knowledge and memories. It was a feat of editing, arranged with the eye of someone to whom social history came naturally.

Walking tours and roads of the spirit

During the 1920s, C.S. Lewis had gone on a number of long walks, and walking tours, with Owen Barfield, along with their mutual friend Cecil Harwood and another anthroposophist, Walter Field. This activity was one of Lewis's greatest enjoyments, not least because it took him away from the burdens of life in his shared household with Mrs Moore and Maureen, the necessity of walking the family dog, and the discomfort of having hands like those of a maid and, later, after moving to The Kilns, a groundsman. After Barfield left for London, Lewis turned for company on these walking tours to his brother, now that he was posted relatively nearby. Upon his retirement, Warnie's constant companionship became a central part of Lewis's life.

At the beginning of January 1931, Lewis and Warnie embarked on the first of an annual series of walking tours up the Wye Valley, beginning near Chepstow beside the Severn Estuary, and taking them about fifty-four miles. It is at their starting point that the River Wye flows into the Severn. Warnie described the extended walk in his diary as "one of the best holidays I have ever had in my life".

In enjoying walking holidays, Lewis, his brother, and his friends were very much of their time. Walking was popular with both the middle classes and the intelligentsia. With the rapid expansion of towns and cities, for many it was part of a new appreciation of nature, which was seen as increasingly precious. Travel books and accounts of journeys on foot and the pedestrian's view of the countryside were popular.

Oxford Professor Valentine Cunningham writes about the presence of this trend in the literature of the thirties:

> Walking and mapping and traversing landscapes couldn't be more fundamental to '30s literature's sense of itself, to the "30s writers" typical envisaging of their art and their politics as being on the road, on the way, into or across new country.... These literary mapmakers seem now, of course, a lot like their immediate predecessors, the Georgian ramblers and walkers, the Hilaire Bellocs and the Richard Jefferies, who obviously engendered the brisk progressions from country pub to country pub that characterized the holidays of C.S. Lewis and his friends, and that came increasingly to attract C. Day Lewis....[4]

C.S. Lewis's friends were drawn into walks, or into many brief or longer vacations that inevitably involved walks or serious walking. In his undergraduate days, as we have seen, he would walk with Nevill Coghill on the Hinksey hills, fervently discussing books and ideas. It is perhaps no coincidence that much of Tolkien's *The Hobbit*, which was being composed in the early thirties, would be made up of a long journey, much of it on foot, by the reluctant Hobbit Bilbo Baggins and a party of dwarves who journeyed through the Shire, and then up and later under the great Misty Mountains. Eventually, the party faced the dangers of Mirkwood and beyond as they trudged through it. Each stage of the journey in *The Hobbit* is beautifully descriptive of the landscape. Lewis had read most of Tolkien's manuscript by the time he wrote *The Pilgrim's Regress* in 1933. The very approach that book was to take – of a journey on foot along mainly rural highways and byways – was of that period as well. Lewis clearly found short or long walks essential for his creativity and the development of his thoughts.

In *The Pilgrim's Regress*, Lewis pictured his route from unbelief to theism to eventual Christian belief as a "main" road that brought him back in touch with what makes us human, with byways and forks leading to the unbalanced follies of either the detached intellect or the unbridled senses. But it was in fact his brother who had been ahead of him on that road. In May 1931, in one of his many weekend visits to The Kilns, something happened that decisively marked Warnie's return to Christian faith, and which he recorded in his diary a few days later:

I started to say my prayers again after having discontinued doing so for more years than I care to remember: this was no sudden impulse but the result of a conviction of the truth of Christianity which has been growing on me for a considerable time: a conviction for which I admit I should be hard put to find a logical proof, but which rests on the inherent improbability of the whole of existence being fortuitous, and the inability of the materialists to provide any convincing explanation of the origin of life. I feel happier for my return to a practice that no material explanation will cover. When I have prepared myself a little further, I intend to go to Communion once again. So with me, the wheel has now made the full revolution – indifference, scepticism, atheism, agnosticism, and back again to Christianity. I hope I manage to retain my faith.[5]

With Warnie's conversion, C.S. Lewis was the only one who was not a professing Christian among those of his circle of friends who would become members of the Inklings in its early years! He had as yet only got as far as admitting the existence of some kind of a God behind the universe. At that time, Lewis considered that there was no way that this God could have personal relationships with humans – just as Shakespeare's Hamlet or Othello, as characters in his plays, could not meet their maker.[6] The only shared characteristics that marked out the Inklings, according to Lewis, were Christianity and a "tendency to write". If Lewis was right, those characteristics were not yet fully in evidence. When the decisive moment for Lewis did occur, later that year, Warnie had a small but important part to play in it.

"A rum thing"

With C.S. Lewis's acceptance of God, the huge battle between his intellectual and his imaginative life began to show signs of an armistice. Perhaps to his surprise, Lewis noticed himself responding to John Bunyan, the seventeenth-century Puritan author. He read Bunyan's account of his inner distress and subsequent conversion to Christianity, recorded in his confession, *Grace Abounding to the Chief of Sinners* (1666). As usual, Lewis shared his reaction with his confidant, Arthur Greeves, in one of his frequent letters: "I should like to know… in general what you think of all the darker side of religion as we find it in old books. Formerly I regarded it as mere devil-worship based on horrible superstitions. Now that I have found, and am still finding more and more the element of truth in the old beliefs, I *feel* I cannot dismiss even their dreadful side so cavalierly. There must be something in it: only what?"[7]

About the time that Lewis, together with Mrs Moore and Maureen, moved into The Kilns in October 1930, he began reading John's Gospel in Greek – it soon became his habit to read some passage of the Bible more or less daily. He also started attending Magdalen College chapel first thing on weekdays and his parish church at nearby Headington Quarry on Sundays. Reading the Gospel of John began to change his picture of the life and person of Christ.

He had also had been reading a Christian writer he much admired, George MacDonald. He had in fact started *Diary of an Old Soul* (1880) early in 1930. He chose this book because Oxford's Hilary (or Spring) term had then started, ruling out private reading except for MacDonald's calendar of brief verses, written after the death of two of his children. In a letter to Arthur, Lewis expressed his satisfaction that there existed many other books of its general type. Significantly, he shared with his friend his view that reading MacDonald's verses was "another of the beauties of coming, I won't say, to religion but to an attempt at religion – one finds oneself on the main road with all humanity, and can compare notes with an endless succession of previous travellers. It is emphatically coming home.…".

Similar thoughts clearly occupied his mind at this time. He had written to another friend, Hamilton Jenkin, on 21 March 1930 about how his outlook was changing. He did not feel that he was moving directly to Christianity, though, Lewis confessed, it might turn out that way in the end. The best way of explaining the change, he said, was this. At one time, he would have said, "Shall I adopt Christianity?" Now it was a matter of whether it would adopt him. Another "party" was involved – it was as if he were playing the card game poker, not patience, as he once supposed. Lewis's letter to Jenkin then and his thoughts to Arthur on MacDonald and Bunyan suggest his brother was right in seeing his sense of alarm around this time as being to do with warning signs of the encroachment of Christianity. Lewis had joked to Barfield that he might have to find him in a monastery. What if he somehow met God here on earth, as if God had stepped into the very world of his own story? It felt, it seems, that he was on the losing side in the last round of poker.

This was not the first time C.S. Lewis had been alarmed by the encroachment of Christianity, and its troubling implication that his life could not be his own any more. It heightened his fears of the divine interferer in his earlier "most reluctant" conversion to belief in God. Some years previously, not long before his first meeting with Tolkien, he had had a conversation with one of his colleagues at Magdalen College that had troubled him. Sitting beside the fire in his college rooms, he and his guest discussed the reliability of the New Testament Gospels. T.D. Weldon was a philosophy don at Magdalen and, according to Lewis, a hard-bitten atheist. To his great surprise this uncompromising atheist suggested that the evidence for the historicity of the Gospels was remarkably good. "Rum thing," Lewis recalled Weldon saying. "All that stuff of Frazer's about the Dying God. Rum thing. It almost looks as if it had really happened once." In his diary that night Lewis noted: "We somehow got on the historical truth of the Gospels, and agreed there was a lot that could not be explained away."[8]

An epiphany in a motorcycle sidecar

One of the great conversions in Christian history was that of the apostle Paul on the way to Damascus from Jerusalem in the early thirties of the first century, when the resurrected Jesus appeared to the fanatical persecutor. Another, in the fourth century, was that of Augustine of Hippo, after he heard a voice that seemed to be a child's calling him to "take up and read" what he took to be the Bible, the book of books. C.S. Lewis's was yet another, and his conversion took place in the sidecar of his brother's motorcycle! Warnie was due to return to Shanghai, and the brothers were making the most of their limited time together. They were on their way to visit the recently opened Whipsnade Zoo, on the Chiltern Hills in Bedfordshire, to the north of London. Mrs Moore and Maureen, together with a family friend and their dog, travelled separately by car. This was on Monday 28 September 1931.[9] Many years later Lewis remembered: "When we set out I did not believe that Jesus Christ was the Son of God, and when we reached the zoo I did."

Lewis's long journey to Christianity had reached a decisive point just a few days before the trip to Whipsnade. On the night of 19 September, as they made their way down Addison's Walk in the grounds of Magdalen College, Lewis had had an intense conversation with Tolkien and someone he had first met the previous year, H.V.D. "Hugo" Dyson, the friend of Nevill Coghill. Dyson and Lewis had become firm friends, after starting to meet around four or five times a year when Dyson was visiting from Reading University. The night-time conversation had turned Lewis upside down. Like Tolkien, Dyson was a devout Christian. Tolkien captured the long conversation on Addison's Walk, and obviously others with Lewis, in his poem *Mythopoeia* (the "making of myth"). Tolkien pictures his friend as a materialist – even though by that time, of course, Lewis had long abandoned atheism and come to believe in a God behind the universe, who was the maker of it. He no longer only believed in a great Spirit that permeated the universe.

With his sparkling wit, Dyson provided a counterpoint to Tolkien's arguments, giving emotional weight to the senior man's more measured words. Tolkien had argued for the Christian Gospels on the basis of the love of story found in all of us and which, for him, was sacramental. His poem *Mythopoeia* gives us an idea of the possible flow of the conversation. Tolkien wrote of the human heart as not being totally corrupted by falsehood, but still receiving nourishment from knowledge that comes from our maker. Though fallen beings, we still remember him, he wrote. He has not abandoned us. Though we are in a woeful state of disgrace, we have traces within us of our mandate to rule as his image-bearers. We create according to the "law in which we're made".

Much later, Lewis effectively filled in the brief outline of the conversation that he had written to Arthur Greeves. This was in one of his most important essays, "Myth Became Fact".[10] He expanded upon the harmony of story and fact in the Gospels: "This is the marriage of heaven and earth, perfect Myth and Perfect Fact: claiming not only our love and

Obedience, but also our wonder and delight, addressed to the savage, the child, and the poet in each one of us no less than to the moralist, the scholar, and the philosopher." He realized that the stories and claims of Christ demand at least as much of an imaginative response as an intellectual one. Lewis would treat this theme more fully in his book *Miracles* (1947).[11]

Tolkien, in his turn, expounded the view he presented to Lewis on Addison's Walk more completely in his essay "On Fairy Stories" (in his expanded 1947 version). His point was that the first-century events recounted in the Gospels are shaped in the real world of things and people by God himself. He is the superlative story-maker, the proper master of all who tell stories. His real world story has a pattern shared with the best human stories. In it, there is a sudden turn from utter catastrophe to the most satisfying of all happy endings. Tolkien created a new word to name this pattern, which has entered dictionaries. The word was "eucatastrophe" – the "good catastrophe". The Gospels, coming from their divine source, enter what Tolkien calls the "seamless 'web' of storytelling". Glimpses of truth that God in his grace gave to the human imagination in its myths are focused and fulfilled in the master story of the Gospels. Myth has become fact. In them, Tolkien said, "art has been verified". Tolkien no doubt had in mind many great myths, but the ones he loved the most were from the pagan world of northern myths. Lewis's loves were broader, encompassing both those and myths of the classical world. Both men, however, appreciated myths wherever they found them.

It was as a result of the long conversation between Lewis, Tolkien, and Dyson, three of the future Inklings, that less than two weeks later Lewis accepted the previously unimaginable and unthinkable. He came to believe that the God behind the universe had entered the universe that he had made as a fully human being – in Lewis's words, that "Jesus Christ was the Son of God".[12] It would take some time for Lewis to work out the implications of this and start to construct his layman's theology that would so captivate millions of his readers. He had accepted, however, what he always would believe was the heart of "mere Christianity": the incarnation of the Son of God. This would remain at the centre of his Christian writings. Tolkien later noted in his diary: "Friendship with Lewis compensates for much, and besides giving constant pleasure and comfort has done me much good from the contact with a man at once honest, brave, intellectual – a scholar, a poet, and a philosopher – and a lover, at least after a long pilgrimage, of Our Lord."[13]

The greatest idea that Lewis took from his discussions with Tolkien was that myths were essential for thinking about and coming into contact with reality: it is a mistake to regard them simply as "lies" or mere fictions. Maria Kuteeva, an expert in language and myth, put it well when she explained that in the making of myth, "a storyteller or 'sub-creator' fulfils the Creator's purpose, and catches fragments of the true light. Therefore, even pagan myths cannot be totally 'lies' since they always capture something of the truth". She understands Tolkien as saying that whereas, in naming things, human "speech is invention about objects and ideas, so myth is invention about truth".[14] It had dawned on Lewis that the truth – Jesus Christ himself – was expressed in the true myth of the incarnation, as recorded in historical documents of the first century.

It was at the point of his conversion that the incarnation became central to both Lewis's thought and his imagination. Though he believed (as he argued with Barfield) that thought is to do with truth and imagination to do with meaning, the two came together in the incarnation, when God became one of us humans. This historical coming together of truth and meaning, the abstract and the tangible, is echoed, sometimes very distantly, in myth. Lewis wrote to Arthur Greeves just a few weeks before his conversion to Christianity:

> I must confess that more and more the value of plays and novels becomes for me dependent on the moments when, by whatever artifice, they succeed in expressing the great myths.[15]

The friendship between Tolkien and Lewis had progressed by many leagues since the two had started to meet regularly around 1929. Tolkien, long afterwards, recalled conversation with Lewis at this period: "C.S. Lewis was one of the only three persons who have so far read all or a considerable part of my 'mythology' of the First and Second Ages…"

When Tolkien lent his friend *The Hobbit* to read at the beginning of 1933, Lewis set down his reaction to the rough draft in another of his frequent letters to Arthur Greeves: "Reading his fairy tale has been uncanny – it is so exactly like what we [would] both have longed to write (or read) in 1916: so that one feels he is not making it up but merely describing the same world into which all three of us have the entry."[16] Lewis had already written to Greeves in great excitement about his friendship with Tolkien. It had much in common, he said, with their own. In a later letter, he offered illumination of the meaning of the literature of "romance", which was important to both Lewis and Arthur. He wrote that Tolkien "agreed that for what we meant by romance there must be at least the hint of another world – one must hear the horns of elfland."[17]

Such a love of romance would also turn out to be a cord that held the Inklings together.

Lewis's circle comes together

Shortly after Warnie took his brother to Whipsnade, he set off for Shanghai, departing from Southampton on the *Neuralia* on 9 October 1931. Jack Lewis saw him off from Oxford railway station. Warnie noted in his diary: "Beastly these partings are, but please God, this will be the last of them."[18] His arrival on 17 November coincided with rising tension between China and Japan. In fact, the Japanese invasion of Manchuria had started in September, before Warnie left England – the army acting without authorization from the emperor. This militarization of Japan would result in its later participation in the Second World War.

One of the letters Warnie received from his brother at this time spoke of his delight in being given a copy of William Law's *Appeal*, intended for those who doubt or disbelieve the "Truths of the Gospel". Lewis enthused to Warnie that "the book is saturated with delight, and the sense of wonder: one of those rare works which make you say of Christianity 'Here is the very thing you like in poetry and the romances, only this time it's true.'"[19] It wasn't until a later letter that Warnie had confirmation of his brother's acceptance of Christianity, when he wrote of taking Communion again at Christmas 1931, after a gap of a great many years. Warren responded to the news in his diary:

A letter from J[ack] today containing the news that he too has once more started to go to Communion, at which I am delighted. Had he not done so, I with my altered views would have found – hardly a bar between us, but a lack of a complete identity of interest which I should have regretted.[20]

Warnie's phrase "a complete identity of interest" applies to all in the circle of Lewis's friends at that time who would become Inklings. As Lewis said, all had Christianity and a tendency to write in common, now that Lewis had capitulated to Christian belief. They would all have regretted it if Lewis had stayed outside, but particularly Tolkien and Dyson, whom, as we have seen, Lewis called the main human means of his conversion. Behind Tolkien and Dyson was all the previous work Owen Barfield had put into trying to persuade his great friend to abandon his materialist worldview.

The Christian and writing element in the Inklings

As a direct result of Tolkien's argument about myth entering real history, C.S. Lewis began to see a new dimension to his varied group of friends, which was to have at least a minor impact on the very history of English literature, and a major one on theology as well. Groups in Oxford that he had belonged to, some of them with Tolkien, were usually made up of dons and other academics, such as professors, and occasionally included students. He now came to value the fact that many of his academic friends, usually shared with Tolkien, were professing Christians, albeit of different persuasions – the distinction of Roman Catholic and Protestant being a central one, epitomized in his "Papist" friend, Tolkien. Though hugely generous with his friendship, much later in life Lewis wrote of his appreciation of having a group of Christian friends in particular. He saw them as participating in a feast in which God "has spread the board and it is He who has chosen the guests".[21]

Those friends who would become Inklings were, however, drawn from a wider circle: while they were all Christians of various hues, and tended to write, they belonged to more than one profession. Significantly, those who were academics were not all teaching at Oxford and, in later years, even taught a variety of subjects; they were not all English language or literature specialists. Barfield is a prime example of an important member of the Inklings who was not in the academic world. He was by then a family solicitor in the City of London. What he was, however, like many of Lewis's friends, revolved around books and poetry: he was a writer.

It was this group of friends, less distinct than the academic clusters Tolkien and Lewis frequented, that was the core of what became the Inklings. In an important sense, Tolkien brought the Inklings into existence by persuading Lewis that he needed to commit himself to Christian faith, making this the integration point of his life. As we saw, he did this with the help of Dyson, and Barfield's solid intellectual groundwork before him. Several of the future Inklings therefore, in effect, played indirect parts in the origin of the group.

The informal club started to take its distinctive shape after Lewis's conversion to Christian belief, as he got together with the friends who were to make up the Inklings. The Coalbiters club had ended in 1933, its very specific purpose fulfilled. An undergraduate club, in which Tolkien and Lewis had participated as the regulation staff members, had also ended with the graduation of its founder, a talented author called Tangye Lean (brother of the famous filmmaker David). They were called the Inklings, and met to read their writings aloud to each other. It may have been in the autumn term of 1933, some months after the ending of the undergraduate club, that the name was transferred to Lewis's circle of Christian friends, at the core of which were the regular meetings of Tolkien and Lewis.

Tolkien's memories of the genesis of the circle consistently imply that the name was adopted soon after the end of the undergraduate Inklings group. John Rateliff is of the opinion that the Inklings "seem to have coalesced as a group during 1933–4."[22] In the very patchy documentation of the highly informal group that has come down to us, the name "the Inklings" does not appear before 1936. On the basis of this lack of contemporary documentation, some believe the group was not named until after 1933, or even after the academic year 1933–1934. It was clearly established, though still characteristically small, by 1936, when Lewis invited Charles Williams to visit the club from London.

For the next sixteen years or so, on through 1949 and perhaps sporadically afterwards, the literary friends continued to meet to read as well as talk, sometimes in later years in Tolkien's spacious rooms at Merton College after his move from Pembroke, but more often in Lewis's rooms at Magdalen, and usually, but not always, on Thursday evenings. By wartime, but most likely even before, Lewis, Tolkien, and others had also begun to gather regularly before lunch on Tuesdays, usually in a snug located in a back room at the Eagle and Child, a public house on St Giles known to the friends as "the Bird and Baby". It may well be that the Inklings didn't meet as regularly as they did in the war years and afterwards, but there were frequent meetings between Inklings friends on other occasions, such as regular meetings between Lewis and Tolkien on Monday mornings in Lewis's college rooms, as already mentioned. After 1932, Warnie would usually be around on these mornings, using one of his brother's rooms for his work on *The Lewis Family Papers* or, later on, for his writing on seventeen-century French social history, and for helping Lewis with his correspondence.[23]

Three of the former Coalbiters, Tolkien, Lewis, and Nevill Coghill, were now in the new group, whether or not it was yet named the Inklings. Coghill must have particularly appreciated its male friendship, with the dissolution of his brief marriage to Elspeth Harley that year, and the beginning of a single life in college accommodation that marked the rest of his career at Oxford.[24] C.L. (Charles) Wrenn helped Tolkien with the teaching of Anglo-Saxon, having joined the university in 1930. At some stage after the formation of the Inklings, perhaps in 1934, he was invited to come along. Warnie records an event attended by Inklings (or future Inklings) at which Wrenn was present, in his diary entry for Thursday 19 July 1934. The occasion was a dinner at Exeter College to celebrate exams being over. Hugo Dyson, who was an examiner, gave the dinner, and invited, among others, Lewis and his brother, Wrenn, Tolkien, and Nevill Coghill. Warnie noted that "everyone was in uproarious spirits – the reaction I suppose after examining. In fact the evening was just a little too high-spirited – too much farce and too little real talk".[25] Such noise and buffoonery, notwithstanding Warnie's disapproval, was as characteristic of get-togethers of Inklings as readings from work in progress, or discussion of the theology of fantasy or of the truth gained by imagination.

Other early members included Revd Adam Fox, and, as often as he could visit Oxford for meetings, Owen Barfield. Another member, Lewis's family doctor, Robert Havard – who was nicknamed "Humphrey"[26] – joined the circle of friends after visiting Lewis to treat him for influenza. The conversation had soon turned to Aquinas and medieval philosophy. It must have been immediately clear to Lewis that his doctor was well read, hence the invitation to the Inklings. In fact, Havard had conducted advanced medical research, and did other writing besides articles for medical journals. As a student at Cambridge University, Havard was co-author of an important study published in 1926 in the *Journal of Physiology*: "The influence of exercise on the inorganic phosphates in the blood and urine."[27] Dr Havard was introduced to the Inklings, he revealed, well before any of the circle were well known outside the academic sphere. This could mean before the publication of *The Hobbit* in 1937 (which had to be reprinted months after publication), and Lewis's *Out of the Silent Planet* in 1938. He woke up one morning, he remembered, to find that members of the group were famous. Interviewed late in his life, Havard recalled his date of joining as 1934 or 1935,[28] but it may have been later. In 1990 he gave a vivid first impression of an Inklings meeting during the early period. Specifically he was remembering his first encounter with Tolkien:

My first meeting with the Professor, or "Tollers" as we all called him, must have been early in 1935 in C.S. Lewis' rooms in Magdalen College, Oxford, during one of the Inklings sessions, to which Lewis had invited me. I gradually became aware of a smallish slender man settled into the depths of an armchair, with a pipe always in his mouth. He spoke relatively little. It was Lewis and Dyson who were in perpetual competition, if not conflict, in the mutual struggle to hold the floor. "Tollers" contributions were usually brief, but witty, and to the point, so far as they could be heard. His speech, always rapid and indirect, presented inspirited difficulties as it escaped between his pipe and closed lips.[29]

Havard soon became one of the central and most appreciated attendees at the Inklings. John Rateliff calls him one of the four who formed the core of the group throughout its existence (the others being Lewis, Warnie, and Tolkien).[30] It says something of his standing with his friends that shortly before the beginning of the Second World War, Lewis asked Havard to replace Warnie on a boating holiday, his brother having been called back into military service. Warnie had planned to take Dyson and his brother up the Thames in the limited space of his small cabin cruiser, the *Bosphorus*. Havard agreed and hastily arranged cover in his medical practice. On the planned route, the river passed under bridges every few miles, the attendant villages usually set back a mile, beyond the flood plain, and featuring at least one convenient public house, and church.

In high spirits, the three set off from Folly Bridge, not far south of Pembroke and Christ Church colleges, where Warnie moored his boat. It was midday on Saturday 26 August 1939. Unknown to them, war would be declared as early as 3 September. The placid waters carried the boat to The Trout at Godstow, a favourite inn, a little before closing time. At this time, Dyson was deep in a discussion with Lewis about the date of the Renaissance. Lewis felt that all periods were times of transition, without clear-cut beginnings. They talked about whether the period started at or before the fall of Constantinople. Havard found his friends' discussion "lit up by flashes of wit and imaginative reconstruction of events"; not "dry and academic" as might be expected. They stopped that first night at Newbridge, where Lewis and Dyson stayed at the Rose Revived pub, while Havard slept on board. The next day they went on early to Tadpole Bridge, where Dyson and Lewis worshipped at an Anglican church while Havard did the same at a Roman Catholic one.

The days continued in talk and the routines of boating. Lewis and Dyson picked up current news from the pubs at which they stayed, being cut off from newspapers. They got upriver as far as the Cotswold town of Lechlade, the highest navigable point on the Thames. On their return downriver the engine eventually failed, making it necessary to tow the small boat. Then the weather turned bad. Tempers were salved by the engine's return to life, and they continued their voyage unaware of increasingly darker news from the European continent. On the first or second of September, remembered Havard, they heard at Godstow of Hitler's invasion of his neighbour, Poland. Their spirits were dashed as they realized that war was inevitable. Lewis quipped, "Well, at any rate, we now have less chance of dying of cancer," which raised a hearty laugh.

The earliest days of the Inklings, however, in the momentous years of the 1930s, had not been shadowed by war. Lewis and his brother were renewed in a Christian faith, Tolkien was delighted by his deeper oneness with his friend, both Tolkien and Lewis were experimenting with prose fiction as well as with the traditional poetry that absorbed their ambitions, and they were surrounded by friends who shared their love of the literature of romance. They looked beyond what they saw as the intellectual wasteland of the merely modern to glimpses of a larger world.

C.S. Lewis celebrated the gift of friendship years later in his book *The Four Loves*:

Those are the golden sessions… when our slippers are on, our feet spread out towards the blaze and our drinks at our elbows; when the whole world, and something beyond the world, opens itself to our minds as we talk;

and no one has any claim on or any responsibility for another, but all are freemen and equals as if we had first met an hour ago, while at the same time an Affection mellowed by the years enfolds us. Life – natural life – has no better gift to give. Who could have deserved it?[31]

CHAPTER 6

The 1930s

Writing books they liked to read

The 1930s saw readings by the Inklings from such works in progress as Lewis's *Out of the Silent Planet* and his poems, and various pieces by Tolkien, including extracts from the unpublished *The Hobbit,* but the Inklings group at that time was very small, with its most prolific writers being Tolkien and Lewis. Dyson would not have had much to offer; Fox and Coghill contributed poems, and Warnie Lewis may have shared research he was doing on seventeenth-century France. Barfield's writing had slowed down because of his absorption into the legal business and, in any case, he could visit Oxford only occasionally. In 1936, when Lewis invited Charles Williams to visit the club from London, it seemed to have few regular attendees (Lewis mentions only the four who had read Williams's *The Place of the Lion*).

Though he reckoned that he was with the Inklings for only about a tenth of all their meetings during the thirties, forties, and fifties, Owen Barfield provides more vivid insights into the readings than many in the group. In a piece called "The Inklings Remembered", he recalled:

… my reminiscences, though vivid enough, are scarce and scattered. I never, to my great regret, heard Tolkien read any of the nascent *Lord of the Rings* but I do recall his reading a poem, in stanza form, with a refrain in which he made us all join. The poem itself has faded, except that the mode was a kind of jovial pastiche Anglo-Saxon. In my recollection, these readings by Inklings authors from their own works were, at least in terms of the time allotted to them, subsidiary to the main business (if what happened can be so described) of the evening. Surprisingly, perhaps not so surprisingly, the reading I do remember well was that of a verse play of my own, *Medea* (in which she turns out to be a werewolf). On this occasion – I do not know if it was so in any other – Lewis had arranged for it to be a proper "reading", with each part allocated to a different reader. The two things that have stuck in my memory are, first, that the reception was favourable but not ecstatic and, secondly, that, when it was over, at least three of those present casually remarked that they had written plays about Medea themselves in the past. Finally, as the conversation drifted farther and farther away from my play, I mildly inquired if there was anybody present who had *not* written a play about Medea! There was also an Inklings meeting at which, on request, I delivered the best account I could of anthroposophy – without, I think, making much impression.[1]

Apart from such tantalizing glimpses, we can only guess at the subjects of their conversations, since there is very little record, especially of the early days. We do know, however, that chapters of *The Hobbit* were read to the group, perhaps as it was being prepared by Tolkien for publication. We can catch a glimmer of some of the ideas discussed and even toasted by the Inklings, because Tolkien gave two lectures in the thirties that may have entered the conversation of the group. One lecture was given in London to the British Academy, and the other at St Andrews University in Scotland for the annual Andrew Lang Lecture. It may be that the supportive spirit of the Inklings spurred him on to say what he did in these addresses, for both put forward a number of brilliant and innovative insights that are discussed to this day. When the lectures were eventually published, they certainly revolutionized the way many thought about myth, fairy story, and poetry. It took some people into the deepest of speculations about the relationship of imagination to thought and to language. One of the outstanding insights Tolkien came out with seemed almost like a throwaway comment: "To ask what is the origin of stories… is to ask what is the origin of language and of the mind."[2] C.S. Lewis thoroughly agreed with his friend's insights, as can be seen in his own literary scholarship and fiction, though Tolkien didn't always see it there!

The thinking that Tolkien put over, particularly on his lecture on fairy stories, had been largely private until he became friends with Lewis, and then expanded his group of friends in the Inklings. It was a big step to air them publicly at St Andrews. Even the lecture on *Beowulf* for the British Academy displayed his very original perspective, drawn from the wells of his private world. The opportunities to give these lectures, so conducive to exploring his concerns, were undoubtedly an important encouragement to Tolkien. After his pledge to Lewis to write on time travel, mentioned in the introduction, he faced a false start and then many more years of labour on *The Lord of the Rings* (the "new Hobbit", as his Inklings friends called it). In giving those lectures, I suspect he was building to some extent on the exchanges and the sharing that were taking place among the Inklings, but in his unique way. Through his influence on C.S. Lewis, he had been one of the important sources of the existence of the Inklings. What he helped to bring into being, therefore, in turn proved to be a help and encouragement to him in both his scholarship and his fiction. The Inklings helped to sustain the vision that powered all his work, just as in his schooldays and in the early part of the First World War he had been inspired by his then group of friends, the T.C.B.S.

Tolkien gave the lecture "Beowulf: The Monsters and the Critics" to the British Academy in London on 25 November 1936.[3] Edith went with him to this important event. The critic Donald K. Fry believed that the lecture "completely altered the course of Beowulf studies". It defended the artistry and overall unity of the early English poem against critics that seemed blind to its extraordinary qualities. Like his later (1939) lecture "On Fairy Stories", the Beowulf lecture opens the door to understanding his work as a scholar, and also as a writer of globally popular fantasy. In 2014, his own prose translation of *Beowulf* was published for the first time, along with extracts from his notes and lectures commenting on the ancient poem, and other related pieces. To understand *Beowulf* through Tolkien's eyes is to understand *The Lord of the Rings*; it is also to see pre-Christian myth in the light of what it heralded, in Tolkien's view.

Beowulf, fairy tales, and other worlds

The following passage from *Beowulf*, in an old translation, speaks of a dragon guarding its hoard, rather like Smaug in *The Hobbit*, and then being outraged by the theft of one of its treasures:

In the grave on the hill a hoard it guarded,
in the stone-barrow steep. A strait path reached it,
unknown to mortals. Some man, however,
came by chance that cave within
to the heathen hoard. In hand he took
a golden goblet, nor gave he it back,
stole with it away, while the watcher slept,
by thievish wiles: for the warden's wrath
prince and people must pay betimes!

In an early draft of the lecture, Tolkien had appreciatively reproduced a poem about a dragon by C.S. Lewis, taken from his *The Pilgrim's Regress*. In the early days of their friendship he had also shown Lewis a draft of his prose translation of *Beowulf*, the manuscript of which contains suggested amendments in what is probably Lewis's handwriting. Tolkien took up several of the suggestions.

In his lecture, Tolkien expresses unhappiness with the existing analysis of *Beowulf* by literary critics. In fact, it had not been criticism proper, he complained, as it had not been directed to an understanding of the poem as a poem, as a unified work of art. Rather, it had been seen as a quarry for historical data about its period. In particular, the two monsters that dominate it – Grendel and the dragon – had not been sufficiently considered as the centre and focus of the poem. Tolkien argued that what he called the "structure and conduct" of the poem arose from this central theme of monsters.

It was clear to Tolkien that the *Beowulf* poet created, by art, an illusion of historical truth and perspective. The poet had an instinctive historical sense, which he used for artistic, poetic ends. Tolkien told his audience that autumn night: "*Beowulf* is in fact so interesting as poetry… that this quite overshadows the historical content…" A literary study of *Beowulf*, Tolkien argued, must deal with a native English poem that is using ancient and mostly traditional material in a fresh way, and thus the focus should not be on the poet's sources, but on what he did with them.

In considering the monsters, which are so pivotal to *Beowulf*, Tolkien explained that this choice of theme actually accounts for the greatness of the poem. The power comes from "the mythical mode of imagination". Tolkien's approach to *Beowulf* is strikingly paralleled in his own stories. For him, the meaning and importance of myth defies abstract analysis. Myth works best when it is allusively rather than explicitly presented in a poem. The *Beowulf* poet had succeeded in making myth "incarnate in the world of history and geography". Tolkien pointed out the danger and difficulty of accounting for this "mythical mode of imagination" in a work like *Beowulf*. Those who defend such a work must avoid killing it by vivisection; instead, they need to capture its life indirectly – or, as Tolkien puts it, its defenders have to account for its power by speaking in "parables". Otherwise, all that is left is "formal or mechanical allegory". The experience of myth is in danger of being explained away as only the result of the poet's artistic and technical skill.

Beowulf was a dragon-slayer. Tolkien saw the dragon as a potent symbol. It is an enemy more malicious than any evil that comes from human foes. Yet it is active in "heroic history", and is present in northern lands that can be recognized by name. According to Tolkien, the creator of *Beowulf* not only used the old legends in a fresh and original fashion, but created a story that interpreted them. In this poem we see "man at war with the hostile world, and his inevitable overthrow in time". The question of the power of evil is at the centre of the story. Beowulf "moves in a northern heroic age imagined by a Christian, and therefore has a noble and gentle quality, though conceived to be a pagan".

The poet who composed *Beowulf* brought together the new Christian north and the ancient pagan one. He does not write allegory; this was developed in later poetry. His symbol of evil, the dragon, captures the ancient force of the pagan northern imagination, while being an essential part of a Christian poem. The author is concerned with "man on earth" rather than the journey to the Celestial City. The northern mood or atmosphere of despair remains as part of the poem, which however carries the poet's Christian hope. The old northern value of valour even in defeat is retained. The poet feels this theme imaginatively or poetically rather than literally, yet with a sense of the ultimate defeat of darkness.

The author of *Beowulf* explored insights that may be found in the pagan imagination. Tolkien would do the same in the *The Lord of the Rings*. In fact, all Tolkien's stories and other accounts of the ages of Middle-earth are set in a pagan, pre-Christian world. His conclusion about *Beowulf* applies also to his own creation: "In *Beowulf* we have, then, an historical poem about the pagan past, or an attempt at one.… It is a poem by a learned man [who] brought probably first to his task a knowledge of Christian poetry.…"

Tolkien gave the annual Andrew Lang Lecture at St Andrews University in March 1939, when his thoughts about his own fiction had developed further. This was entitled "On Fairy Stories". It set out Tolkien's basic ideas concerning imagination, fantasy, and what he called "sub-creation". The creation of the primary world by God is at the heart of Tolkien's understanding of story. Mankind, bearing God's image, employ their imagination in making art, including stories. These are to varying degrees subordinate or secondary creations, or "sub-creations", full of meaning imaginatively drawn from the primary world, given that humans bear the image of God. The situation has been distorted, however, by the fall of humanity. Tolkien put forward a case that stories can nevertheless become very effective sub-creations in that they have the artistic advantage that their medium is language itself. Languages have a unique ability to carry mythologies, and myth itself can be about truth without losing particularity and therefore becoming only abstract. Imagination is able in some sense to perceive real things and therefore meanings, and imagination is at the root of all language. It is a condition of thought itself.

Tolkien expressed such ideas very elegantly and tangibly in his Andrew Lang Lecture, drawing upon a rich and extensive knowledge of mythologies, folk tales, myth, fantasy, and fairy tale. At this time, the Inklings had been meeting for perhaps as long as five years or more. As well as hearing his friends read, Tolkien had read from *The Hobbit*, and early drafts of what would become *The Lord of the Rings*. C.S. Lewis tells us that one of the subjects that were constantly before their minds was the art of narrative. As academics by trade, both Lewis and Tolkien were also, by practice as well as knowledge, developing their narrative skills, helped by the advice and responses they got from fellow Inklings. It is likely that many of the themes that Tolkien explored in his lecture that day in Scotland were part of the lively and informed conversations of the Inklings.

Tolkien, who had by then written much of the basic matter of *The Silmarillion*, and published *The Hobbit* (in 1937), attempted to set out patterns underlying good fairy tales and fantasies, demonstrating that they were worthy of serious attention.

High in importance was that fairy stories offer a secondary world, with an "inner consistency of reality"; this was all to do with being sub-creations. A good fairy tale in Tolkien's view has three other key structural features. Firstly, it helps to bring about in the reader what Tolkien called recovery. The story brings us back to the primary world with fresh vision. There is a restoration of meaning. We are able to see again something of the glory of ordinary and humble things and qualities that make up human life and reality, things such as stones and rivers, trees and hills, woodland, love, friendship, food and drink. Related to this recovery, the good fairy story secondly offers escape from the prison of narrow and distorted views of life and meaning. Tolkien is careful to point out that this is the escape of the prisoner rather than the flight of the deserter. Thirdly, the good story offers consolation, leading to joy (similar to the experience Lewis would chart in his autobiography, *Surprised by Joy*). Such consolation, Tolkien was to argue in his later version of the lecture, had meaning only because good stories pointed to the greatest story of all, the Gospel narratives. For him, this first century account had all the structural features of a fairy tale, myth, or great story, and, in addition, it was true in actual human history – the greatest storyteller of all had entered his own story. Tolkien believed in fact that God himself came to earth as a humble human being, a king like Aragorn, in disguise, an apparent fool, like Frodo, who risks his life in order to destroy the ruling Ring. These ideas were essentially the same as those Tolkien had been putting to C.S. Lewis while walking with him and Dyson in Addison's Walk years before.

Lewis on the origin of romantic love in poetry

For Tolkien, the ancient poem *Beowulf* and fairy tale in general belong to the literature of "romance". Lewis defined "experiences which are called romantic" as "the most serious and ecstatic experiences either of human love or of imaginative literature".[4] Given the common interest among the Inklings in the literature of romance, we could try to take elements of a group manifesto from Tolkien's two lectures. Tolkien was certainly defining his own attitude to stories of romance, and their implications on all levels, including theological.

Being an informal group, however, the Inklings did not operate according to a conscious manifesto or mission statement. It is more that Tolkien's central concerns in the lectures hint at a tacit worldview held in common with his friends that stood against the cultural mainstream. A look at C.S. Lewis's ideas as expressed in his scholarship at this time also points to a worldview that he had in common at least with Tolkien, and in all likelihood also with the other Inklings. As the 1930s developed, Lewis built on Tolkien's idea that fantasy, fairy tale, and other "romance" literature were adult fare, and had always been so, and were not primarily for children. He also defined his concerns (and surely Tolkien's) as the "rehabilitation" of an older world for his contemporaries. This rehabilitating concerned far more than the influential syllabus that he had helped Tolkien establish in the Oxford undergraduate honours course in English, which effectively concluded in 1830 (with only a nod to even the Victorian period in an optional exam paper). In effect, that syllabus had championed and spotlighted a premodern period which Lewis later called the "Old West", as we have seen.

Lewis read far more widely and eclectically than Tolkien, who was increasingly focusing his attention on the English West Midlands in the Middle Ages, both in his fiction and in his linguistic work at Oxford. The fruit of Lewis's wide but close reading was many literary essays over the years, most of them collected posthumously. It also included major studies such as *The Allegory of Love: A Study in Medieval Tradition* (1936), on the growth of allegory and the developments of romantic love, and *English Literature in the Sixteenth Century, Excluding Drama* (1954), Lewis's contribution to the *Oxford History of English Literature*. Lewis began writing the sixteenth-century history in 1935 at the suggestion of Professor F.P. Wilson, one of the series editors, who had been Lewis's tutor when he was an undergraduate. Lewis also continued to work on an author he loved, Edmund Spenser, who lived at the same time as Shakespeare and wrote the great poem *The Faerie Queene*. The results of Lewis's study of Spenser were scattered throughout many books and academic papers. David L. Russell perceptively comments that "most literary criticism is dated within its generation, but Lewis' remains highly readable, provocative, and, perhaps more significantly, in print… a forceful testimonial to his powers as a scholar".[5]

Subtitled "A Study in Medieval Tradition", *The Allegory of Love* is among the outstanding works of literary criticism of the last century. Lewis traced the concept of romantic love from the beginnings of allegory through Chaucer and Spenser. In the process, he depicted the long struggle between its earlier manifestation, the romance of adultery, and its later incarnation, the romance of married love between the sexes.

As we have noted, *The Allegory of Love* was published in 1936, the year Lewis and Charles Williams met. Williams had developed a complex theology of romantic love, and their common interest in this subject was an important element in their friendship. Tolkien, too, was exploring this theme in his then unpublished fiction, in the love of Beren and Lúthien, and Aragorn and Arwen, and other instances. Lewis would explore it in other writings, such as his novels *Till We Have Faces* and *That Hideous Strength*. In the biblical tradition, shared knowledgeably by Lewis, Tolkien, and Williams, romantic love is distinctively explored in the histories of Jacob and Rachel, David and Bathsheba, and poetically in The Song of Songs.

The Allegory of Love draws attention to the fact that the Middle Ages provide the key and the background to both Lewis's thought and his fiction, just as they do to Tolkien's. It is evident that much of Lewis's scholarly work centred on that period, and, additionally, he regarded writers of the sixteenth century, and the entire Renaissance, as part of the same intellectual and imaginative world (as we saw in the introduction to this book). His science-fiction stories would celebrate the medieval picture of the cosmos he loved, as would his Narnian tales. *The Allegory of Love* can be seen as part of his concern to rehabilitate the imaginative and intellectual insights of this vast period for the contemporary reader.

The Allegory of Love demonstrates the historical approach that Lewis took to literature. We can see this in his concern to help the reader enter as fully as possible into an author's intentions. He liked to do this by concentrating as much as he could on textual criticism, which he said he valued above other types of critical activity, as a later comment makes clear: "Find out what the author actually wrote and what the hard words meant and what the allusions were to, and you have done far more for me than a hundred new interpretations or assessments could ever do." Lewis was committed to the *author*ity of the author. It also expresses his hallmark focus on the Christianization of paganism (in this case, as evidenced in the history of romantic love in medieval times).

An extract can take us into a theme that had already become central to Lewis's view of the imagination: the use of what he called "stock" images, and archetypes, in poetry and other imaginative writing, and the reliance of human thought on metaphors. Both Tolkien and Barfield can be heard speaking along with him.

Allegory, in some sense, belongs not to medieval man but to man, or even to mind, in general. It is of the very nature of thought and language to represent what is immaterial in picturable terms. What is good or happy has always been high like the heavens and bright like the sun. Evil and misery were deep and dark from the first. Pain is black in Homer, and goodness is a middle point for Alfred no less than for Aristotle. To ask how these married pairs of sensibles and insensibles first came together would be great folly; the real question is how they ever came apart, and to answer that question is beyond the province of the mere historian.[6]

Critic Harry Blamires points out that Lewis "revived the genre of historical criticism by his work on Medieval and Renaissance literature in *The Allegory of Love* (1936) and *English Literature in the Sixteenth Century* (published in 1954)". His rehabilitation of this genre, in Blamires's view, may be even more significant than the works themselves.

In the preface to *The Allegory of Love,* references are made to three Inklings: Tolkien, Hugo Dyson, and Owen Barfield. The book itself is dedicated to Barfield, to whom Lewis acknowledges the greatest debt, after his father, Albert:

C.S. Lewis and his brother, Warren Lewis, on vacation in Annagassan, Ireland, around 1949 (© The Marion E. Wade Center).

Formal portrait of Charles Williams, 39 years old, taken the year before C.S. Lewis invited him to an Inklings meeting (© The Marion E. Wade Center).

J.R.R. Tolkien and Hugo Dyson, Merton College, 1954. From the collection of Harry Lee Poe.

_c._ 1947. An Inklings gathering, seated on the low stone wall of terrace at the Trout Inn, Godstow, with the River Thames behind them. L. to R: Commander James Dundas-Grant, Colin Hardie, Robert E. "Humphrey" Havard, C.S. Lewis, and Peter Havard (son of Dr Havard). (© The Marion E. Wade Center.)

Dorothy L. Sayers, a friend of Charles Williams and C.S. Lewis. The mystery writer, dramatist, and popular theologian had strong affinities with the Inklings, though not a member (© The Marion E. Wade Center).

Owen Barfield, taken in the USA, probably while visiting Wheaton College, Illinois (photograph by Douglas R. Gilbert © 1973).

Nevill Coghill directing Richard Burton, in the Oxford University Dramatic Society production of Christopher Marlowe's *Doctor Faustus* in 1966 (© Terrence Spencer/The LIFE Images Collection/Getty).

Leeds University, where J.R.R. Tolkien was first Reader then Professor of English Language between 1920 and 1925 in a highly productive period.

Lord David Cecil, as President of the Jane Austen Society, in conversation with a member at the 1968 annual meeting. Cecil, in the 1930s, pioneered Austen studies. From the collection of Harry Lee Poe.

Pembroke College, Oxford. Tolkien was a fellow here from 1925 to 1945, while university Professor of Anglo-Saxon.

Exeter College, where J.R.R. Tolkien was an undergraduate until 1915, as were Nevill Coghill and H.V.D. Dyson a few years later.

Coghill was elected a research fellow here in 1924, and official fellow and librarian in 1925.

Exeter College quad with the notable gothic chapel (within which is a commemorative bust of J.R.R. Tolkien).

Merton College, front quad. The Inklings sometimes met in Tolkien's college rooms here after he became Merton Professor of English Language and literature in 1945. Hugo Dyson became a fellow and tutor in English Literature here, also in 1945. In 1957, Nevill Coghill was elected Merton Professor of English Literature.

Merton College seen from Christ Church Meadow.

New Building, Magdalen College, rear view. Here the Inklings met in C.S. Lewis's rooms for many years. The room they usually used overlooked the deer park.

Magdalen College tower from Addison's Walk.

Addison's Walk, Magdalen College, where J.R.R. Tolkien, Hugo Dyson, and C.S. Lewis had a long night conversation that changed Lewis's life. Lewis often took a circular walk here from the college.

Opposite page:

Top: The Kings Arms was a popular meeting place for Inklings members in twos or threes, or for more regular gatherings. It is located conveniently close to the Bodleian Library, used for research.

Middle: The tiny White Horse pub, in Broad Street, was a meeting place for the Inklings. It is beside Blackwell's Bookshop, much used by members. On one occasion in 1944, Tolkien read a draft chapter of *The Lord of the Rings* here to C.S. Lewis and Charles Williams.

Bottom: The Eagle and Child in St Giles, known by the Inklings as "the Bird and Baby", is the pub most associated with the group.

Top right: When the Eagle and Child was extensively modernized, the Inklings crossed over St Giles for a new venue for gatherings, adopting the more suitable Lamb and Flag pub.

Middle right: Eastgate Hotel, near Magdalen College, which Lewis and Tolkien would often adjourn to after meeting together in Lewis's college in the early years of their friendship.

The Kilns, home to C.
Lewis and his brother
Warnie, was set in
eight acres, including
woodland and a floo[
quarry (suitable for
punting and swimmin[
Close friends would
visit from time to time
This photo was taken
in 1930, around the
time that Lewis move[
into the house with N[
Moore and her daugh[
Maureen (© The Ma[
E. Wade Center).

Among the Inklings,
Tolkien and C.S. Lew[
most particularly wer[
inspired in their fictio[
by the landscapes
they knew. Here, the
meeting of the rivers
Trent and Sow near t[
Essex Bridge in Great
Haywood, Staffordsh[
inspired the confluen[
of two rivers near the
Bridge of Tavrobel in [
early story concernin[
Middle-earth.

Vale of the White Horse, Oxfordshire. Some of the Inklings shared in long walks and walking holidays
enjoyed by C.S. Lewis in the countryside of England and Wales. Oxfordshire and Berkshire offered
many fairly local walks.

There seems to be hardly any one among my acquaintance from whom I have not learned. The greatest of these debts – that which I owe to my father for the inestimable benefit of a childhood passed mostly alone in a house full of books – is now beyond repayment; and among the rest I can only select…. Above all, the friend to whom I have dedicated the book, has taught me not to patronize the past, and has trained me to see the present as itself a "period". I desire for myself no higher function than to be one of the instruments whereby his theory and practice in such matters may become more widely effective.

The dedication reads: "To Owen Barfield, wisest and best of my unofficial teachers."

Lewis as a literary controversialist: *Rehabilitations*

Lewis's collection of essays, *Rehabilitations* (1939), is something of a snapshot of his concerns throughout the 1930s. It bears the marks of ideas shared by and having affinities with his Inklings friends, which comes out, I believe, in what Lewis calls "a certain unity" in various "beliefs about life and books which are implicit throughout". Lewis's diversity of essays – held together, he believed, by a tacit view of life and books – may well echo the diversity, yet possible underlying unity, of the Inklings.

In his brief preface Lewis states that much of his book praises what he loves but which is under attack, especially in English studies. Six of the nine essays are, he says, provoked by these attacks. Two, he points out, "defend great romantic poets against popular hatred or neglect of Romanticism".

Two other essays defend "the present course of English studies at Oxford" (based on the syllabus set up by Tolkien, with Lewis's help). Another essay partly defends so-called lowbrow books (such as some of those by Rider Haggard, John Buchan, Beatrix Potter, and P.G. Wodehouse), which, he believes, have "so greatly increased my power of enjoying more serious literature as well as 'real life'; but it is much more a defence of disinterested literary enjoyment against certain other dangerous tendencies in modern education".

Another supports the study of alliterative verse, so native a feature of early English poetry – a genre he later on mentions as being employed by Tolkien. Thinking probably of his friend's poetic and unfinished version of the story of Túrin Turambar,[7] from the "matter" of Middle-earth, Lewis writes: "Professor Tolkien will soon, I hope, be ready to publish an alliterative poem." One essay in the collection, "Bluspels and Flalansferes", draws heavily on the insights of Owen Barfield's *Poetic Diction* (1928). The essay focuses on perceiving reality through meaning rather than abstractly through thought. Lewis celebrates the imagination as the organ of meaning, involved in all human knowledge of reality; for him the imagination provides a sensing, perceiving, feeling knowledge that can be objective but personal (or participatory). A human facility with image and metaphor is a necessary condition of winning knowledge. Typically, Lewis states, "a man who says *heaven* and thinks of the visible sky is pretty sure to mean more than a man who tells us that heaven is a state of mind".[8] Lewis tops off the book with all guns blazing by exploring the relationship between Christianity and literature, revelling in the importance that unoriginality held in the imaginative richness of premodern times.

"Christianity and Literature" represents C.S. Lewis's early thinking on the subject. It reflects, I believe, the Christian dimension of his friendship with Tolkien and the other Inklings. He begins his essay by pointing out that Christian literature is just like any literature – to be good rather than bad it relies on essential qualities such as suspense, variety, and apt choice of words. Where there is poor Christian writing, as in a bad hymn (a pet hate of Lewis's), at least some of the reason for its poorness will be confusion of thought or bad taste in its sentiments. But it is not so much these structural norms about which he is concerned. Rather, he finds himself out of kilter with central notions to be found in the literary criticism of his day. This is a conflict of attitudes rather than of precisely spelled out concepts. He picks out some of these keywords of modern criticism. They are words such as *creative*, *spontaneity*, and *freedom*. The bugbear concepts of the critics are scorned. They are the opposites: *derivative, convention*, and *rules*. For modern critics, Lewis was convinced, great authors are heroes; they are innovators, pioneers, explorers. Bad authors lack courage. They cling together in accepted schools and have to follow models.

While the New Testament says nothing explicitly about literature, he pointed out, it does reveal quite a different attitude. For Lewis, this emphasis is found in the apostle Paul's passage in one of his letters (in 1 Corinthians 11) about imitation, derivation, and mirrored glory. Paul writes about the woman being the glory of a man, as a man is the glory of God. The pattern is that man is derived from God in Adam, and woman derived from man in Eve ("the Son of Adam and Daughter of Eve" in Narnia). Man imitates God, and woman imitates man. This reflects a higher pattern within the Godhead. There the Son imitates the Father (something that also happened quite literally, in Lewis's view, when Jesus, as a boy, copied what Joseph was doing as a carpenter–builder). There is a pattern here of imitation that is found throughout human culture (as when learning takes place).

"In the New Testament," writes Lewis, "the art of life itself is the art of imitation." The mentality this naturally leads to, Lewis argues, is the very opposite of the ruling values of contemporary criticism, such as originality. "'Originality', in the New Testament," he writes, "is quite plainly the prerogative of God alone." The fulfilment of our humanity, in fact, seems in the New Testament to lie in a completely opposite direction. Our maturity exists "in acquiring a fragrance that is not our own but borrowed, in becoming clean mirrors filled with the image of a face that is not ours". The goodness of our humanity is a "derivative or reflective... good".

The vision underlying the essays in *Rehabilitations*, and indeed touching all of the writings of Lewis and Tolkien in this period, involves restoration in three main areas:

1. The fairy story and fantasy.
2. "Learning" and education against a modern overemphasis on "training".
3. Reintroducing the values of what Lewis called the "Old West", such as sacrifice, chivalry, hierarchy, freedom, goodness, dignity, beauty, wonder, holiness, friendship, and fellowship.

So what was it about "fairy stories" and fantasy that led Tolkien and Lewis in particular to want to rehabilitate them for a modern audience?

Their reasons for this interest were both personal and professional. Personally, they had both read and enjoyed such stories when young, in collections by the Brothers Grimm and Andrew Lang. Both had been captivated by George MacDonald, as in the stories of Curdie and *The Golden Key*. Professionally, they studied and taught the literatures of medieval romance, and in Tolkien's case, he was immersed in the richness of Norse myth. They knew therefore that it was only quite recently that such tales had been regarded as "children's stories". These were tales told and enjoyed by grown-ups through much of history. Even strong warriors enjoyed them, rejoicing in their triumphant moments, weeping at tragic turns of events. These stories told them important things about reality: about who they were and what the world was like, and about the realm of the divine.

Both men realized that there was a need to create a readership for these books again – especially for an adult readership, as we saw in the introduction. Lewis's space trilogy came out of this same impulse to write the sort of stories that he and Tolkien liked to read. He felt he could say things in science fiction that he couldn't say in other ways. In the case of Tolkien, he had been expressing this growing realization for years when the two men met – ever since convalescing in the First World War, he had been writing hundreds of pages of his cycle of myth and legend from the early ages of Middle-earth.

Concerning education, Lewis argues in *Rehabilitations* that learning is the mature stage of education. It is an activity for people who have already been humanized by the educative process. Learning is marked by a desire to know: it is intentionally aimed at knowledge as a good in itself.

C.S. Lewis believed that we live today in a world that is fractured from the older world by what in later years he would call a Great Divide, which ushered in the age of the machine, as we saw. Our new age is dominated by a persistent idea of progress, in which the past is superseded.

Lewis's approach in his fictional writings would become increasingly eclectic (a characteristic of an older poet he admired, Edmund Spenser); he drew freely and widely on the images and stories of the whole of the "Old West". Tolkien had interests that were, and would steadfastly remain, more focused on the early English period of literature and northern mythology, but his aims were similar to Lewis's. It is evident that he wished to encourage contemporary people to appropriate this important older history for themselves through his stories. He wanted them to take what Lewis called Old Western values and virtues into their contemporary lives instead of simply absorbing the narrow myths and presuppositions of modern thought and culture. Tolkien and Lewis wished to open a door that would awaken desires and allow the experience of sensations yet unknown, pointing to a reality beyond "the walls of the world". Though Barfield was preoccupied at that time with the grinding work of a solicitor, he still did a little writing and one day would have the leisure to write many books that continued his unique exploration of the importance of imagination in knowledge, a theme central to the Inklings. Charles Williams, with his characteristic emphasis on the theology of romantic love, would soon be a distinctive presence in Inklings meetings.

Of all the Inklings, perhaps Lewis most clearly saw the strategic importance of rehabilitating, for people of the new world, the virtues and values of the long-ago world of the West. He hoped that an enjoyment of his stories would encourage a recognition and exploration of the books, stories, and attitudes of this older world. He felt that this vast older world embodied a remarkably consistent wisdom about the nature of our very humanity. (Lewis would use the ancient term the *Tao*, borrowed from Eastern thought, to name the way of life of these values.[9]) He was concerned that the dominant worldviews of the twentieth century propagated values that would lead inevitably to the "abolition of man" (the title of a philosophical tract that he would one day write on modern education[10]).

Lewis would write many more stories in the future, including *The Chronicles of Narnia*, as part of a strategy to rehabilitate these essential human values. It was natural for him to draw on the imaginative resources and symbolic languages of this earlier, premodernist period. Like Tolkien and Barfield, he was convinced that the future of the contemporary Western world would be exceedingly bleak without the vision of humanity embodied in those values. Charles Williams's writings reinforced such a desire, even if he was perhaps more content than Lewis, Tolkien, and Barfield simply to work out the traditional Christian doctrines in arresting and often shocking forms of fiction, and highly experimental poetry based on the Old Western theme of King Arthur.

A minor Christian renaissance at this time?

C.S. Lewis and his friends in the Inklings were not as isolated at that period as he felt they were, as he faced the self-chosen task of rehabilitating stories of "romance" for adults (the kind of books he, Tolkien, and his friends enjoyed reading, such as Charles Williams's supernatural thriller *The Place of the Lion* – a blend of Platonism and the book of Genesis the like of which perhaps hadn't been seen since the Middle Ages). Along with writing, and encouraging the writing of, such stories, Lewis became conscious of an urgent need for a defence of increasingly cast-off values and virtues that he felt were germane to our very humanity.

The 1930s in fact marked a "minor renaissance" of Christian themes in English literature. This is according to Harry Blamires (a former student of Lewis's, author, and critic). The writers among the Inklings at that time were very much part of this small but significant movement.

The beginnings of this resurgence go back to 1928 when George Bell, who was Dean of Canterbury Cathedral, thought that it was time to bring drama once again into churches. He started the Canterbury Festival, which was then closely connected to the recently formed Friends of Canterbury Cathedral. The most notable play to appear in the festival was T.S. Eliot's verse drama, *Murder in the Cathedral*, which was premiered there in 1935. The following year, festival-goers were presented with Charles Williams's *Thomas Cranmer of Canterbury*. The year after came Dorothy L. Sayers's *The Zeal of Thy House*. Her retelling of the Faust story, *The Devil to Pay*, was performed in 1939.

Harry Blamires makes the point that writers such as Lewis, Tolkien, and Williams did not exist in splendid isolation. It is clear from what he describes that the Inklings were part of an important current in the literary milieu of the 1930s. He writes:

Lewis began writing just at the point when this minor Christian Renaissance in literature was taking off. His *Pilgrim's Regress* came out in 1933. And the 1930s were a remarkable decade in this respect. Eliot's *Ash Wednesday* came out in 1930, *The Rock* in 1934, *Murder in the Cathedral* in 1935 and *Burnt Norton* in 1936. Charles Williams's *War In Heaven* was published in 1930, *The Place of the*

Lion in 1931, *The Greater Trumps* in 1932, and his play
Thomas Cranmer of Canterbury in 1936. Helen Waddell's
Peter Abelard came out in 1933. Meanwhile on the stage
James Bridie had great popular successes with his biblical
plays *Tobias and the Angel* (1930) and *Jonah and the Whale*
(1932). Then by 1937 Christopher Fry was launched with
The Boy with a Cart. That same year saw Dorothy Sayers's
The Zeal of Thy House performed, and David Jones's *In
Parenthesis* and Tolkien's *The Hobbit* published. Lewis's *Out
of the Silent Planet* followed in 1938 along with Williams's
Taliessin through Logres and Greene's *Brighton Rock.* Eliot's
Family Reunion followed in 1939, Greene's *The Power and
The Glory* in 1940. During the same decade Evelyn Waugh
was getting known and Rose Macaulay was in spate.
Edwin Muir, Andrew Young, and Francis Berry appeared
in print.

So when the literary historian looks back at the
English literary scene in the 1930s and 1940s he is going
to see C.S. Lewis and Charles Williams, not as freakish
throwbacks, but as initial contributors to what I have
called a Christian literary renaissance, if a minor one.[11]

Looking back decades later, it is easier for us to see such a
pattern emerging. Of more significance at the time for Tolkien
and Lewis, of course, was the informal club they had started
in the early thirties.

CHAPTER 7

The war years and the Golden Age of the Inklings

There is very little documentation on the early years of the Inklings, before the Second World War. What there is suggests that the group had settled into a pattern of the two types of meeting, one of a reading group, usually in C.S. Lewis's rooms at Magdalen College, and the other mainly a conversational group, meeting in favourite pubs, normally the Eagle and Child in St Giles. Warnie Lewis in later years considered the latter supplementary to what he called "the Inklings proper", those meetings with a focus on readings. Owen Barfield,[1] however, seems to have considered the conversations that took place as integral to the group's essence, and certainly Hugo Dyson did, as he actually much preferred talk to readings of work in progress.[2]

The group may not have met as frequently in the early days as we know they did in the war years – that is, twice weekly during term time and often more.[3] Furthermore, before the war the evening meetings may have been more common than morning gatherings in pubs. In addition, it must be said, Tolkien and Lewis met often, perhaps out of term time as well as in it, with Warnie Lewis tending to be around at these meetings too after 1932. What we do know is that a good amount of reading took place between Inklings members in one way or another before the war. The documented readings to the whole group include Tolkien's *The Hobbit*, Lewis's *Out of the Silent Planet* (read as a serial, according to Tolkien), and various poems.

The war years, 1939–1945, up to the death of Williams (which occurred just after VE[4] Day), form a highly significant part of a discernible phase in the life of the Inklings circle – something of a "golden age", in fact. Williams's arrival in Oxford in September 1939 marks its beginning, in that it took place at the very start of what turned out to be another world war. In this period the second type of meeting became more customary – that is, the Tuesday-morning gathering. Williams added an extraordinary new dimension to both types of gathering. A note by Lewis of meetings with Charles Williams clearly shows the pattern of the two types of gathering during wartime. He records that from September 1939 "until his death [in 1945] we met one another twice a week, sometimes more: nearly always on Thursday evenings in my rooms and on Tuesday mornings in the best of all public-houses for draught cider".[5]

The number of those documented as being part of the group within the Charles Williams period, either regularly or intermittently, is larger than before the war: C.S. Lewis, Warren Lewis, Tolkien, Charles Williams, Hugo Dyson, Owen Barfield, Dr "Humphrey" Havard, Nevill Coghill, Adam Fox (perhaps until 1942),[6] and Lord David Cecil. Warnie Lewis was absent for the first part of the period on war service (which meant that we have references to Inklings meetings in Lewis's letters to him). Owen Barfield could visit only from time to time from London. Hugo Dyson attended quite frequently from Reading and returned to teach in Oxford in 1945. Guests are recorded as being invited to evening Inklings meetings during this period: the poet Roy Campbell (after the Inklings came across him in the Eagle and Child pub the Tuesday before) and the fantasy author E.R. Eddison (who made two visits during this time).

The intensified life of the Inklings group in wartime seems to have resulted from two main factors. The first is the war. It created a greater appreciation of the club among its members, as they, like people in Britain in general, were drawn together in response to the crisis. Most of the Inklings had served in the previous world conflict, which had ended just over twenty years before, and thus had a very realistic view of the consequences of war. They were deemed unnecessary for military service, either simply because of their age or because their civilian work was important.

Warren Lewis, as an experienced professional solder, was the exception. He was called up out of retirement to reprise his previous role in military supplies. His war service was short-lived, however, and he returned to the UK shortly before the Dunkirk evacuations from France in 1940. The other main factor was related to the war. Charles Williams, who had met the Inklings probably three years before, was evacuated to Oxford along with other staff from the London branch of the Oxford University Press. He would soon become a treasured, regular member, and then also a familiar lecturer in the university's English School. These responsibilities were on top of his publishing duties, performed in a makeshift office. Lewis would remember him as "my friend of friends, the comforter of all our little set [the Inklings], the most angelic man …".[7]

Charles Williams's lectures were highly popular with students. In his published memories of his time as an undergraduate in the English School, John Wain devotes a number of pages to him. For Wain, Williams was one of the truly inspiring figures at Oxford.[8] His hold on students can be witnessed by the occasion when his lecture on *Hamlet* filled the lecture hall. Tolkien, as it happened, was lecturing at the same time, but his most of his students deserted him to hear Williams. The only student who remained for Tolkien's lecture on Anglo-Saxon was one who had been sent to take notes. Tolkien was left to lecture to that single student, but he magnanimously had a drink with Charles Williams afterwards. Such success created no ill feeling between the two friends. It was only his interest in the occult that troubled Tolkien, and perhaps there was a certain jealousy, as Williams took a central place in Lewis's affections that Tolkien had had in earlier years.[9]

C.S. Lewis captures the vitality of Inklings gatherings of various sorts (including walking excursions) in some blurb that he wrote about himself in 1943 for the American publisher of his science-fiction story *Out of the Silent Planet*, which was appearing Stateside for the first time: "My happiest hours are spent with three or four old friends in old clothes tramping together and putting up in small pubs – or else sitting up till the small hours in someone's college rooms talking nonsense, poetry, theology, metaphysics over beer, tea and pipes." This tantalizing glimpse of his enjoyment of his friends at this time also indicates the very small size of meetings of the Inklings, whether the evening meetings devoted more to reading, or their more informal companionship on walking holidays. It is interesting that he makes this comment on the jacket of *Out of the Silent Planet*, a story that features Lewis himself as a character who helps the hero, Dr Elwin Ransom, to write up his adventures on Malacandra (Mars). Furthermore, Ransom is loosely based on J.R.R. Tolkien. In a small meeting perhaps characteristic of the Inklings at this time, Lewis and Tolkien might represent as much as 40 per cent of the gathering.

Most of our picture of the Inklings in wartime – as they group together in those days of foreboding, with a growing sense of the whole world being in danger – is gained from such scraps as that brief blurb. These morsels come from letters, such as those written by Lewis to his brother at the beginning of the war while Warnie was on active service in England and France, or Tolkien's letters to his son Christopher, on flight training with the RAF in South Africa, the land of Tolkien's birth. They also come from Warnie's beautifully written diaries and brief diary entries by others, or from memories of Inklings members or visitors to meetings recorded long after in interviews, or written down in brief memoirs. One American visitor, Chad Walsh, wrote of a Tuesday-morning Inklings in the very first study of Lewis's thought and writings in 1948 (*C.S. Lewis: Apostle to the Skeptics*):

> Only in retrospect did I realize how much intellectual ground was covered in these seemingly casual meetings. At the time the constant bustle of Lewis racing his friends to refill empty mugs or pausing to light another cigarette (occasionally a pipe) camouflaged the steady flow of ideas. The flow, I might add, is not a one-way traffic. Lewis is as good a listener as talker, and has alert curiosity about almost anything conceivable.[10]

Here is a selection of glimpses of meetings of the Inklings as a twice-weekly group, or in twos or threes elsewhere. As Lewis emphasized walking tours in his book blurb (in fact, *Out of the Silent Planet* opens with Ransom's walking holiday), we might begin there, even though they are outside the informal pattern of Tuesday and Thursday meetings.

Walking tours in wartime

As we have seen, walking tours or brief walking breaks, preferably in the company of friends, were one of Lewis's great delights. In his science-fiction story *Out of the Silent Planet*, the protagonist is on a solitary walking tour during the summer vacation. For a spring walk, Lewis liked a southern tour, perhaps in Dorset, where he remembered the season as being remarkably far on, the woodland nearly green, primroses evident in "great cushiony clumps", and the sea glimpsed in the distance. Such a walk would be punctuated by halts or "soaks", perhaps lying down in barns or on sun-facing hill slopes.[11]

His letters and diaries, together with the diaries of his brother, give details of many walking holidays. The plan was usually for friends to make their way to a starting point by train or car and then to walk for several days, putting up in small hotels or country inns, which provided a hot supper, a bed for the night, and breakfast. In April 1927, for instance, Lewis had walked with Cecil Harwood (who was never a member of the Inklings) and Owen Barfield across the Berkshire Downs. At this period Harwood planned the walks, and in a letter to him in 1931 Lewis called him "Lord of the Walks". When Warren retired early and joined Lewis's household at The Kilns, an annual walking tour for the two was soon institutionalized, as we have seen. There were eight such tours during the thirties – the last taking place early in 1939 – to the Wye Valley, to Wales and Aberystwyth, to the Chiltern Hills, to the Derbyshire Peak District, to Somerset, and to Wiltshire.

In a letter to Warnie while he was still with the British forces in France, Lewis recorded a four-day walking holiday on Exmoor in the spring of 1940. It lasted from Friday 5 to Monday 8 April.[12] Cecil Harwood lived at the time in Minehead in Somerset, beside Exmoor, so the idea was for the three, and another friend, Walter Field, to meet there. Field was an anthroposophist, like Barfield and Harwood. In Minehead, Lewis met Hugo Dyson, who, unknown to him, was staying with in-laws there, together with his wife, Margaret, who was laid up with measles. Lewis was delighted to find Dyson in Minehead, and made sure that most days the walk ended up back there, so he could see something of his great friend, who couldn't walk with them. Much to Lewis's surprise and pleasure, Field and Dyson got on well together; he hadn't anticipated that they would have much in common. Lewis said that this was despite the fact that Field talked incessantly about a then fashionable view of economics that championed social credit. Lewis clearly enjoyed the unusual sight of Dyson being reduced to silence by Field's determination to explain the theory.

Lewis had visited the area three months earlier, in January, to walk with Harwood. The walks began and ended in Minehead, to save expense for Harwood, who had a large family. (One of his children, Laurence, was Lewis's godson.[13]) Lewis had also been there for rather similar walks ten years before, accompanied at that time by the same friends, Barfield, Harwood, and Walter Field. As far back as 1920, while an undergraduate, he had visited that same locality with Mrs Janie Moore, when they had stayed in Old Cleeve and had cycled together into the countryside from Dunster.

In his long letter to Warnie, Lewis beautifully described the walks and the sights that he saw: wooded ridges, the variety and tone of weather, visiting a church (where Lewis was urged by the others to read a passage from the pulpit Bible), the merits of various bars, rising fields and slopes of heather, and climbs rewarded with the prospect of "hills on hills on hills to the end of the world". On one high top, marked by its cairn of stones, Barfield recited a sonnet. Places visited included Dunkery Beacon, the village of Wootton Courtenay (where Lewis read from the Bible), a farm called Cloutsham, the "beautiful" village of Dunster, Croydon Hill, the villages of Luxborough, Bridgetown, and Winsford (where they stayed one night), and Timberscombe (where there is an old coaching house called The Lion Inn) in the valley of the River Avill.

Lewis wrote that one evening they had a "splendid" time "telling a story". This, he explained to Warnie, was "an old diversion on these walks in which each player invents a chunk in turn: the natural tendency of each to introduce new characters and complications and then to 'hand the baby' to the next man, produces the fun. Dyson proved specially good at it..." Though of the Inklings only Lewis, Barfield, and Dyson were present, it is sufficient to give a glimpse of the enjoyment of each other's company that was so characteristic of the circle. Lewis obviously wanted his absent brother to partake in that enjoyment via the long letter.

It wasn't until Lewis's return to Oxford, after sharing much of the train journey back with Barfield (as far as Reading on the London-bound train), that he read on a newspaper billboard the shocking news of Hitler's invasion of Denmark. This was the second seizure of a country by the Nazis, the first being Poland.

Further glimpses of Inklings meetings[14]

A revealing session of the Inklings took place on Thursday 9 November 1939, less than two months after Charles Williams arrived on the scene, a meeting that illustrates the flavour or atmosphere of wartime Inklings sessions, at least the overtly literary ones.

After dining at Oxford's Eastgate Hotel, favoured by the Inklings, the group listened to Tolkien reading from the first book[15] of what would become *The Lord of the Rings* (the "new Hobbit"), Williams from a Nativity play, and Lewis from a chapter of the book he was writing on the problem of pain. Lewis described, in a letter to his absent brother, the ever-talkative Dyson as "a roaring cataract of nonsense". The piece read by Tolkien may have been a reworked section – he was making substantial changes, to do with the nature of the Ring of power and the identity of Aragorn (who not long before had been a Hobbit called "Trotter"!). Whatever it was that Tolkien read, it was likely to have brought in the nature of evil. Lewis, later in his letter to Warnie, described the subject matter of the readings that evening as having "formed almost a logical sequence". His own chapter from *The Problem of Pain* almost certainly expounded on this theme. Williams's verse drama – *The House by the Stable* – directly concerned the battle to win the human soul to evil. It effectively presents the upside-down perspective of hell. Two allegorical characters – Pride, in the form of a pretty woman, and Hell, her brother – seek to elicit the precious jewel of the soul from the breast of Man. They are interrupted by the figures of Joseph and Mary seeking shelter for the night, marking divine intervention in history.[16]

At another Inklings meeting two and a half months later, on Thursday 25 January, the "usual party" enjoyed rum and hot water on a cold evening, and heard Tolkien read a new chapter of what became *The Fellowship of the Ring*. The "usual party" was presumably Dyson, Charles Williams, Revd Adam Fox, and Lewis – Havard had been unable to attend so far that term "by various accidents" (common of course in icy conditions[17]) that presumably needed his medical attention. Warnie was still in France, Coghill's attendance was increasingly erratic, and Barfield could rarely come. The rest of the evening was spent in talk, regrettably with no details of the conversations noted.

Humphrey Havard was, however, able to attend an Inklings session on Thursday 1 February 1940. It was, wrote Lewis to the absent Warnie, "the usual pleasant party... with the welcome addition of Havard". The doctor read a short paper on the clinical experience of pain, prepared as an appendix for use in full or in part in Lewis's book *The Problem of Pain*. Lewis added: "We had an evening almost equally compounded of merriment, piety, and literature." He didn't forget to note that they drank rum with hot water again, and observed that the Inklings was[18] now very well provided with the "estates",[19] almost all of them: "Fox as chaplain, you as army, Barfield as lawyer, Havard as doctor." What was lacking, he wrote, was "anyone who could actually produce a single necessity of life, a loaf, a boot, or a hut".

Shortly after this, on Thursday 15 February, Owen Barfield was able to attend an Inklings meeting while over from London, which greatly pleased Lewis. At the next week's meeting, on 22 February, a great storm blew up. Lewis records in his weekly letter to Warnie that "we had a furious argument about cremation". He admits that he had hitherto been unaware of the "Papal dislike of the practice", which was clearly evident in Tolkien and Havard's emotional reaction, which greatly surprised him. The two Roman Catholics were convinced that it was a fact that atheists supported cremation, and that even as a corpse, the lifeless body was "the temple of the Holy Ghost". Lewis's retort – "but a vacated temple", adding that it was surely reasonable to destroy a church building to stop it "being defiled by Communists" – didn't go down well.

Just a week later, Hugo Dyson, up from Reading, attended the Thursday-evening Inklings on 29 February 1940. All were present except for Warren Lewis and Owen Barfield. During the meeting, Adam Fox read a poem on Blenheim Park in winter. We do not know if there were other readings, but this is likely, with writing by the Inklings being very active during the war. The conversation turned to Charles Williams's recent lecture to Oxford English undergraduates in the setting of the Divinity School, where he celebrated the theme of chastity and the doctrine of virginity in Milton's *Comus*. On being told of this, Dyson remarked, to the amusement of the group, that Williams was "becoming a common chastitute".[20]

Lewis had been constantly aware of his brother's absence in France as Nazi forces advanced but, to his relief, Warnie, as mentioned, had been safely evacuated in early May 1940 before the main retreat of the British army from Dunkirk.[21] The two brothers had spent a few days together before Warnie, his leave over, joined his unit at Wenvoe Camp in Cardiff. Lewis explained in a long letter to him later in the month that his handwriting might be illegible because his arms were trembling after the effort of cropping with a heavy scythe in the extensive grounds of The Kilns (scything the "nettles by the hen run and the grass and weeds in the neighbouring plantation"). Lewis was also missing Warnie and grieving over the news from the Netherlands. Enemy forces had started marching towards the neutral country, forcing the Dutch queen, Wilhelmina, to flee to England. Despite a strong defence, the nation had fallen to the occupiers by 15 May. He told Warnie that one of his students was in very low spirits when he attended a tutorial with him. He was German Jewish, and his parents were in Holland.[22]

According to that letter to Warnie, there was the usual evening Inklings meeting on Thursday 16 May. Lewis sat in the north room of his accommodation in Magdalen College, looking out at the hawthorn in the grove, as he awaited the arrival of the other Inklings. He much regretted the fact that his brother "had passed from the status of a sense-object to that of a mental picture". Dr Humphrey Havard was the first to arrive, then Charles Williams, and then Tolkien. As he went into the south room with them (which looked over the lawns towards the Cloister and Great Tower) he noticed "the exquisite smell of the wisteria pervading the whole room". Charles Wrenn turned up later in the evening, and after that they went around the walks in the extensive grounds of the college. All of them had asked for news of Warnie, and expressed their gladness that he had survived France. Lewis added no details of the readings or conversation.

Later in 1940, Warnie Lewis, now discharged from the army, returned permanently to Oxford and The Kilns, so the informative letters from Lewis to him ceased. Later in the war, however, Tolkien's letters to his son Christopher record impressions of Inklings meetings. One of these was on Thursday 13 April 1944. Tolkien wrote, in an episodic letter, that he was going to Magdalen that night. He anticipated that those attending would be the Lewis brothers, Charles Williams, Lord David Cecil, and probably Dr Havard (who is "still bearded and uniformed" after returning from a period of military service). Tolkien mentioned that Major Lewis was writing a book, adding that this activity "was catching". In the event all turned up as expected except David Cecil, and they stayed until midnight. The best part of it, according to Tolkien, was Warnie's chapter on the subject of the court of Louis XIV. He was not so partial to the concluding chapter of Lewis's *The Great Divorce*, which was read out that evening.

We also catch glimpses of Inklings meetings in memories recorded years later. Humphrey Havard vividly recalled the setting of the club of friends, and the reception of Lewis's *The Screwtape Letters* as instalments were read:

> The usual procedure, after drinks and gossip had been exchanged, was to settle into armchairs and then for someone to be invited to read a recent manuscript. The rest then commented, led nearly always by Lewis. Criticism was frank but friendly. Coming from a highly literate audience, it was often profuse and detailed. The universal complaint from the speaker actually holding the floor was that everyone else spoke so much that it was barely possible to get his own ideas in edgeways. True enough, the informality of the group led occasionally to several trying to speak at once. As the only nonliterary and nonteaching member, my chief contribution was to listen. The talk was good, witty, learned, high hearted, and very stimulating. We all felt the itch to join in.
>
> It was in this way that the early *Screwtape Letters* first saw daylight. They were greeted hilariously. We heard several of Lewis's poems... and chapters from the *Problem of Pain* and *Miracles*.[23]

A substantial proportion of the "new Hobbit" was read to the Inklings over ten years or more. At times, the reading was to Lewis alone, or to two or three members outside Inklings hours. In his regular Monday-morning meeting with Lewis on 29 May 1944, Tolkien read out the two latest chapters from *The Lord of the Rings*, "Shelob's Lair" and "The Choices of Master Samwise". Tolkien noted that Lewis approved of them with unusual fervour, and was moved to tears by the second chapter.

One of the Inklings who benefited from sharing work in progress was Charles Williams. Episodes from what was to be his final novel, *All Hallows' Eve*, became a feature of the meetings for a while. On Thursday 28 October 1943, for instance, at a meeting of the Inklings in Lewis's rooms, Williams read from it and evoked an exclamation from Lewis that it was much the best thing that he had done. Some months later Charles Williams recorded in a letter to Michal, his wife, that "Magdalen" (i.e. the Inklings) "thinks it 'tender and gay' among all the melodramatic horrors". In later years, Tolkien remembered: "I was a sort of midwife at the birth of *All Hallows' Eve* read aloud to us as it was composed, but the very great changes in it were I think mainly due to C.S. Lewis."[24]

Charles Williams illustrates the complex nature of the dynamics of the Inklings. Not only did he join with what he called "the Magdalen set" or just "Magdalen" for the Thursday or sometimes Friday evenings, but often he met just with Lewis, or with Lewis and Tolkien, or even simply with Lewis's brother, Warnie. It looks as if the Inklings were a bit like the Christian church: where two or three were gathered, there the group existed. Lewis vividly described the scene of an occasion when Williams read to Tolkien and him from a study of Arthurian legend, which was to be curtailed by his sudden death. The reading took place sometime in 1944:

Picture to yourself… an upstairs sitting room with windows looking north into the "grove" of Magdalen College on a sunshiny Monday Morning in vacation at about ten o'clock. The Professor and I, both on the Chesterfield, lit our pipes and stretched out our legs. Williams in the armchair opposite to us threw his cigarette into the grate, took up a pile of the extremely small, loose sheets on which he habitually wrote – they came, I think, from a twopenny pad for memoranda, and began [reading].… [25]

John Wain, a member of the Inklings for a time, recalls this period and the evening meetings in Lewis's college rooms with a novelist's eye:

I can see that room so clearly now, the electric fire pumping heat into the dank air, the faded screen that broke some of the keener draughts, the enamel beerjug on the table, the well-worn sofa and armchairs, and the men drifting in… leaving overcoats and hats in any corner and coming over to warm their hands before finding a chair. There was no fixed etiquette, but the rudimentary honours would be done partly by Lewis and partly by his brother, W.H. Lewis, a man who stays in my memory as the most courteous I have ever met.[26]

"The Inklings can never be the same again"

Charles Williams's wartime evacuation to Oxford, and his admittance into the Inklings, deepened his influence on C.S. Lewis. After Lewis's death, Tolkien was to describe his friend as being under Williams's "spell"; Lewis was "too impressionable", he felt. Tolkien also referred to the Inklings in these later years as Lewis's séance, alluding to Williams's taste for the occult. These late memories are in sharp contrast to Tolkien's reception of Williams at the time. From his wartime comments, it is clear that Tolkien benefited from Williams's friendship and was encouraged by his friend's positive and perceptive responses to readings from *The Lord of the Rings*.

The day after war in Europe ended on Tuesday 8 May 1945, Charles Williams was almost alone in the temporary offices of the Oxford University Press for the last day that he would work. That evening he walked the Oxford streets with Anne Spalding (at whose house he was lodging). Victory bonfires were burning everywhere. There was a sense of ending as revellers went wild. The following day Williams could not work; he was gripped with pain. Later in the week he was taken to the Radcliffe Infirmary, located nearby on the Woodstock Road. Florence Williams arrived by train from London after hearing of the emergency, and stayed in Oxford.

After the weekend, Williams was operated on for a condition that had troubled him years before, but he never fully recovered consciousness. All that Lewis had heard was that he was to have minor surgery. The evening of the day of Williams's operation, Lewis gave a talk on "Resurrection" at the Socratic Club. Hope in the resurrection of the body after death was a central tenet of his Christian belief. The day after, on Tuesday 15 May, Lewis made his way to the Radcliffe, carrying a book he wanted to lend Williams, intending to join the others as usual in "the Bird and Baby" a few minutes' walk away. He was stunned to find that his great friend had passed away. The shock persisted as he sleepwalked down to St Giles and the Eagle and Child pub, where the Inklings had gathered – unprepared, as he had been, for the news.

Warnie Lewis, working in Lewis's college rooms on his book on French history, received a phone call at 12:50 for his brother with the message "Mr Charles Williams died in the Acland this morning".[27] That evening Warnie recorded the unexpected death in his diary: "And so vanishes one of the best and nicest men it has ever been my good fortune to meet. May God receive him into His everlasting happiness." He added: "The Inklings can never be the same again." Warnie recalled how someone in the group would casually say, "'Well, goodbye, see you on Tuesday Charles.'… He passes up the lamplit street, and passes out of your life for ever."

Charles Williams was buried in St Cross churchyard, Holywell, in Oxford, not far from the grave of Kenneth Grahame. Michal Williams would one day share the grave, and nearby would be the remains of Hugo Dyson. In Dorothy L. Sayers's detective novel *Busman's Honeymoon*, Lord Peter Wimsey and Harriet Vane, in great happiness, are married in the church of St Cross.

As the dingy war years passed, the Inklings had dreamed of having a "Victory Inklings", a week's holiday of talk, beer, and books after the conflict was over, totally ignoring any clock. With the loss of Charles Williams, the actual event in mid December 1945 was a much reduced affair. A few of the Inklings arrived at their location in the Cotswold Hills in dribs and drabs. Barfield had to call off coming because of illness. That just left the Lewis brothers, Tolkien, and a delayed Humphrey Havard in the party. It was just after the end of the Michaelmas term. The depleted group settled in a homely pub called The Bull, by the marketplace in Fairford, a small town on the River Coln, west of the Thames.

The celebration lasted four days, days hard-won from their work and family responsibilities and commitments. The first day, before the others arrived, Warnie patiently walked with Tolkien, who would constantly stop to look at wildflowers or whatever else caught his attention. As usual, Warnie recorded the events in his diary. The quiet reading and the activities of the group interested him equally. The long-promised Inklings victory event became more of an opportunity to dream of the future than to dwell on the past. With war over, a season of peace and possibility lay ahead. In The Bull, Warnie wrote in his diary,

> [w]e were very cosy in our own lounge in the evening where I read Lewis Carroll's *Life* by [S.D.] Collingwood, and Tollers my Dr. J.[ohn] Brown's *Letters*. J[ack] arrived, without Barfield who was ill, by 9.35 on Wednesday, and Humphrey [Havard] turned up to lunch by car; after which we had one of the best winter walks I ever took… On Thursday… [i]n the afternoon we walked through Horcott and Whelford… Whelford, a mere Hamlet, has a simple little Church where we all felt that God dwells; nothing to "see" in it. There, to my surprise and pleasure, Tollers said a prayer. Down on the river was a perfect mill house where we amused ourselves by dreaming of it as a home for the Inklings…[28]

One day they drank beer at the unusually named Pig and Whistle at Coln St Aldwyn, "a dream village". When they returned to Oxford, Warnie recorded that he and his brother dined at the Royal Oxford Hotel with Christopher Tolkien, back from South Africa and, at twenty-six, one of the youngest of the Inklings. The dreams of the Inklings had not died.

CHAPTER 8

The close of the Golden Age

After the war the ranks of Inklings swelled. They now included a new generation of members, who were invited along from time to time: Christopher Tolkien, back from his RAF service with his pilot's wings, and John Wain, the poet, novelist, and critic (and future Oxford Professor of Poetry). Wain graduated from St John's College in 1946 and was invited to attend the Inklings by Lewis, who had tutored him. The other members documented during this period were Lewis, Tolkien, Warnie Lewis, Hugo Dyson, Humphrey Havard, Owen Barfield (still an occasional visitor from London), Charles Wrenn, and Lord David Cecil, as well as new members: Colin Hardie, a classicist at Magdalen College with a deep interest in Dante, Gervase Mathew, a medievalist and writer, R.B. McCallum, a fellow in History at Pembroke, J.A.W. ("Jaw") Bennett, a fellow and tutor in English at Magdalen (like Lewis), James Dundas-Grant, in charge of a residential home for Roman Catholic students in Oxford, and C.E. "Tom" Stevens, a fellow and tutor in ancient history at Magdalen.

Not everyone listed here was invited to attend the literary Thursday nights (the usual etiquette) or, when brought along by an existing member, was welcome there.[1] Some attended only the Tuesday-morning meetings. Guests were sometimes invited. One recorded as attending a Thursday-night meeting was Stanley Bennett of Cambridge University, who would eventually be one of those behind an invitation to Lewis from that university to take on the new Chair of Medieval and Renaissance literature. Another guest, Gwynne Jones, Professor of English at Aberystwyth, visited on 24 April 1947 with Tolkien, and, according to Warren Lewis's diary entry for that night, read "a Welsh tale of his own writing, a bawdy, humorous thing told in a rich, polished style".[2] At first, those there were annoyed that Tolkien had brought along Professor Jones, but they soon warmed to him.

John Wain tells us that following Charles Williams's death, the most proactive Inklings on the reading evenings were once again reduced to two: Tolkien and Lewis. Wain claimed that "[w]hile C.S. Lewis attacked [the whole current of contemporary art and life] on a wide front, with broadcasts, popular-theological books, children's stories, romances, and controversial literary criticism, Tolkien concentrated on the writing of his colossal 'Lord of the Rings' trilogy. His readings of each successive instalment were eagerly received, for 'romance' was a pillar of this whole structure".[3] Lewis, in a letter to the journal *Encounter*,[4] challenged Wain's account of the Inklings, which made them seem like a cabal or cell. The idea of the group being driven by a strategy, warlike on Lewis's part, was alien to him. He supremely valued the fact that the Inklings were a group of freely chosen friends.

Dyson certainly valued the fact that conversation between friends was central, as he saw it, to the Inklings. His preference for talk over listening to work in progress appears to have grown more marked after he left Reading University and became a don at Merton College in 1945. At a "Bird and Baby morning", as Warnie tended to call it, Lewis drew humorous attention to Dyson's love of talk and reticence in writing (and also to Tolkien's somewhat notorious inaudibility). This was on one autumn Tuesday in 1950.[5] At the gathering were the Lewis brothers, Tolkien, James Dundas-Grant, and Colin Hardie. Warnie recorded in his diary that night, "A good and quite unintentional *gaffe* by J[ack]: the question was propounded whether Tollers' voice production or Hugo's hand writing gave more trouble to their friends. J[ack:] 'Well, there's this to be said for Hugo's writing, there's less of it.'"[6]

Dyson gained some notoriety by starting to exercise a veto against further reading by Tolkien of instalments of *The Lord of the Rings*. After an evening that was well attended, Warnie wrote that Tolkien and his son Christopher, he and his brother, Humphrey Havard, and Gervase Mathew settled down to listen to an instalment of the "new Hobbit". At that point Hugo Dyson "came in just as we were starting on [it], and as he now exercises a veto on it – most unfairly I think – we had to stop".[7] The irony was that during this early period of his appointment at Merton, Dyson frequently missed meetings because of apparent carelessness or by simply forgetting about them.

Hugo Dyson's vetoing of Tolkien's reading of *The Lord of the Rings* appears to suggest that one of the important Inklings discouraged rather than encouraged the making of stories (one of the key features of the Inklings' interests).[8] Though Dyson famously preferred talking to reading (and so presumably the pub meetings of the Inklings were more congenial), he was an active and treasured member. And though his output was very small, he did write for example on the Augustans and Romantics in literature. As we have seen, he backed Tolkien up strongly during the conversation with Lewis in 1931 that convinced the latter of the truth of Christianity and that myths and stories could become fact. The apparent anomaly of his irritation with Tolkien's reading was more than likely due to its scale and duration. When Lewis, in contrast, was reading from *The Screwtape Letters,* the other Inklings were convulsed with laughter, according to Dr Havard – on at least some occasions those present when Lewis was reading these fictional letters would have included Dyson. There is no record of Dyson vetoing any other reading, including Tolkien's of *The Notion Club Papers* (see below), in what must have been a number of extracts, given its length.

The Notion Club

A fictional character in one of Tolkien's stories is based partly on Dyson, as others are on C.S. Lewis, Dr Havard, and even Tolkien himself. This story is the futuristic *The Notion Club Papers*, which seems to have started as a play on the Inklings club, poking a certain amount of fun at them, but which then became a much more serious and intense exploration of the way language carries a mythology – one of the central concerns behind Tolkien's scholarship and fiction.[9]

On Thursday 22 August 1946, Warnie Lewis's diary recorded "Tollers" reading "a magnificent myth which is to knit up and conclude his Papers of the Notions Club". This would have been an account of the catastrophic end of Númenor (Tolkien's new version of the myth of Atlantis), published long afterwards as "The Drowning of Anadûnê".[10] In a letter to his publisher, Stanley Unwin, in July 1946, Tolkien had mentioned having written three parts of his story about the Notion Club. He said that it took up material employed in the unfinished *The Lost Road,* but in an entirely different frame and setting. Like *The Lost Road,* it is a time-travel book, having the purpose of introducing the tales of Númenor. The Inklings meetings at that time (much larger than in earlier days, of course) provided the inspiration for the setting of a largish and informal literary group. The text is made up of papers supposedly found early in the twenty-first century, constituting the minutes of discussion of the Notion Club in Oxford between 1986 and 1987 – the period leading up to and including a great storm of much significance.

Tolkien wrote the unfinished papers between 1945 and 1946. They are a second attempt (the first being *The Lost Road*) at time travel, in response to the challenge that Lewis and Tolkien had set themselves to write a time- or space-travel story, as we saw in the introduction to this book. Lewis's response in the form of a space-travel book was his *Out of the Silent Planet*, admired by Tolkien.

The Notion Club Papers idealizes the Inklings but only hints at actual people within the group, and the very like-minded scholars differ in important ways from the real Inklings. Nevertheless, with their strong emphasis on conversation and a community of minds, the Notion Club reach to the very soul of the Inklings. The papers concern the discovery of clues to the lost world of Númenor through strange words that contain clues for philologically aware people, people exceptionally sensitive to language. The work appreciates the value of a group or community of people in building up together an imaginative picture of the past. The insights into the past achieved imaginatively are in a curious way as objective as the seemingly hard facts of traditional history. This objectivity is dramatically demonstrated by the intrusion of a great storm in late twentieth-century Oxford that derives from the calamity that befell Númenor long before, in an early period of Middle-earth's history. The world of Númenor –

specifically its terrible destruction – in fact intrudes into the future Western world in the summer of 1987. By a remarkable coincidence, there *was* a great storm – of hurricane force – in Britain in the autumn of that year, which had a devastating impact. Tolkien was only a few months out with his storm!

As well as language, the Inklings-like discussions of the Notion Club concerned the status of dreams, and time and space travel via that medium. Behind them is an exciting exploration of the place that imagination has in putting us in contact in some way with objective reality, resisting the view that imagination is purely about the inner world and not about fact at all.

"No one turned up"

Evening meetings of the Inklings continued at least to the autumn of 1949, about the time Tolkien finished writing *The Lord of the Rings*. Then, in Warnie Lewis's diary entry for Thursday 27 October, he wrote: "Dined with J[ack] at College... No one turned up after dinner..." This marks the end of at least regular evening gatherings of the Inklings. Some are recorded after this time without indication that any reading took place. There were occasions, for instance, of what the Inklings called "ham suppers"– meals in Lewis's college room enjoying ham and other foods sent by a generous American admirer, a distinguished surgeon called Dr Warfield M. Firor, to help in this period of post-war austerity.

In retrospect, Warnie Lewis writes of the Thursday-evening Inklings:

> The ritual of an Inklings was unvarying. When half a dozen or so had arrived, tea would be produced, and

then when pipes were well alight Jack would say, "Well, has nobody got anything to read us?" Out would come a manuscript, and we would settle down in judgment on it – real unbiased judgment, too, since we were no mutual admiration society: praise for good work was unstinted, but censure for bad work – or even not-so-good work – was often brutally frank. To read to the Inklings was a formidable ordeal, and I can still remember the fear with which I offered the first chapter of my first book – and my delight, too, at its reception.[11]

The petering out of the Inklings as a reading as well as a conversational group was not the end of the circle, as we'll see in the next chapter. The emphasis now became almost entirely on conversation, however – though it seems likely that there were occasions when Inklings did still read their work to each other without the institution of the familiar evenings in Lewis's or Tolkien's college rooms. We know of one meeting where reading took place in a pub. This is documented back in 1944, at the White Horse pub (on Wednesday 12 April). The ending of reading evenings, regrettably, meant that the group lost much of its glory. Had they continued, for instance, it might have encouraged Tolkien to complete at least parts of *The Silmarillion*, the medley of writings about the creation and earlier ages of Middle-earth, such as its four great stories, including the tale of Beren and Lúthien.[12]

The conversations that took place among the Inklings were highly valued. It would be a mistake to think that it effectively finished as a definite group in 1949 and that the next fourteen years can be ignored as irrelevant. Owen Barfield made no secret of the fact that he felt the Inklings discussions to be of great importance. His book *Worlds Apart:*

A Dialogue of the Sixties reads somewhat like one of Plato's dialogues transposed to the twentieth century. Tolkien's *The Notion Club Papers* is made up largely of dialogue.[13] It is no accident, I think, that Humphrey Carpenter's reconstruction of an Inklings evening conversation, even though one Inkling thought it entirely unreal,[14] is remembered by all who read his *The Inklings*. He had recourse to the memories of existing Inklings in a unique way, and it was natural to create a vignette of a meeting in imagined conversation. The importance of conversation to the group is paralleled in many other past literary or artistic groups, such as the Bloomsbury Group (and, relatedly, Lady Ottoline Morrell's literary parties), the Pre-Raphaelite Brotherhood,[15] the friendship of William Wordsworth and Samuel Taylor Coleridge (and Coleridge's "conversation" poems), Dr Johnson's The Club, and the Blue Stockings Society.

One hugely significant factor that affected the lives of the Inklings increasingly in their Golden Age was their Christianity, or perhaps their response to Christianity if they did not completely share that faith with their friends. What some of Lewis's university colleagues called his "hot gospelling" – his popular lay theology – also disturbed Tolkien, and eventually contributed to a gradual cooling of their relationship, though they never ceased to be deeply rooted friends and to acknowledge the importance of the friendship. Their bond had also been tested by Lewis's devotion to what Tolkien considered the strange Charles Williams, and in later years by Lewis's marriage to a divorcée, Joy Davidman.[16] The common faith of Tolkien and Lewis, in fact, was part of their motivation to write popular fiction for adults, even though Tolkien couldn't follow Lewis's path into writing popular theology.

The Inklings and the popular touch

In Oxford circles, it was still generally felt in the period of the Inklings' Golden Age that shoemakers should stick to their lasts. Dons writing outside their specialism, especially at a popular level, went against the Oxford grain. This applied also in the world of fiction. Dons writing crime and detective stories were tolerated – this provided amusement for other dons, after all. Writing fantasy was another matter (unless written for children), and the related fledgling genre of science fiction was considered as more or less pulp fiction. Both Tolkien and Lewis, among the Inklings, were particularly vulnerable to criticism from their peers, Tolkien especially in writing *The Lord of the Rings* and Lewis most blatantly in his writing and public speaking as a lay theologian.

For many years, Tolkien's meticulous work in creating the world of Middle-earth, with its convincing geography, languages, history, and attendant stories of gods, Elves, and men, was limited to being a private hobby, shared only with intimates such as C.S. Lewis, and rarely elsewhere. *The Hobbit*, rather coyly, started to open the "hobby" up to the wider world, unintentionally in its early stages of writing. The writing of a sequel for adult readers, begun soon after the publication of the children's book, much more consciously exposed Tolkien's vast creation. He acknowledged that without the encouragement of Lewis, he would never have completed the task of many years' duration. As we have seen, he also acknowledged his debt to the Inklings in nurturing his writing of it, in his dedication to them of the first edition of the initial volume of *The Lord of the Rings* in 1954.

Following their pact, in 1936, to write a story about time or space travel – the kind of story they liked to read – Lewis and Tolkien were committed, as one, to writing for adults. They wished to rehabilitate stories of "romance" – stories that evoked a world beyond the material one in capturing qualities of experience and sensation that set humans apart from merely physical existence.

When it came to Lewis's involvement in writing lay theology, which began in the war years, a serious division began to emerge between the two men, which to some extent reflected their different churches. Tolkien essentially felt that explaining Christian teaching should be left to those who carried authority in the church, with theological training behind them. He was not entirely rational in his position, but held to it rather emotionally. After all, he admired G.K. Chesterton, one of the great lay theologians of the last century, who had converted to Roman Catholicism. Also, although understated, there is some powerful lay theology of Tolkien's own in the revised version of his essay "On Fairy Stories", which appeared in 1947 in the Inklings' posthumous tribute to Charles Williams.[17]

It is likely that Tolkien's unease with his friend's forays into theology grew slowly. The strong theology underlying Lewis's *Out of the Silent Planet* was satisfactorily unobtrusive for Tolkien. He did everything in his power to help his friend to find a publisher. But as months of war passed by, and the great theological issues of good and evil and the frailty and value of human life opened up, Lewis the Oxford English don was invited to write a book on the problem of pain for the general public. There were plenty of good theologians around, but Ashley Sampson, the editor of The Christian Challenge Series, went to Lewis.[18]

This small book ranged far and wide. Lewis, in his distinctive voice, which combined clear logic and rich imagery, discussed

God's control over all human events, including suffering, the goodness of God, human wickedness, human and animal pain, and heaven and hell. Lewis read from it to the Inklings as it was being written. His pithiness and his flair for communicating often complex ideas effectively and engagingly to a popular readership attracted one reader in particular. This was James Welch of the BBC's religious programming department, who quickly wrote an invitation to Lewis to consider broadcasting.

Before long C.S. Lewis was a household name in Britain, his voice familiar to thousands of listeners as he gave several series of radio talks on what Christians believe.[19] He later called the talks "Mere Christianity" when all of them were gathered into one collection for publication. This must had added even more to Tolkien's unease about, and many of his Oxford colleagues' dislike of, Lewis's very popular lay theologizing. Lewis the evangelist didn't go well with Lewis the stalwart of the English School, especially as his earlier support of Tolkien's English syllabus reform was unforgotten and unforgiven by many.

The BBC talks took place between August 1941 and April 1944. For those who felt negative towards Lewis the lay theologian, the news got worse. Most would not have known of the talks on Christianity that the RAF invited Lewis to give to its flight personnel, mainly in Bomber Command (where crews had a very short life expectancy). What soon became well known throughout the university, however, came about as a result of an invitation in 1941 from a pastoral worker in her thirties who was with the Oxford Pastorate. She was called Stella Aldwinckle. The Pastorate was attached to the Anglican church of St Aldate's, but worked independently of it. She wished to set up a club as a forum for discussion between Christians and those without faith, following the principle of the philosopher Socrates to follow the argument wherever it led. In C.S. Lewis's words, the Socratic principle was applied "to one particular subject matter – the pros and cons of the Christian Religion".[20] It would become one of the most popular and vibrant undergraduate clubs at Oxford. Lewis was asked to be president, and agreed. Stella would be chairman.

Stella Aldwinckle was Chaplain for Women Students from 1941 to 1966, and won the affection of many. One such was the philosopher and novelist Iris Murdoch, who had studied at Somerville, then a women's college:

> Those of us (including myself) who were then Marxists were, as I recall, though certainly not "converted", well-disposed, recognizing in her a thoroughly serious pure-hearted person, a thinker with a cause at least analogous to our own. Stella… taught by what she was, by her presence, her faith and her concern. Also, wherever she went she promoted argument.… I left Oxford in 1942, just after the Socratic Club was founded, and returned in 1948 to find the Club flourishing and indeed famous, and Stella as busy as ever in her "parish" carrying her faith into all its corners. The Socratic Club was unique among Oxford Societies, attracting speakers with strongly-held and very diverse views. Its pioneering discussions raised philosophical and theological issues which became more explicit later on.[21]

The Oxford University Socratic Club, with its focus on intellectual difficulties with Christian belief, was supported by several of the Inklings and indeed by others of Lewis's Christian friends outside the group, such as the Revd Austin Farrer. One of the brightest theologians in Oxford, he was to become an important influence on Lewis. Another Christian friend who joined the fray on one occasion was Dorothy L. Sayers.

The very first meeting of the club, on Monday 26 January 1942, was held in the East Junior Common Room of Somerville College. The speaker was Dr Humphrey Havard, and his subject was "Won't Mankind Outgrow Christianity in the Face of the Advance of Science and of Modern Ideologies?" In her introduction to this initial meeting of the club, Stella explained, according to the minutes: "The speakers of the Socratic Club were to be chosen to introduce subjects of which they have made a careful study and about which they are willing and competent to attempt to answer questions."

Dr Havard's talk was not reproduced verbatim in the *Socratic Digest*, but quite a full precis was. From this we learn that Havard, who had considerable experience in medical research, led off by revealing "that he had himself deserted Christianity, in the face of the advance of science, for some years". He then set out his views during that period of unbelief, followed by "the reasons for his changed point of view". As a scientist he had mistaken Nature's uniformity for an "absolute principle", making him abandon all the elements of the supernatural in Christianity, though he continued to admire its ethical views. It was after studying the beliefs of the Roman Catholic Church that his views altered. He came to see that abandoning the traditional Christian interpretation of the events in the New Testament Gospels led to more intellectual problems than if you believed them.

Many of the speakers at the club were famous atheists or agnostics, very often eliciting a response from C.S. Lewis. One distinguished atheist, Antony Flew, among a number of leading philosophers who addressed the club, late in life became a theist. Helen Tyrrell Wheeler, a student at the time, remembered an early meeting:[22] "I have a strong visual memory of these evenings, always associated with lamplight inside and total blackout without, of a big sprawling comfortable room with as many people sitting on the floor as in the old-fashioned immense armchairs and C.S. Lewis hurrying over Magdalen Bridge from his rooms to preside. He always established an immense, though rather impersonal, geniality and with his bright eyes and ruddy farmer's cheeks looked not unlike a medieval illustration of a fiery seraphim, though dressed in decent academic black."

Charles Williams also gave his support by speaking at the Socratic Club. As someone who had a whole theology based on romantic love, it was appropriate that he was chosen to speak on a subject that was very pertinent in the wartime student world: "Are There Any Valid Objections to Free Love?" He gave the talk on Monday 2 March, a matter of weeks after Dr Havard's talk. The hall was well filled. Again, we have only a precis of his presentation, recorded in the *Socratic Digest*. Williams argued the need for a "pattern" (not necessarily just the Christian pattern) to give meaning to both freedom and love. The precis notes him as saying: "It was impossible to be 'adult' in love unless the moments or the moment could be accepted or rejected at will. Fidelity was the mark of such power of will. Unless it operates under fixed conditions all that we mean by love would cease to be. If 'Freedom' in 'Free Love' meant freedom to be ruled by the emotions of the moment, and the 'Love' meant the conscious pursuit of conscious felicity Mr. Williams emphasized that it was neither 'Free' nor 'Love'."[23]

As usual, there was discussion after the talk. That evening the discussion rather rambled until Lewis in the chair directed that the meeting must decide whether it wanted to discuss the predilections of bees or those of humans. Afterwards Lewis invited his pupil Derek Brewer and two or three others back to his rooms to meet Charles Williams and partake of a drink. Williams, Brewer jotted down afterwards, was wearing a very old blue suit, and, while he talked in his animated way, he vigorously flicked cigarette ash down his long-suffering waistcoat. During the conversation, Lewis and Williams were in agreement that it was just as difficult to avoid pleasure as pain in life. Lewis at one point retrieved his copy of Williams's *Taliessin Through Logres* from his shelves and urged the poet to read from it. Williams read from his verse with gusto.[24] A secret of appreciating Charles Williams's Arthurian poetry is to read it aloud, or to hear it read, as perhaps Lewis realized.[25]

Also from the Inklings, Gervase Mathew addressed the club on the subject of "Christian and Non-Christian Mysticism", on Monday 4 June 1945, a few weeks after the death of Charles Williams. His talk was not reproduced in the *Socratic Digest*, but it did contain a very detailed reconstruction of the talk. Mathew covered a wide span in his talk. He included the importance of mystical elements in traditional Christianity, a closer look at the mystical theory and doctrines of the Middle Ages, an application of this theory and these doctrines outside Christianity (including Sufism and "tendencies within Hinduism"), and, finally, a consideration of the very opposite views that account for mystical writings as coming from literary conventions or "pathological factors". Taking into account Gervase Mathew's membership of the Inklings, a significant part of his fascinating talk explored "knowledge by means of friendship". The reconstruction in the *Socratic Digest* tells us:

Mystical experience was knowledge through friendship, as it is alternatively phrased, "*cognitio per modum amoris*"[knowledge through the way of love] or "*per modum compassionis*" [by way of compassion]. Understanding of this doctrine is dependent upon an understanding of the medieval approach to friendship. By "*amicitia*" [friendship] was meant self-giving, the union of two souls who know each other intuitively, in whose relationship there is not, as there is in acquaintanceship, the need for one to use inference or discursive reason in his knowing of the other. If this intuitive knowledge is possible between man and man, is it also possible between man and God? It was answered, that it was made so in the Incarnation, in which Christ had united man with the Godhead. Through Grace a man might, as a member of His mystical body, share in the divine Life. So there was, through grace, a possibility of friendship between man and God. Charity in fact was "*amicitia*", the love of friendship between man and God, made possible solely through the Grace given at the Incarnation.

This share in Christ's life increases with the growth of charity, "*caritas*", that love of God for His own sake which reflects Christ's love for us, and the love for others which reflects Christ's love for them.[26]

A similar vision of friendship growing into friendship with God through divine love is found in a book Lewis wrote towards the end of his life – *The Four Loves*. Its insights were built upon his reflections on friendship, enriched by his experience over the years, particularly of groups of friends such as the Inklings. Perhaps as Lewis listened to his friend and fellow Inkling Gervase Mathew speaking, further seeds of that future book were sown.

As we are about to see, the Socratic Club acted as a catalyst that helped to change the direction of Lewis's work. As a result, he put more emphasis on his imaginative writing, which really was closer to the bias of Tolkien's own writings. Ironically, this happened when the friendship was cooling, which meant that Tolkien was probably unaware of the shift that was taking place in Lewis's strategy as a Christian writer. The circumstances of the change have turned into a myth that is misleading, and needs dispelling.

The routing of Lewis, the Christian defender of the faith?

In 1947 Lewis had published *Miracles*, which defended supernaturalism (as against naturalism, or materialism – the position he had held as an atheist). Supernaturalism, by definition, does not rule out the possibility of miracles, but holding to such an outlook does not in itself make a person uncritical of any claims to miracles. The following year, philosopher Elizabeth Anscombe challenged Lewis's basic argument against naturalism as put forward in chapter three of that book – he claimed that a materialist view was self-refuting as it undermined any validity to human thought itself. A Roman Catholic, Anscombe was a member of the Socratic Club. She would in the future translate and edit works of the eminent philosopher Ludwig Wittgenstein (1889–1951), under whom she had studied while a research student at Cambridge. She is often interpreted as being responsible for what was a defeat that led Lewis into serious self-doubt about his whole approach to the intellectual defence of Christian faith. Anscombe's paper, however, simply aimed to clarify and to bring out some confusion in the argument Lewis had used in *Miracles*.

Dr Anscombe pointed to a number of words or phrases that Lewis had used either unclearly or uncritically – such as "validity", "irrationality" of causes, "reason", "cause and effect" in reasoning, and "explanation". Lewis did acknowledge afterwards that he was unclear in his argument, but neither he nor Anscombe regarded it as anything less than essentially robust. In response to the debate, Lewis rewrote the chapter for a later edition.

Elizabeth Anscombe was interested in the reaction to the debate on the part of some of Lewis's followers. These considered it an utter defeat, and interpreted Lewis's response as one of despondency. She wondered if it might have been a case of psychological projection (that is, they were projecting their own fears and uncertainties onto Lewis). This view that Lewis was soundly defeated in battle – by a cheroot-smoking young woman at that – has continued among later interpreters of Lewis, such as biographer A.N. Wilson. According to this widely accepted view, Lewis was so confounded by Anscombe's logic that he abandoned his role as eminent Christian apologist and turned to more devotional books and writing for children – that is, *The Chronicles of Narnia*.

This does not, however, fit the facts. In the first place, Lewis continued in his high-profile position as president (and iconoclast) of the Socratic Club – the scene of his apparently ignominious defeat – for another seven years, until his move to Cambridge University. As for the writing of the *Chronicles*, this was, in fact, part of a natural development in Lewis's imaginative approach to the defence of Christianity that had begun with *Out of the Silent Planet* and which became increasingly important to him as he saw how such books were received. It does have a grain of truth in it, as his encounter with someone who went on to be a leading British philosopher in the analytical movement did help Lewis to change course strategically in his writings. There was nothing second best, however, in his shift to more imaginative writing.[27]

Rather than destroying Lewis's confidence, and forcing him to turn away from an intellectual defence of Christianity, what he did eventually acknowledge was that philosophy had become increasingly specialized and analytical. He did not object to such analysis, but felt that if he tried to continue in that more and more rarefied world, he would only be communicating with a smaller and smaller audience. The impact of the new analytical philosophy, especially if combined with logical positivism (a mix Anscombe did not make), was so great that the intellectual world of Lewis's formative years in Oxford, dominated by philosophical idealism, effectively dissolved.[28]

As a gifted philosopher, Elizabeth Anscombe's critique was powerful, and she intended it to be constructive. She felt that Lewis responded to it in an honest and serious way, evidenced by the fact that he did substantially revise the third chapter of *Miracles*[29] (for the 1960 paperback edition). The debate she had with Lewis was not a parochial matter, but a challenge for any serious philosopher concerned about the validity of human thought.

After Lewis's death, the debate was rerun, with Elizabeth Anscombe once again putting forward her concerns, and the philosopher John Lucas holding forth with Lewis's case. According to the Oxford philosopher Basil Mitchell (who took over as president of the Socratic Club after Lewis), Lucas was able to uphold Lewis's argument.[30] The conclusion was not that Lewis's case had no philosophical foundation, but rather that he wasn't equipped to deal with the techniques used by the analytical approach in the immediately post-war period. In a sense, it was hard for him to see it as genuine philosophy, judged by what he had himself taught in philosophy tutorials in the 1920s. Now, over six decades after Lewis and Anscombe debated, a lot of people would agree with him that the purpose of philosophy is much wider than mere analysis of language.

An interesting footnote is a letter Lewis wrote to Stella Aldwinckle a couple of years after the debate, which was about the future programme of the Socratic Club. In it, he suggested that Miss Anscombe give an address to the club, called "Why I believe in God". He would be very much behind this. Half-jokingly he added: "The lady is quite right to refute what she thinks bad theistic arguments, but does this not almost oblige her as a Christian to find good ones in their place: having obliterated me as an Apologist ought she not to *succeed* me?"[31]

Lewis was aware of the general public's reception of his wartime broadcasts, reflected in sales of his books such as *The Screwtape Letters* and *The Great Divorce*. He increasingly felt that his calling was to a broader readership. After this realization, he did take a much less direct approach to communicating Christianity. But it was a considered strategic move, not a retreat. He followed in the spirit of his friend Tolkien, even if not in the letter. Tolkien was content to write *The Lord of the Rings* with not a single mention of God, and yet the book embodies divine providence and other theological elements throughout. It is likely that Lewis began writing *The Lion, the Witch and the Wardrobe* in 1948, after the debate with Elizabeth Anscombe, and did not intend that book, or the subsequent other volumes about Narnia, to be allegory – that is, to have an explicit, almost one-to-one correspondence with Christian doctrine. This allusiveness, to various degrees, also applied to further works of lay theology that Lewis would write, such as *The Four Loves* (1960) and, even more so, *Letters to Malcolm: Chiefly on Prayer* (published in 1964 after his death).

CHAPTER 9

The Final Years

C.S. Lewis continued his work as a fellow and tutor in English at Magdalen College throughout the Inklings' Golden Age and into the 1950s. This was the post he had taken up in 1925. Without promotion, he dutifully tutored his pupils and carefully prepared lectures that inspired students across the university.

J.R.R. Tolkien had started teaching at Oxford the same year as Lewis, as we saw. His first post was the senior position of Rawlinson and Bosworth Professor of Anglo-Saxon, and fellow of Pembroke College. In 1945, he moved to another, broader Chair, Merton Professor of English Language and Literature, which he retained until retirement in 1959. Some of his academic work did not appear in print until after retirement. He conscientiously supervised generations of postgraduate students, but his lectures became famous among some of his students in later years for his poor enunciation. He was at his best performing texts; his rendering of *Beowulf* and one of Chaucer's *Canterbury Tales* really brought them to life.

Charles Williams came to Oxford at the outbreak of war in his role as a senior editor at Oxford University Press, London branch. Through the efforts of Tolkien ("the lord of the strings") and Lewis, he was recruited to do some lecturing to undergraduates in the Oxford English School and given an honorary MA, and his friends even hoped that he might get a permanent post. His premature death in 1945 meant that the final part of his trilogy of Arthurian poems was unrealized. The central characters of his final novel, *All Hallows' Eve* – which benefited from being read to the Inklings – walked the streets of a twilit London after their deaths, caught in a struggle between powers of good and evil that encompassed the living and the dead.

Owen Barfield spent the 1930s, 1940s, and most of the 1950s in the self-imposed tedium of his family's law business in London. He had little time to write, but, when he did, the pieces often but not always related to anthroposophical teaching. When he could, he wrote poetry and fiction, including his verse drama, *Orpheus* (which was staged in Sheffield, at the Little Theatre, in September 1948). On one occasion, he used his legal expertise to save his client C.S. Lewis from bankruptcy, when Lewis incurred an enormous tax bill that, in his ignorance, he hadn't expected. He had generously given away all the royalties from his increasingly successful books, such as *The Screwtape Letters*.[1] When Lewis was appointed to the Cambridge Chair, he tried (unsuccessfully) to procure his position at Magdalen College for Barfield. It was only in 1959, when he was able to retire from the law firm, that Barfield started an astonishing second life of scholarly and imaginative writing, which included extensive lecturing, much of it in the United States.

In her lengthy obituary of C.S. Lewis for the British Academy in 1965, Dame Helen Gardner reflected on his emphatic Oxford presence, and also on the way he was snubbed by the university establishment:

In the early 1940s, when I returned to Oxford as a tutor, Lewis was by far the most impressive and exciting person in the Faculty of English. He had behind him a major work of literary history; he filled the largest lecture room available for his lectures; and the Socratic Club, which he founded[2] and over which he presided, for the free discussion of religious and philosophic questions, was one of the most flourishing and influential of undergraduate societies. In spite of this, when the Merton Professorship of English Literature fell vacant in 1946, the electors passed him over…

Helen Gardner explained:

In [passing Lewis over] they probably had the support of many, if not a majority, of the Faculty; for by this time a suspicion had arisen that Lewis was so committed to what he himself called "hot gospelling" that he would have had little time for the needs of what had become a very large undergraduate school and for the problems of organization and supervision presented by the rapidly growing numbers of research students in English Literature. In addition, a good many people thought that shoemakers should stick to their lasts and disliked the thought of a professor of English Literature winning fame as an amateur theologian…[3]

Cambridge University came to Lewis's rescue in 1954 with the offer of a new Chair of Medieval and Renaissance literature that seemed tailor-made for him, as detailed in the introduction to this book. With a little help from Warnie, Tolkien fervently persuaded Lewis to take the post, even though he had declined it twice, in the face of the Cambridge Vice-Chancellor's persistence. Lewis is most commonly associated in people's minds with Oxford: he was an undergraduate at University College, and a fellow of Magdalen College for nearly thirty years, and, together with Tolkien, had helped to shape the curriculum of the Oxford Honours English School. He would, however, be closely associated with Cambridge University for over eight years, from late 1954 until his early retirement due to ill health in 1963. During those years he would stay in his Cambridge college mid week during term time, while continuing to live at The Kilns. He would write several important literary books at Cambridge, including *Studies in Words*, *An Experiment in Criticism*, and *The Discarded Image*.

While a consensus in Oxford disparaged Lewis, there were also many who responded to his writings on lay theology, particularly his theological fiction such as *The Screwtape Letters* and *The Great Divorce*. In 1947, the American *Time* magazine had published a cover feature on C.S. Lewis entitled "Don v. Devil", taking *The Screwtape Letters* as its theme, which boosted his continuing appeal in the USA. This was an indicator of Lewis's place in people's minds as a popular communicator of the Christian faith. His success as a lay theologian and as a writer of popular books outside his literary world was directly proportional to a growing dislike of such activities felt by many of his peers. As we have seen, even his close friend Tolkien was unhappy about Lewis being a popular spokesman on Christian belief, although he supported the promotion that his friend deserved. Many of his Inklings circle, however, were unruffled by his high profile as a lay theologian, with some participating in the popular Socratic Club as lead speakers.

The 1950s were a period of trial and tribulation for Lewis, with contrasting times of great joy in his personal life, and satisfaction with the growing and widening response to his writings. *The Lion, the Witch and the Wardrobe* was published on 16 October 1950, after the Inklings had seen and discussed the proofs earlier in the year in the Eagle and Child pub. Soon a generation of children in Britain, the United States, and elsewhere was added to Lewis's readership and a number of them wrote to him, invariably receiving a personal reply.[4]

With the cooling of his friendship with Tolkien and the ending of regular readings in Inklings gatherings, Lewis had turned elsewhere to seek criticism of his writings in progress. A young writer, Roger Lancelyn Green, had helped to inspire Lewis's *The Lion, the Witch and the Wardrobe* after lending him his unpublished children's story. Soon Lewis was reading the burgeoning tales of Narnia to Green or passing him handwritten manuscripts on them to read. Green came up with the series title, *The Chronicles of Narnia*. Lewis even spoke to Green of the possibility of his becoming his literary biographer.[5]

The decade had started with the lifting of the increasing burden of care for his "adopted mother", Janie Moore, when she died in early January 1951 after a long decline. Lewis had already started to enjoy the luxury of the company of other women friends, such as the poet Ruth Pitter. He also enjoyed responding to his witty new penfriend, Joy Davidman Gresham, who had been writing from New York State since the beginning of 1950. She became the third of his American admirers to make their way across the Atlantic to visit him (the earlier being Chad Walsh and Lewis's benefactor Dr Warfield M. Firor).

Joy Davidman was a poet and novelist who had been converted to Christianity from Marxism partly through reading Lewis's books. A relatively short time after making his acquaintance, Joy had come to live in England with her sons, a dramatic move. She and Lewis now gradually grew closer. Joy, in fact, not only brought a new dimension of companionship to Lewis, who had been mainly used to male friendship, but she also became an important collaborator on some of his writing, most significantly his novel *Till We Have Faces*.

Joy was also to bring tragedy. As their friendship turned slowly to love, she was found to have terminal cancer. As with Janie Moore, Lewis reached out to a woman in great need, and in this case married Joy, at first in a civil ceremony in April 1956. This was ostensibly to secure British nationality and protection for her and her two young sons, but it had soon become a full marriage of reciprocal love. A bedside Christian wedding ceremony took place nearly a year later, on 21 March 1957, after they had learned of the cancer.

After a clergyman friend had prayed for her healing at the time of the Christian ceremony, Joy had an unexpected reprieve. Her diseased bones rejuvenated against all medical expectations. Lewis called it a miracle. By July that year Joy was well enough to get out and about. Throughout this period her sons David and Douglas were away during term time at boarding school.

The next year Joy and Lewis were able to have a whole fortnight's holiday in his old country, Ireland, and other holidays followed. Nevill Coghill remembers Lewis quietly telling him: "I never expected to have, in my sixties, the happiness that passed me by in my twenties."

The cancer returned to defeat Joy, but not before the Lewises had snatched a brief but memorable trip to Greece in the spring of 1960. Roger Lancelyn Green and his wife, June, holidayed with them to help provide necessary care for Joy. The happiness that had come to Lewis so late in life was followed by bitter bereavement, captured in his memoir of the experience, *A Grief Observed*.[6] Joy died on 13 July 1960, just two months after enjoying the wines and olive trees of Greece, where the ancient myths haunted the ancient ruins. After her death he wrote, "Her mind was lithe and quick and muscular as a leopard. Passion, tenderness, and pain were all equally unable to disarm it. It scented the first whiff of cant or slush; then sprang, and knocked you over before you knew what was happening."[7]

Over the years following the end of Inklings reading evenings, Lewis took on yet another burden of care. This was a result of Warnie's affliction, as he fell deeper and deeper into alcoholism and made increasingly desperate attempts to stay dry. He spurned any involvement with Alcoholics Anonymous, and willpower simply wasn't enough, despite his greatest efforts. After an urgent call, Lewis would find himself rushing to Drogheda, in Ireland, where Warnie had been admitted to hospital while "holidaying". The Sisters of the Convent Hospital of Our Lady of Lourdes never failed to care for the seriously ill drunk. Many of Warnie's Protestant prejudices about Roman Catholic institutions were removed because of his sojourns there. The roots of his alcoholism may have lain in his military service overseas, and the attraction of the officer's mess to relieve the tedium. Warnie's addiction, as has been noted, was the main obstacle to Lewis's accepting the Cambridge Chair in 1954. Tolkien had carefully and kindly reassured Lewis that he could take it without neglecting his dependent brother.

The club in the snug

As with the earlier years of the Inklings, documentation of the final years of the group is patchy and limited. What there is does not support a view that the group was effectively dead after the reading evenings ceased as an institution around the autumn of 1949. Attendance at the Eagle and Child on Tuesdays (then on Mondays after Lewis started at Cambridge) was often higher than it was for the evenings of reading, and the conversation was wide-ranging and nearly always intellectually engaged, it seems. The Inklings met in a closed snug at the back of the pub, called "The Rabbit Room", as they had done in the Golden Age. Lewis attended until his death, except for periods of illness (his own, and presumably Joy's). When he was not present, the meetings were just not the same. Around the time of the death of his wife, Lewis was absent for a short period. James Dundas-Grant remarked: "Attendance dropped and, to me at least, stars ceased to sparkle. When he did come back, he was the same old Jack. Our spirits rose; attendance rose."[8]

Those recorded as attending in this period – permanently, frequently, or occasionally – included Lewis, Tolkien, Christopher Tolkien, Warren Lewis, Dr Humphrey Havard, Lord David Cecil, Owen Barfield, R.B. McCallum, J.A.W. Bennett, Colin Hardie, Charles Wrenn, Gervase Mathew, Hugo Dyson, James Dundas-Grant, and C.E. "Tom" Stevens. Roger Lancelyn Green was able to drop in only very occasionally – after 1950, he lived in his ancestral home, Poulton Hall, in Cheshire.

As had been the case with evening meetings, attendance appears to have been by invitation. Dr Havard was a mutual friend of Lewis and Dundas-Grant, so Lewis asked his opinion on whether "D. G." should be invited to the Tuesday gathering at the Eagle and Child. Havard was clearly supportive, as Dundas-Grant was invited and eventually got to know Lewis and became a friend. He remembered:

We met every Tuesday over a glass of beer. Warnie, his brother, was there; McCallum of Pembroke; Father Gervase Mathew, O. P., from Blackfriars; Tolkien of Merton and Havard. Others came and went. We sat in a small back room with a fine coal fire in winter. Back and forth the conversation would flow. Latin tags flying around. Homer quoted in the original to make a point. And Tolkien, jumping up and down, declaiming in Anglo-Saxon. Sometime, in the summer, after we had dispersed, Havard would run Jack and me out to The Trout at Godstow, where we would sit on the wall with the Isis flowing below us and munch cheese and French bread.[9]

What jottings and memories that exist of the meetings in the 1950s give us glimpses of what subjects the wide-ranging conversations turned to, but with little detail about the content. If we wish to get an idea of the content of Lewis's own contributions to conversations, the best source is his correspondence, now collected by Walter Hooper and published in three large volumes. Lewis's beautifully written letters are the closest we can get to his conversation, though we can get other tastes of it in his many essays. These, like his letters, contain his distinctive voice. In his letters, he is in conversation with his recipient. His essays also bring his reader into the conversation, as when he writes memorably about heaven in his essay-sermon "The Weight of Glory".[10]

On Thursday 22 June 1950, the conversation in the Eagle and Child was likely to have included Lewis's forthcoming *The Lion, the Witch and the Wardrobe*. He handed around the galley proofs to the gathered Inklings. If Tolkien was there, as he often was at that time, he may have commented on the book. He had heard Lewis read, or had read himself, at least a few early chapters during the previous year, and had expressed his dislike of the story to Lewis. Later he had commented to Roger Lancelyn Green, when he learned that Lewis had lent him the manuscript to read, words to the effect of: "It really won't do, you know! I mean to say: *Nymphs and their Ways, the Love-Life of a Faun*. Doesn't he know what he's talking about?"[11] There is no record of why the meeting was on Thursday rather than the usual Tuesday.

Roger Lancelyn Green met C.S. Lewis on a number of occasions to discuss various Narnian stories in manuscript form. He offered valuable criticism of structure and details, to which Lewis responded: he postponed the completion of *The Magician's Nephew* in the light of Green's comments and made important structural changes. When circumstances permitted, Green made a number of visits to the Inklings meetings on Tuesdays. One significant occasion was Tuesday 13 February 1951, shortly after Lewis's bid to become Oxford Professor of Poetry. Green recorded in his diary: "To 'Eagle and Child' to meet C.S. L.: a grand gathering – Tolkien, McCallum, Major Lewis, Wrenn, Hardie, Gervase Mathew, John Wain, and others whose names I didn't catch. Discussion on C. Day Lewis (who was elected Professor of Poetry last week, beating C.S. L. by nineteen votes): Lewis praised his *Georgics* but considered his critical work negligible."[12] Unfortunately, Green records no more of the conversation. It was likely that it was dominated by the news of Lewis's defeat.

On another visit to the Inklings in the Eagle and Child, Roger Lancelyn Green did note some of the topics of conversation in his diary. This was on Tuesday 9 October 1954. The first volume of *The Lord of the Rings* had been published the previous July, bearing a dedication to the Inklings. Green recorded: "To 'B.[ird] and B.[aby]' to meet Lewis; his brother,

McCallum, Tolkien, Gervase M.[athew] there as well. Very good talk, about Tolkien's book, horror comics, who is the most influential and important man in various countries: decided Burke for Ireland, Scott for Scotland, Shakespeare for England – but there difficulties arose, Pitt and Wellington also being put forward."[13]

As Tolkien's second volume, *The Two Towers*, was published two days later, it is not clear which of the books was discussed. In the biography he co-authored with Hooper, Green indicates "the book" simply as *The Lord of the Rings*.[14] Tolkien's affectionate tribute in the first volume is to his sons and daughter, and "to my friends the Inklings. To the Inklings, because they have already listened to it with a patience, and indeed with an interest, that almost leads me to suspect that they have hobbit-blood in their venerable ancestry. To my sons and daughter for the same reason, and also because they have all helped me in the labours of composition".

C.S. Lewis made reference to the Inklings group late in the fifties. He was responding to a letter from Nathan Comfort Starr, who had visited a Tuesday meeting of the group at the Eagle and Child in 1948, eleven years before, and wished to see them again during a visit to England. Lewis wrote: "There is still a weekly meeting at the Bird and Baby: but whether you can call it the Old Group when there is a new landlord and Charles Williams is dead and Tolkien never comes is almost a metaphysical question, and one you will discuss much better on the spot." Lewis may have had in mind the philosophical puzzle of identity. If you stand by a river looking at it as the water flows by, it remains that river though the waters before you change. (The opposite view seems to be held by the Greek philosopher Heraclitus: "You cannot step twice into the same river; for fresh waters are ever flowing in upon you.")[15] Similarly, your self or "I" remains constant, as your reference to your identity, though all the cells in your body change every few years. Likewise, has the Inklings remained the Inklings through all its changes of members, and other changes?[16]

When the Eagle and Child was renovated by the "new landlord" and the door to the snug removed, the Inklings reluctantly switched to the Lamb and Flag across the road. Here a private corner was usually available. This is where Green found himself on Monday 17 June 1963. He noted in his diary: "To 'Lamb and Flag' about 12, there joined Jack. Several others – Gervase Mathew, Humphrey Havard, Colin Hardie, and a young American, Walter Hooper, who is writing some sort of book or thesis about Jack…"[17] We don't know the topics of conversation, but it was shortly after this that Hooper provided Lewis with secretarial help during Warnie's absence on an alcoholic binge. This led, after Lewis's death later that year, to his many years of labour in editing and bringing Lewis's writings to publication, culminating in the three large volumes of his collected correspondence.

Sometime between 19 and 24 August 1963, Father John Tolkien took his father to The Kilns to see C.S. Lewis, who had resigned from his Cambridge post because of ill health. Tolkien had expressed a wish to see his friend. John Tolkien remembered: "We drove over to The Kilns for what turned out to be a very excellent time together for about an hour. I remember the conversation was very much about the *Morte d'Arthur* and whether trees died."

A few days before his death, Lewis in a letter referred to the group in diminished terms: "Once a week I attend a reunion of old friends at one of the Oxford taverns. (*Beer* thank goodness is not on the list of things denied me.)"[18] What remained of the Inklings was their eternal core of friendship, that dynamic of difference and shared way of seeing: as Lewis once put it, the "What! You too?" factor.

Friends tried to continue the meetings without Lewis, with little success. Truly, the group came to its earthly end with his death. Tolkien confessed in a letter to his daughter, Priscilla, after Lewis's funeral: "So far I have felt the normal feelings of a man of my age – like an old tree that is losing all its leaves one by one: this feels like an axe-blow near the roots. Very sad that we should have been so separated in the last years; but our time of close communion endured in memory for both of us. I had a mass said this morning, and was there, and served; and Havard and Dundas-Grant were present."[19]

It would be a mistake to overemphasize the cooling of the friendship between Lewis and Tolkien. The bonds between them clearly persisted. Tolkien went through negative periods that affected his perceptions, as was sometimes evident when he looked back as an old man on earlier events. It can be seen distinctly in his views on Charles Williams, as we saw. Documents from the war years, when he knew Williams, show clearly that he appreciated him deeply, not least because of Williams's warm and perceptive responses to hearing readings from *The Lord of the Rings*. There is no denying, however, that the obscurity in William's writings could be frustrating, and his use of occult and magical symbolism could be distasteful to more delicate palates. His greatest novel, *All Hallows' Eve*, was substantially improved artistically by being subjected to comments from the Inklings – particularly, Tolkien pointed out, to those from Lewis. Tolkien was probably jealous, in some way, of Williams for taking up attention that he had been used to from Lewis. This would have been exacerbated by the strong marks of Williams's influence on some of

Lewis's writing from the publication of *That Hideous Strength* (1945) onwards.

An issue that puts in context the degree of cooling of the friendship between Tolkien and Lewis is what we know of his actual relationship with Lewis and the Inklings in the final years, after the ending of the evening sessions of reading.[20] It was during that period that Tolkien dedicated *The Lord of the Rings* to the group. He also played a very active part in his friend's appointment to the Cambridge Chair in 1954, and the two corresponded with as well as met each other. To give some examples from the sparse documentation of Tolkien's meetings with Lewis and with the Inklings: on 19 September 1950 he met Lewis and other Inklings at the Eagle and Child pub, and spent an evening in Lewis's college rooms with them; on 13 February 1951 he met with fellow Inklings at the Eagle and Child, and dined with Lewis and his brother, Warren; and on 7 February 1952 he attended a ham feast with the group. On 28 April 1953, Lewis wrote an endorsement of *The Fellowship of the Ring* at Tolkien's request, even though Tolkien knew that an endorsement from his friend might have a negative impact on the book's reception. And at some stage during this period, Tolkien was worried about Lewis's health.[21]

A richness of books

The publication of *The Lord of the Rings* was one of a number of significant publications by Inklings in this final period. Williams's unexpected death had meant that his cycle of Arthurian poems was never completed. Lewis did what he could by lecturing on the existing poems and publishing his study of them, along with an unfinished portion of a book by Williams on the Arthurian legends in *Arthurian Torso*, in 1948.

Although Owen Barfield would be tied to his work as a lawyer until his retirement in 1959, he did publish in 1957 a major book on the history of ideas, *Saving the Appearances*, which was much admired by C.S. Lewis. It explores the relationship between science and religion. Rather than a traditional history of ideas about the momentous rise of modern science, Barfield is concerned with the evolution of human consciousness (see chapter three, where we looked at some of Barfield's developing ideas). Changes in how we explore the natural world, he argues, correspond to changes in our consciousness. Today we are the inheritors of an alienation between ourselves and nature as a result of idolatry. There is now a lamentable disparity between human consciousness and the mind of the scientist. Barfield is concerned with an all-important human participation in nature as a historical process. Our need, in this age of separation, he says, is for a final participation, so as to bring ourselves to oneness with God and nature.

A sequel, *Worlds Apart*, published six years later, continued the exploration of these themes in the form of a many-sided conversation between a narrator who is intentionally Barfield-like, a rocket research engineer, a theologian, a retired schoolmaster, and a physicist. The participants meet over a weekend with the intention of resolving the current fragmentation between the intellectual disciplines. The narrator, Burgeon, is a solicitor, and another character, Hunter, is a professor of historical theology and ethics and – according to a letter Barfield sent to a friend – "three parts C.S. Lewis". Lewis sent a letter to Barfield near the end of his life with his thoughts on the manuscript of *Worlds Apart*, in which he clearly knows of his "relation to Hunter" and says he has enjoyed the book.[22]

The Chronicles of Narnia were also published during this period, with a book appearing each year between 1950 and 1956. Although Tolkien was very negative about the first chapters, the books owe an enormous debt to him, not least for the way that Lewis embraced his idea of sub-creation in inventing the secondary world of Narnia, and for drawing their inspiration from the medieval world and pre-Christian mythology. Like *The Lord of the Rings*, the books would be translated into many languages, and be adapted into audio dramas and some into films. It was in creating Middle-earth and Narnia that its two best-known authors captured the essence of the kind of stories that were greatly admired by the Inklings. Tolkien appeared to mellow in later life in his attitude to the Narnia books. He certainly did not hate them, as some like to think. On one occasion when his granddaughter Joanna Tolkien[23] was staying with her grandparents, her grandfather pulled out the Narnia books from his bookshelf as recommended reading![24]

One of C.S. Lewis's best works of fiction was published in the same year that the final Narnian story appeared. This was *Till We Have Faces*, a retelling of the classical myth of Cupid and Psyche, a story that had haunted Lewis for many years. As mentioned earlier, he wrote it partly in collaboration with Joy Davidman in the period before their marriage. He benefited from her skills as a novelist, and the help she could give in writing the narrative from a woman's perspective.[25]

Till We Have Faces reflects the interest the Inklings had in myth (in a literary and philosophical sense), seen as an imaginative capturing of truth that allows what are normally abstract ideas to be made tangible and concrete, preferably in a historical setting, whether the history is real or invented. This is what Tolkien had tried to do with the imagined history and geography of Middle-earth in *The Lord of the Rings*. In Lewis's case, he set his story in an imagined kingdom of the classical world, in which a highly educated Greek slave serves as one of the central characters. Ironically, given Tolkien's apparent antipathy to all things Narnian, this novel of Lewis's has a great affinity with his friend's creation, being set, for instance, in a pre-Christian world in which there are only unfocused anticipations of what the two friends – and most of the Inklings – considered the greatest story of all, the Gospel narratives where, for them, myth had most fully and clearly become fact.

Lewis's *Till We Have Faces* in many ways builds on what he had done in writing *Perelandra* in the war years, another of his best works of fiction for adults. This was the second of his science-fiction stories. Inspired by the scholarly work he had been doing on John Milton's *Paradise Lost*, and aided by insights from Charles Williams on Milton's poem, Lewis made his first attempt to retell myth not as falsehood, but as an imaginative grasp of truth and fact. In this case, instead of simply retelling the temptation of the first humans in the Garden of Eden in the Genesis setting, Lewis portrays the temptation of the first humans on another planet, in the paradisiacal world of Perelandra (the planet Venus) at the beginning of its history. Both stories are beautiful outcomes of the pledge Tolkien and Lewis made in 1936 to write for adults the kind of books they (and their Inklings friends) liked, though of the two only *Perelandra* is science fiction; *Till We Have Faces* is literary fiction, and has never enjoyed the success of his science fiction and his theological fiction (*The Screwtape Letters* and *The Great Divorce*). But then it takes quite a bit of thought to recognize *The Lord of the Rings* as time-travel fiction!

During the final years of the Inklings, this period of extraordinary fruitfulness for Lewis, he also published in 1954 his magnum opus, *English Literature in the Sixteenth Century, Excluding Drama*, for the *Oxford History of English Literature* (or "Oh Hell" as Lewis called it in the long years of writing it). He also brought out in 1955 a book that has come to be grouped with great works of Christian confession or conversion stories – like St Augustine's *Confessions* or John Bunyan's *Grace Abounding to the Chief of Sinners*. This was his memoir of his life up to his conversion to Christianity from atheism and other forms of unbelief, and he called it *Surprised by Joy: The Shape of My Early Life*. "Joy", remember, was his technical term for an inconsolable longing that no human experience could satisfy. Some of his Inklings friends, however, spotted a double entendre. We do not know if this play on words was deliberate, but the name "Joy Davidman" came to their lips – "Surprised by Joy Davidman". The book was in fact dedicated to her.

After the Inklings

By 1963, Tolkien had not attended an Inklings gathering for a considerable time; no one knows how long. The gratitude he had expressed to the group in his foreword to *The Fellowship of the Ring* in 1954 is unlikely to have gone away, but he and Edith, his wife, would inevitably have been experiencing the natural decline caused by aging.

In retirement, Tolkien had suffered the loss of his college rooms in Merton. The solution to where to put his books was solved by converting the garage at his house on Sandfield Road into a rambling study. When Philip Norman visited Tolkien to interview him for *The Sunday Times*, he thought the house looked like a church rectory. It was so close to the grounds of Oxford United Football Club that the street was swamped with supporters at match time. (It is unlikely that the estate agent had mentioned that fact when Tolkien was buying the house.) Norman was rather struck with the study within the garage, which, he wrote, was "filled with books and the smell of distinguished dust".

Sales of the three red clothbound volumes of the *The Lord of the Rings* continued to be excellent, so the Tolkiens could afford to live comfortably. They were able to take holidays, and the Mirabar Hotel in Bournemouth became a favourite place to visit. For the sake of Edith, who was unhappy living in Oxford and suffered increasing ill health, the couple eventually bought a large bungalow and moved there. As he had done since retirement, Tolkien worked (albeit more slowly) on the plethora of drafts relating to the stories, histories, and other aspects of the earlier ages of Middle-earth that can be glimpsed tantalizingly in the background of events in *The Lord of the Rings*.

It was in the mid-sixties that the "Tolkien phenomenon", as it has been called, really began. An important element in its origin was the publicity given widely in the USA to an unauthorized paperback edition of *The Lord of the Rings*, made possible by a loophole in US copyright law. Readers and fans of Tolkien were asked to support an authorized edition, from which the author would benefit in royalties. The sales were a publisher's dream: Tolkien became the J.K. Rowling of the later 1960s. His mythology of Hobbits and Elves entered mainstream culture, with bands such as Led Zeppelin alluding to him, and the Beatles even considering a film version of *The Lord of the Rings*, in which they would star.

Though Tolkien was bewildered by his new celebrity status, he devoted much of his time to painstakingly answering the queries about Middle-earth that came in his large postbag from readers. A secretary had to be employed to handle the torrent of mail. This didn't, however, help him in the daunting task of organizing his material of fifty years about the earlier ages of Middle-earth. He dreamed of publishing *The Silmarillion*, having lost the power to accomplish it. His fears were captured in a beautiful story, the last published in his lifetime, called *Smith of Wootton Major*. Tolkien described it as "an old man's book, already weighted with the presage of 'bereavement'".

Tolkien did not lose his spirit, however. When Clyde S. Kilby, a great supporter of his work and that of other Inklings, offered to spend one summer vacation helping him with putting *The Silmarillion* together, he gladly accepted. Kilby spent the summer of 1966 trying to get his head around the material. Though he gained a powerful understanding of what Tolkien was attempting to accomplish, he failed to move him forward. There was another person, however, who was in a unique position to prevent the background material of Middle-earth from falling back into being merely Tolkien's hobby. This was another member of the former Inklings circle, his son Christopher Tolkien. More than with any other person, Tolkien had shared his tales, annals, peoples, and geography of early Middle-earth with him.

Edith Tolkien died in 1971, and Tolkien himself in 1973. Within two years, when he was just over fifty, Christopher Tolkien had resigned from his Oxford teaching to devote himself to editing his father's unfinished work, turning it into a form that could be published. Enlisting the help of a young writer of fantasy, Guy Gavriel Kay, he succeeded in producing a concise version of the material, which was published as *The Silmarillion* as quickly as 1977. Christopher created a book, faithful to his father's vision, that was a coherent compendium of stories, annals, legends, and other related elements. *The Silmarillion*, in fact, provided a narrative map or key to the variety of publications that followed, such as *Unfinished Tales* and the twelve volumes of *The History of Middle-earth*. As a scholar of Old and Middle English himself, through his editing and his knowledgeable commentary Christopher also enabled publication of his father's translations of narrative poems such as *Sir Gawain and the Green Knight* and *Beowulf*.

As we have seen, the unpublished writings of C.S. Lewis

also gained a resourceful and committed editor in the form of the young American whom Lewis had met at the end of his life – Walter Hooper. With great determination, Hooper embarked on a course that saw at least twenty books of Lewis's published posthumously. Most were collections of letters or essays, but others were his diaries and poetry collections. By collecting Lewis's letters together in three large volumes, published between 2000 and 2006, Hooper made it difficult to doubt that Lewis was one of the great letter writers of the twentieth century.

Owen Barfield was one of the many friends at Lewis's funeral as winter hovered in 1963. He was well into his second life as writer and speaker, with invitations coming in from all over North America and a growing readership for his books in literary and intellectual circles. His fiction, which had not previously been published beyond specialist or esoteric channels, now began to explore more mainstream contemporary topics such as the environment. He, like Tolkien, knew what he had lost in Lewis. In a talk he gave at Wheaton College, Illinois, less than a year after Lewis's death, he said:

> Now, whatever else he was, and, as you know, he was
> a great many things, C.S. Lewis was for me, first and
> foremost, the absolutely unforgettable friend, the friend
> with whom I was in close touch for over forty years,
> the friend you might come to regard hardly as another
> human being, but almost as a part of the furniture of my
> existence.[1]

The Wheaton talk belongs to the period of Barfield's enthusiastic reception in North America. He had never had a popular appeal, though some of his recently published fiction is much more accessible than most of his writing. The year of his talk – 1964 – marked a spell as Visiting Professor at Drew University in New Jersey. This was the first of several similar posts at universities in North America that lasted into the 1980s, when he was entering his eighties. One of his many books of this period, *Speaker's Meaning* (1967), was made up of lectures that he had given at Brandeis University, near Boston. Over a decade later, his seminal book, *History, Guilt and Habit* (1979) grew out of lectures he gave in Vancouver, British Columbia.

Towards the end of his life, Barfield thought back over the decade or more of his fruitful visits to the USA. He was the only one of the central figures in the Inklings, apart from Warnie Lewis, to set foot in the New World.

I first went to America in 1964.… Quite a lot was happening, I was writing a lot of articles, I suppose – but then it was rather like starting a new life in America. Although I had no reputation in England, a certain part of the academic world in America, the English departments, quite lot of people… were already interested in my books. It was a strange experience, rather like the "ugly duckling"!… "I've read your books, of course" – that sort of thing, you know. And of course it was useful from a financial point of view; they paid you awfully well. I had no responsibilities other than teaching. That went on until 1974–5.… The last time was at SUNY [the State University of New York]… It went on for over ten years. I was going fairly regularly to America.[2]

214

As with the paperback publication of Tolkien and the rise of the Tolkien phenomenon, Barfield's timing was exactly right. Intellectuals of the counter-culture of the sixties, and others deeply interested in the direction Western culture was taking, were looking for an alternative to modernism (what Barfield called the "materialist paradigm" and Lewis had called "the Age of the Machine"). Postmodernism was already in the air, and it was air that he could breathe. Barfield, like Lewis and Tolkien, both of whose reception was growing at that period, were in a sense premodern. They could live imaginatively in the ideas and images of a premodern culture such as the medieval period or classical times, and help their contemporaries, through their insights and vision, to have a perspective on the modern world that was not, in Barfield's phrase, idolatrous. The modern person could be freed from what Lewis, under Barfield's influence in the 1920s, called "chronological snobbery", which we encountered earlier.

Warnie Lewis survived his brother by ten years, continuing his battle against alcoholism. He prepared a biography of C.S. Lewis that he interspersed with his letters, the original of which is now housed, unpublished, in The Marion E. Wade Center at Wheaton College, Illinois. His manuscript was drastically cut down by a publisher's editor and became *The Letters of C.S. Lewis*, with Warnie's reduced biography at the beginning as a memoir, and snippets from it as explanation of the letters throughout. With the combination of his biography and his brother's letters in the original manuscript, it is likely that Warnie thought of it as a combined venture. It may have helped him to feel that the brother he had lost was a little closer. He continued to keep his diary, though lamenting that he had not recorded more of Jack's conversation.[3]

Warnie recorded a visit from Owen Barfield on Tuesday 29 July 1969, soon after his visit to Southern California, where the retired solicitor had spoken about the Inklings. Barfield had come to have dinner with Warnie and spend the night. Warnie found it pleasant to have "a long chat" with him again. He noticed that Barfield still had his old mental alertness, but grumbled about not remembering names, and forgetting whether or not he had just met someone, "in the case of casual acquaintance". They soon got into deeper water:

> In the course of our talk it emerged that he is that baffling thing, a practising Christian who is a believer in reincarnation; I objected that if there is reincarnation, the essential *me*, WHL dies, and therefore it amounts to the atheist belief that death ends everything. This he would not have, holding that in each life you add something fresh to the basic *you* from which you started. But what about the endless reincarnation of your ancestors, from which you inherit? I doubt if either of us understood the other, but I found it an interesting evening.[4]

Warnie discovered that Barfield now partook of whisky and hot water at night. He abstained, but inwardly congratulated himself that in preparation for Barfield's visit, he had purchased a "half bottle" earlier in the day "just in case".

CHAPTER 11

Just a Group of Friends?

Did the Inklings have some kind of "group mind"? Were they a cabal, or merely a group of Lewis's friends? Were they a movement of cultural and literary change? Will they be remembered, like the Bloomsbury Group or other intellectual, cultural, or artistic groups, such as the Clapham Sect, the Blue Stockings Society, or the Pre-Raphaelite Brotherhood? Will they soon be considered of little importance?

I've come to the conclusion that it is equally mistaken to see the literary club simply as a group of friends, or as a doctrinaire group driven by a highly defined common purpose. A set of aims does not neatly distil when we zealously tidy up the seeming randomness and chaos of what we know of the group's life. Something stronger emerges, however, relating to the group's identity, when we get to know the group as best we can, which is what this book has tried to do. Owen Barfield, a particularly important member of the group, speculated about the Inklings. Speaking in California in 1969, he talked about this something, or quiddity, at the heart of the Inklings when he looked at the circle, as perhaps a distinct moment in the history of the Romantic Movement. We'll return to this suggestion below.

In trying to focus on any kind of common purpose in the Inklings, there is the danger of labelling. In 1966 Warnie Lewis responded to the tag "the Oxford Christians", used by Charles Moorman in his book *The Precincts of Felicity: The Augustinian City of the Oxford Christians,* by writing – correctly I think – that the name "Oxford Christians" "strikes the wrong note... by suggesting an organized group for the propagation of Christianity, while in fact the title is justified only in the most literal sense, i.e. that we nearly all lived in Oxford and were all believers".[1]

If someone had said that the group was for the defence of Christianity, the title "the Oxford Christians" might perhaps have been a little closer to the mark, though this would still suppose some kind of agenda or constitution, which the Inklings never had. It might have been closer still if it were claimed that the group existed to defend the values of the "Old West", which takes us back to our introductory chapter. Maybe the Inklings were fellow dinosaurs with Lewis – valuable relics of a bygone age.

The Inklings and "Romantic Religion"

In his 1969 talk Barfield took as his starting point the no longer fashionable label "the Oxford Christians", which was still being used sometimes of the core thinkers: himself, Tolkien, C.S. Lewis, and Charles Williams. Barfield was surprised to be considered a core member at all, given how infrequently he had been able to attend the meetings. Six years had passed since the death of Lewis, and Barfield was in the process of making a detailed study of the Romantic poet and thinker Samuel Taylor Coleridge, so he was very much aware by then of the historical context of the Inklings. He speculated:

When I first began to realize, coming over here [to the USA] upon two years in succession and from reading that people here and there were talking about – oh – titles like "the Oxford Christians",… "Romantic Theology", "the School of Romantic Religion" in reference particularly, perhaps exclusively, to… Lewis, Charles Williams, and Tolkien, and, apparently, myself as… an accredited member… I found it rather amusing when I first began to hear people talking about this, and found that they were writing dissertations and so forth. But I have been beginning to wonder, to put it crudely, whether there isn't something in it!

He continued:

The question would be, did something happen… to the heritage of the Romantic Impulse in connection with this group of people and their writings? Was there something like… a development that was also a kind of christening of that heritage taking place in that period in Oxford through the minds of these men? Was something happening that hadn't quite happened before?… with these Oxford Christians?

If yes (the direction in which Barfield was inclined to go), the recognizable strands, he speculated, were joy or romantic longing (associated with Lewis), the increasing presence, or immanence, of the divine in the human (Barfield's interest), the idealization of sexual love (Williams's concern), and the eucatastrophe or very opposite of tragedy (a strong feature of Tolkien's thought and work).[2]

Barfield usefully picked out four themes that represent

different aspects of a religious quality associated with four writers considered to be leaders or shapers in their thought and work. He associates this quality with the Romantic Movement, which in English literature has its origins mainly in Wordsworth, Coleridge, and other poets of that time, greatly influenced by the German Romantics. It can thus be seen as "Romantic Religion". C.S. Lewis argued strongly that such experiences of romance had theological implications. Writing specifically of Charles Williams after his death, Lewis said that the term "romantic theologian" was invented by him. He explained:

> A romantic theologian does not mean one who is romantic about theology but one who is theological about romance, one who considers the theological implications of those experiences which are called romantic. The belief that the most serious and ecstatic experiences either of human love or of imaginative literature have such theological implications and that they can be healthy and fruitful only if the implications are diligently thought out and severely lived, is the root principle of all his [Williams's] work.[3]

A common purpose in the Inklings?

If they were not working to an explicit agenda or manifesto of some sort, how were the Inklings able to have a purpose? The creative and constantly unexpected composition and output of the group, it appears, was possible only because of its informal nature and commonality of strong affinities rather than identical beliefs. This commonality, though it is contemporary in some sense at least (as witnessed by the global popularity of Lewis and Tolkien), might be labelled "Old Western", using Lewis's term from his inaugural lecture in Cambridge.[4] The affinities the Inklings shared are held in common in at least some respects with post-war writers who used parable and symbol in their fiction, such as William Golding, George Orwell, and T.H. White, science-fiction writers such as Arthur C. Clarke and Ursula Le Guin, and fantasy writers including J.K. Rowling and Diana Wynne Jones. These authors have a variety of beliefs (just one of them is a fairly straightforward confessing Christian, like those at the heart of the Inklings).

The founding fathers of the Inklings were orthodox Christians, or had Christianity as a vital reference point. The intellectual climate of the club was one marked by its interest in the fulfilment of pagan insights in Christianity. This climate was created by Lewis and Tolkien, inspired perhaps, or at least focused, by Barfield's insights. It was captured in Tolkien's essay "On Fairy Stories" and Lewis's essay "Myth Became Fact". Lewis and Tolkien are sometimes regarded as "modern medievalists" seeking to rehabilitate lost insights from that period, in for instance *The Lord of the Rings* and the Narnian Chronicles.[5]

Having looked at Owen Barfield's insights into what made the Inklings distinctive, it is worth considering the thoughts of another Inkling, the distinguished literary scholar and biographer Lord David Cecil. While Cecil considered himself to be outside the main Christian beliefs of the group, there was, he felt, something distinctive about the group that greatly attracted him. By good fortune, he was asked to review Humphrey Carpenter's important study *The Inklings*, which evoked thoughts that he had developed over many years about the group, and about his friends in it. Cecil had noticed that individuals within the Inklings had very definite opinions on a range of matters, which were different from each other. These differences went as far as to determine their practice of Christianity and their churchmanship.

Cecil writes that the "meetings were... occasionally attended by persons who did not share The Inklings' distinctive point of view but who liked spending an evening in their company. I myself was one of these; I found such evenings enjoyable and stimulating; and all the more because the spirit of The Inklings was in piquant contrast to those of the Oxford circles in which I spent most of my time".

He tried to pin down what made the group distinctive:

> The qualities, then, that gave The Inklings their distinctive personality were not primarily their opinions; rather it was a feeling for literature, which united, in an unusual way, scholarship and imagination..... To study a book in translation or without a proper knowledge of its historic background would have been to them unthinkable; they were academic in the best sense of the word. But – and this made them different from most academics – they also read imaginatively. The great books of the past were to them living in the same way as the work of a contemporary....

Cecil explained that Lewis would talk about Edmund Spenser and Charles Williams about Milton as other critics would talk about modern writers like T.S. Eliot or D.H. Lawrence. He added: "Yet they did not try to bring them up-to-date. Simply they read their books in the spirit in which they were written. And they could communicate their sense of this spirit to their hearers so that, for these also, these great books sprang to fresh, full life. This was a unique achievement in the Oxford of their time."

The way that the Inklings could enter fully into these old books was echoed in their imaginative creations. Ancient northern worlds could come alive in Tolkien's Middle-earth and the splendour of the medieval universe could enchant modern children who read the Narnia stories. This may have been what Cecil was thinking when he wrote in that review: "The Inklings' imagination displayed itself more freely in their purely creative writing…"[6]

Loyal Narnians, Christian friends, a commonality

In his early description of the Inklings to Charles Williams, in 1936, Lewis pointed out that one element that the group had in common was the Christian faith. He clearly felt that one purpose of the club was to enjoy as much as possible its shared faith. Lewis, in his understanding, stood against the modern world, which displayed and championed what he saw as its post-Christian character. Like the loyal Narnians in *Prince Caspian*, who kept alive the memory of Aslan and Old Narnia, Lewis and his friends in the Inklings cherished the virtues and values of the Old West, and sought to rehabilitate them. The very friendship and fellowship that he perceived as holding the group together was, for him, a vestige of that older world, which he called the "Old West".

Lewis spoke of the "What! You too?" factor in the forming of friendships. He wrote in *The Four Loves*: "Friendship is born at that moment when one man says to another: 'What! You too! I thought I was the only one…'"[7] Central to Lewis's perception of the Inklings was the sharing of a common purpose and vision amid all the diversity and individuality of its members. Integral to this was a Christian faith (even if not always orthodox) that explored the relationship between myth and reality, and delighted in the imagination. John Wain pointed out that literature of myth and the "fine fabling" that invented it was regarded highly within the Inklings. Work that involved what Tolkien called "sub-creation" was particularly prized – the secondary worlds of Middle-earth, Malacandra, and a medieval Europe displaying the symbolism of the human body were enjoyed by the Inklings as stories and poems were read. The approach to the degree or kind of truth that the imagination could capture varied between the individual Inklings. The diversity ranged on a scale from Barfield's view (that the imagination discovered truth) to that of Lewis (that the imagination only captured meaning, but was admittedly a necessary precondition for the capturing of truth).

All of them seemed convinced that myth had the ability to generalize without losing contact with the individual character of natural things and, at its highest level, historical fact. This was one of the bases of the argument employed by Tolkien and Hugo Dyson in the autumn of 1931 to convince Lewis of the truth of the Christian claims. For them, at a particular point in real history, myth had become fact, fulfilling countless prefigurements in human storytelling and making of myths. The telling of their stories and their making of myth was high on the agenda of their literary meetings. Evidently, even those who could not spin a story (such as Dyson and Warnie) encouraged those who could (Lewis, Tolkien, Williams, and, when he could attend, Barfield).

Diana Glyer, in her study of the Inklings as a writing group,[8] argues the danger of simply seeking similarity between the texts of those who participated in the Inklings to find commonality. She comments: "Influence is greater than imitation, and to a large extent independent of it." The emphasis in a merely comparative treatment is on a finished work, rather than on the act of composition. Influence, however, bears upon the actual process of writing, editing, redrafting, and rewriting, which is the stuff of a writing group like the Inklings.

What was read at Thursday-evening gatherings could, of course, have an impact on the other Inklings meeting the following Tuesday at the pub only while both existed. The pattern of discussion and conversation after 1949 in the Eagle and Child would by necessity have been different – more free-ranging. My understanding of the dynamics of two groups in parallel, as was the case with the Inklings, was deepened by my membership a few years ago of a writing group – the Leicester Writers' Club. Usually, an evening session between 7 and 9 p.m. was devoted to manuscript readings, where published and aspiring writers read from work in progress, and received extemporary criticism from the group (which together had a very wide experience of genres and publication). Afterwards, a number would then move on to a hotel bar nearby for an informal gathering, very much friendship-based. Sometimes the conversation was entirely general, but often it referred back to what had been read earlier in the evening. Sometimes all of the group would participate in conversations, and sometimes several conversations would go on at once, between twos, threes, and more.

Diana Glyer, as we saw, argued that influence is far more than similarity in finished texts. "The Inklings were not a coterie nor a cohesive literary movement nor a mere group of friends. They had much in common, but were by no means men of one mind. They were knowledgeable peers,

225

writers who met on an ongoing basis to discuss written works in progress. They read their work aloud to one another and offered specific, substantial suggestions to one another. By doing so, they influenced each other and each other's writing."[9]

Mutual influence is therefore the key to the literary identity of the Inklings. Karen LeFevre, quoted by Diana Glyer, sets out four roles that are common when writers interact socially: they function as editors, resonators, collaborators, and opponents. "Writers often invent by involving other people: as editors and evaluators whose comments aid further invention; as 'resonators' who nourish and sustain the inventor as well as the invention; as collaborators who interact to create new ideas; and as opponents or devil's advocates who provide challenges and alternative perspectives to work against."[10]

Diana Glyer gives an excellent example of Tolkien's need for social help in the writing process of *The Silmarillion*. Dr Clyde S. Kilby of Wheaton College, Illinois, offered assistance and Tolkien responded: "If I had the assistance of a scholar at once sympathetic and yet critical, such as yourself, I feel I might make some of [*The Silmarillion*] publishable. It needs the actual presence of a friend and advisor at one's side, which is just what you offer."

In the event it was another of the Inklings, Tolkien's son Christopher, who made it publishable after Tolkien's death, along with a vast amount of other material that he had left unfinished.

Some conclusions

The Inklings will be remembered mainly as a very significant literary group. Their readings of work in process were only part of the picture. While the meetings in pubs, which were undoubtedly important, continued the literary impact informally, they reinforced the dynamics of gatherings of friends and nurtured conversation. The members constitute a literary group that is very much part of mainstream twentieth-century literature. In the Inklings there is a guiding vision of the relationship of imagination and myth to reality, and of a Christian worldview in which a pagan spirituality is seen as prefiguring the advent of Christ and the Christian story. In this respect Tolkien's "On Fairy Stories" and C.S. Lewis's "Myth Became Fact" are among the nearest things to manifesto essays for the group, but in an open-ended way. They certainly reflected the conversations of the group, and not simply Lewis and Tolkien as writers in isolation. They are a living rebuttal of individualism and of a modern obsession with originality and the new.

Ironically, it was as writers in community – even when only one other person shared in the creativity, as with Lewis and Roger Lancelyn Green or Tolkien and Lewis – that the latter two in particular added their distinctive voices to literature. That need for community was part of their embrace of an older world that they wished to rehabilitate for modern readers, enriching their lives as they were enabled to appropriate the past for their present and future.

The pattern of friendship

C.S. Lewis believed that friends open up aspects of each other, and saw this process embodied in the Inklings. In this view he was influenced by the ideas of Charles Williams, particularly his concept of "Co-inherence". It follows that both major and lesser members of the Inklings would be important in this process. Lewis memorably expresses this in his chapter on "friendship" in *The Four Loves*. In this extract "Ronald" is John Ronald Reuel Tolkien, and "Charles" is Charles Williams. Lewis points out the way in which friendship, in his view the love least susceptible to jealousy, expands:

> In each of my friends there is something that only some other friend can fully bring out. By myself I am not large enough to call the whole man into activity; I want other lights than my own to show all his facets. Now that Charles is dead, I shall never again see Ronald's reaction to a specifically Caroline joke. Far from having more of Ronald, having him "to myself" now that Charles is away, I have less of Ronald. Hence true Friendship is the least jealous of loves. Two friends delight to be joined by a third, and three by a fourth… each bringing out all that is best, wisest, or funniest in all the others.

This pattern of friendship fostered a mutual influence among the Inklings. Influence of course can take as basic a form as simple encouragement and discouragement. Lewis encouraged Tolkien to complete *The Lord of the Rings*, and Dyson at times discouraged him by exercising a veto on his reading from chapters in progress. Tolkien was discouraging to Lewis over the early chapters of *The Chronicles of Narnia*, but encouraging over the writing of *Out of the Silent Planet*. There was clearly great affection between the members of the Inklings, evidenced for example by what each wrote about the other. Lewis included characters in his science-fiction stories that were based on the Inklings. Tolkien did similarly in his unfinished *The Notion Club Papers*, and wrote verses about some of the group. Barfield fictionalized Lewis in his books. Lewis eulogized Williams both before and after his death.

So were the Inklings simply a circle of C.S. Lewis's friends? They *were* a circle of Lewis's friends, but not simply that. For Lewis and his friends, friendship itself was a rich and complex relationship, with roots in an older world, and with the power to enable what is best in our humanity, if not misused. How ought friendships to be lived? That question was at the heart of the work and concerns of the Inklings, however imperfectly they practised and embodied friendship.

An Inklings gallery

Owen Barfield (1898–1997) was born in London, and after graduating from Oxford with a BA in English he undertook a postgraduate B.Litt, upon which his book *Poetic Diction* was eventually based. In 1925 he published a children's book, *The Silver Trumpet*; the following year, his study *History in English Words* came out. Around 1929 Barfield returned to London, to begin training in his father's law firm. Because of this he could only attend Inklings meetings from time to time. He remembered visiting Oxford at least once a term, and this sometimes enabled a visit to an Inklings gathering. After his retirement at the age of sixty he had a new lease of life, extending for nearly forty years of writing and lecturing, in the process making a significant impact via various English departments throughout North America. There he was praised by scholars and writers, including novelist Saul Bellow and historian Theodore Roszak.

J.A.W. ("Jaw") Bennett (1911–1981) was a New Zealander, and, from 1947, a fellow don with Lewis at Magdalen College, Oxford. In 1964 he filled the position of Professor of Medieval and Renaissance literature at Cambridge left vacant when Lewis resigned owing to illness.

Lord David Cecil (1902–1986) taught English literature and modern history at Wadham College, Oxford. After an absence during which he devoted himself to writing, he became a fellow of English at New College. He was the author of many books, his subjects including William Cowper, Jane Austen, Samuel Palmer, Edward Burne-Jones, and others.

Nevill Coghill (1899–1980) This aristocratic Irishman read English at Exeter College, though his studies at Oxford University were postponed by service in the First World War. He and C.S. Lewis became close friends as undergraduates. Later, in 1924, he was elected a fellow at Exeter, a year before Lewis became a fellow of Magdalen. In their student days, the atheist Lewis was impressed by the fact that his brilliant friend could be a devout Christian. His theatrical productions were renowned, with one of his star pupils being Richard Burton. He was also admired for his translation of Chaucer's *Canterbury Tales* into modern English couplets. He became Merton Professor of English Literature at Oxford (1957–1966).

Commander James Dundas-Grant (1896–1985) After being affected by poison gas in the First World War, "D.G.", as he was later dubbed, became an underwriter at Lloyd's of London, and enlisted in the Royal Naval Volunteer Reserve. He was recalled to military service at the outbreak of the Second World War. In 1944 he was appointed Commander of the Oxford University Naval Division, taking up residence in Magdalen College, where he met Lewis, who he felt looked like a gentleman farmer in his scarecrow clothes. D.G. was invited to a Thursday Inklings, and later to the Tuesday gatherings at the Eagle and Child.

Henry Victor ("Hugo") Dyson (1896–1975) served in the First
World War and read English at Exeter College. He helped
Tolkien to persuade C.S. Lewis of the truth of Christianity.
He initially lectured in English at Reading University, near
enough to Oxford to keep in touch with fellow Inklings.
(Reading University had close links with Oxford University.)
There he developed an innovative Combined Humanities
course in 1930. He also helped in the creation of a School
of Fine Arts. Like Charles Williams, he gave lectures to the
Workers' Educational Association. Dyson was a memorable
and outstanding lecturer. He preferred teaching to writing – he
had few works published. He moved permanently to Oxford
in 1945, when he was elected fellow and tutor in English
Literature at Merton College, the same year that Tolkien
became Professor of English Language and Literature there.
Dyson retired in 1963. A member of the Inklings throughout
its existence, his preference was for conversation rather than
the reading of work in progress.

Adam Fox (1883–1977) was one of the earliest members of
the Inklings. C.S. Lewis got to know him over breakfasts
at Magdalen College, where Fox was a fellow and Dean of
Divinity from 1929. As a result of string-pulling by members
of the Inklings, he was elected in 1938 as Professor of Poetry
at the university. In 1942, he moved to war-torn London to
become Canon of Westminster Abbey. As well as a book of
poetry, his publications included *Plato for Pleasure* (1945), *Meet
the Greek Testament* (1952), and *Dean Inge* (1960).

Colin Hardie (1906–1998) studied at Edinburgh Academy
before going to Balliol College, Oxford. From 1930 to 1933 he
was a fellow and Classical tutor of Balliol. For three years he

was Director of the British School in Rome, before becoming a fellow and Classical tutor at Lewis's college, Magdalen. Before the war they found a common interest as members of the Oxford Dante Society, which both Tolkien and Charles Williams later joined. It was not until after the war, it seems, that he joined the Inklings. Hardie became the Public Orator of the University of Oxford from 1967 until 1973.

Dr Robert Emlyn "Humphrey" Havard (1901–1985) His father was an Anglican clergyman, but Havard joined the Roman Catholic Church when he was thirty-one, under the influence of Ronald Knox, the writer, priest, and Bible translator. One of the most faithful of the Inklings, he attended the club regularly, with a period away on naval service during the war. He also had to cope with occasional medical emergencies. Affectionately known by the Inklings as the "Useless Quack", in 1934 he took over a medical practice with centres in Headington and St Giles, not far from the Eagle and Child pub. Lewis placed him as a minor character in *Perelandra*. During the Second World War he spent time as a surgeon with the Royal Naval Reserve. When he had to return to Oxford (his wife having been diagnosed with breast cancer), he was dubbed "the Red Admiral" by Lewis because he now had an arresting red beard and turned up to a meeting in naval uniform. The innovation of Havard's beard was made more dramatic by its contrast with his shock of white hair (it had turned white in his thirties). It was Hugo Dyson who called him "Humphrey" because he couldn't remember his real name. Havard had five children. He lost his wife to the cancer in 1950.

Clive Staples ("Jack") Lewis (1898–1963) C.S. Lewis was born in Belfast on 29 November 1898. Jack (as he called himself) and his older brother, W.H. "Warnie" Lewis, were devoted to each other. Their mother, Flora, died when Jack was nine. Their father, Albert, unable to bear his loss, dispatched Jack and his brother to an abusive boarding school in Watford, England. He was wounded in battle in France during the First World War. By 1923 Lewis had been awarded a Triple First at Oxford University. In 1925 Magdalen College appointed him a fellow and tutor in English, and he met J.R.R. Tolkien later that academic year. He remained in this position without promotion until 1954, when Cambridge University honoured him with the prestigious new Chair of Medieval and Renaissance literature. In 1953, Lewis first met an American poet and novelist, Joy Davidman, with whom he had corresponded for some time. They eventually married, their lives overshadowed by her cancer, which eventually claimed her life in 1960. Lewis died at his Oxford home, The Kilns, on 22 November 1963, just short of his sixty-fifth birthday.

Warren Hamilton ("Warnie") Lewis (1895–1973) was Lewis's only sibling. He was one of the earliest members of the Inklings (indeed, Lewis may have formed the group partly for his benefit). Like many of them, he was a gifted writer, eventually bringing out books on French history. His diaries give important and vivid insights into his brother's life, as well as into meetings of the Inklings. He had a military career from the onset of the First World War to his early retirement in 1932, achieving the rank of major.

Ronald Buchanan McCallum (1898–1973) Born in Paisley, Renfrewshire, he served in the First World War before studying Modern History at Worcester College, Oxford. He was a historian and fellow of Pembroke College, Oxford until 1955, when he was elected Master of Pembroke. He wrote many books, including *Asquith* (Duckworth Great Lives series, No. 70, 1936). After C.S. Lewis died, he attempted, and failed, to keep the Inklings going. Finally, he conceded its end: "When the sun goes out there is no more light in the solar system."

Gervase Mathew (1905–1976) contributed to *Essays Presented to Charles Williams*. He studied at Balliol College, Oxford. In 1928, he joined the Catholic order of Dominicans, being ordained a priest in 1934. He remained in Oxford to lecture in modern history, theology, and English, and wrote books on Byzantium and medieval England.

Courtenay E. "Tom" Stevens (1905–1976) was fellow and tutor in Ancient History at Magdalen College, Oxford, from 1933, where he was an inspiring teacher. While a schoolboy at Winchester, he acquired the nickname "Tom Brown Stevens", after the hero of the popular story *Tom Brown's Schooldays*. He studied under the historian R.G. Collingwood at New College, Oxford. During the Second World War he served as an intelligence officer. One of his many publications was the book *The Building of Hadrian's Wall* (1966).

Christopher Tolkien (b. 1924) The third son of J.R.R. Tolkien, he was born in Leeds during his father's time as Reader then Professor of Anglo-Saxon at the university there. During the Second World War, Christopher trained as a pilot with the RAF. He studied at Trinity College, Oxford and lectured in Anglo-Saxon, Middle English, and Old Norse at several Oxford colleges, eventually becoming a fellow of New College. In 1975, after his father's death, he resigned his academic duties to devote himself to editing his father's vast body of unfinished work for publication.

John Ronald Reuel Tolkien (1892–1973) was born in South Africa to English parents, but from 1895 was raised in Birmingham. He went up to Exeter College, Oxford in 1911. After finishing his studies in 1915, he served with the Lancashire Fusiliers, and married Edith Mary Bratt in 1916, before fighting in the Battle of the Somme. He spent the remainder of the war serving in England, as he recuperated from a severe form of what was called "trench fever". They had four children, John, Michael, Christopher (a member of the Inklings after the Second World War), and Priscilla. Tolkien met Lewis in 1926, and in 1929 they began meeting weekly to read to one another and talk. This was a seed of the Inklings. As well as holding three professorial Chairs, one in Leeds and two in Oxford, Tolkien was the author of *The Hobbit* (1937), *The Lord of the Rings* (1954–1955), and many books published after his death, edited by his son Christopher.

John Wain (1925–1994) was one of Lewis's more famous pupils. He was a poet, critic, and novelist, serving as Professor of Poetry at Oxford from 1973 to 1978. His autobiography, *Sprightly Running*, tells evocatively of his experiences of Oxford in wartime: "Once a week, I trod the broad, shallow stairs up to Lewis's study in the 'new building' at Magdalen. And there, with the deer-haunted grove on one side of us, and the tower and bridge on the other, we talked about English literature as armies grappled and bombs exploded." With Christopher Tolkien, he was one of the youngest members of the Inklings. In 1947 John Wain joined the English Department at Reading University for a period of teaching that lasted until 1955. His early novel *Hurry on Down* (1953) was followed by further successful novels. He also published books of criticism and poetry.

Charles Walter Stansby Williams (1886–1945) Poet, novelist, biographer, theologian, and literary critic, he was born in Islington, London, and joined the Oxford University Press, eventually becoming a senior editor. He married Florence "Michal" Conway in 1917. He gave popular adult evening classes in literature for the London County Council, and wrote a series of seven supernatural thrillers, including *The Place of the Lion*. When Williams was evacuated with the OUP to Oxford, he, in John Wain's words, "gave himself as unreservedly to Oxford as Oxford gave itself to him". Oxford University recognized Charles Williams in 1943 with an honorary MA, and his writings were admired by T.S. Eliot, C.S. Lewis, Dorothy L. Sayers, and W.H. Auden.

Charles L. Wrenn (1895–1969) As well as a member of the Inklings, Wrenn was a family friend of the Tolkiens. He studied at Queen's College, Oxford and from 1917 to 1930 he was a university lecturer at Durham, Madras, Dhaka, and Leeds. Then he returned to Oxford to take up the post of university lecturer in Anglo-Saxon, working closely with Tolkien. During the Second World War he held the Chair of English language and literature at the University of London. In 1946, he went back to Oxford to take up the post of Rawlinson and Bosworth Professor of Anglo-Saxon, which Tolkien had vacated to become Merton Professor of English Language and Literature.

A select Inklings chronology

1917: Tolkien begins writing the tales that will become *The Silmarillion.*

Autumn 1919: Lewis and Barfield meet as undergraduates and survivors of the war.

1925: Tolkien is elected to the Chair of Anglo-Saxon at Oxford University; Lewis becomes a fellow and tutor in English at Magdalen College.

Tuesday 11 May 1926: The first recorded meeting between Tolkien and Lewis. They meet at the four o'clock "English Tea" – a meeting of the Oxford English School faculty – at Merton College.

18 September 1926: Lewis's narrative poem *Dymer* is published.

1928: Lewis begins his twice-weekly lectures on "The Prolegomena to Medieval and Renaissance Studies", which soon make him one of the most popular lecturers in Oxford.

1928: Barfield's *Poetic Diction* is published, the ideas in which have an enormous impact, first on Lewis and then on Tolkien.

27 May 1928: Lewis has just obtained a copy of Barfield's *Poetic Diction*, and immediately writes to him: "I think in general that I am going to agree with the whole book more than we thought I did. We are really at one about imagination as the source of meanings i.e. almost of *objects*. We both agree that it is the *prius* [antecedent] of truth."

1928: In an undated letter to Barfield, perhaps written in 1928, Lewis observes that Tolkien had told him that Barfield's "conception of the ancient semantic unity had modified his whole outlook". He had been reading Barfield's *Poetic Diction*.

November 1929: One Monday evening, after one of many meetings Lewis attends, Tolkien comes back with him to his college rooms and sits talking of northern myths by a bright fire in the larger sitting room. He leaves at 2:30 in the morning, in the wind and rain.

1929: Publication of Lord David Cecil's biography of the poet William Cowper, called *The Stricken Deer.*

6 December 1929: Lewis reads Tolkien's poetic version of the tale of Beren and Lúthien, lent to him from his collection of writings about Middle-earth, during the evening. His response is enthusiastic.

Late December 1929: Lewis stays in London for four days at the Barfields' home. For two of the days Maud and their adopted baby are away, giving Barfield and Lewis an "uninterrupted feast of each other's society".

1930: Tolkien begins to write *The Hobbit.* Charles Williams publishes *War in Heaven* and *Poetry at Present.*

21 March 1930: Lewis writes to his friend A.K. Hamilton Jenkin, telling him how his outlook is changing. He does not feel that he is moving exactly to Christianity, though, he confesses, it may turn out that way in the end.

1931: Tolkien's reformed English School syllabus is accepted, backed by C.S. Lewis, bringing together "Lang." and "Lit.". Whipsnade Zoo opens.

9 May 1931: Warnie Lewis returns to belief in Christianity.

19–20 September 1931: After a long night-time conversation with Tolkien and Hugo Dyson on Addison's Walk in Oxford, Lewis starts to become convinced of the truth of Christian belief, especially the doctrine of the incarnation of Christ.

28 September 1931: Lewis returns to Christian faith while riding to Whipsnade Zoo in the sidecar of his brother's motorbike.

1 October 1931: Lewis writes to Arthur Greeves that he now believes in Christ and Christianity.

22 November 1931: Lewis writes to Warnie in Shanghai about his meetings with Tolkien: "This is one of the pleasant spots in the week. Sometimes we talk English school politics: sometimes we criticize one another's poems: other days we drift into theology or 'the state of the nation': rarely we fly no higher than bawdy and 'puns'."

1932: Lewis reads the draft of *The Hobbit.*

16–29 August 1932: Lewis writes *The Pilgrim's Regress* while holidaying in Northern Ireland.

April 1933: On Easter Sunday Lewis has an idea for a book (probably while in church), which he outlines to Warren, who records it in his diary: "A religious work, based on the opinion of some of the [Church] Fathers, that while punishment for the damned is eternal, it is intermittent: he proposes to do sort of an infernal day excursion to Paradise." Many years later the idea becomes the book *The Great Divorce.*

End of Hilary (Summer) Term, 1933: The undergraduate club called "the Inklings" disbands.

Michaelmas (Autumn) Term, 1933: This marks the possible beginning of Lewis's convening of a group of friends specifically to share their writing and discuss, eventually called "the Inklings," using the name of the former undergraduate club.

Monday 4 December 1933: Owen Barfield is up from London and staying at The Kilns. Barfield and Warren drive into town, where they are joined by Lewis at half past ten. Warnie is secretly miffed when he discovers that Lewis has arranged to go for a walk with Tolkien that afternoon. It seems to him that he sees less and less of his brother every day.

Monday 26 March 1934: Lewis, Warren, and Tolkien meet at Magdalen College to read the script of *The Valkyrie.* Lewis and Tolkien read in the German, and Warren in English. He finds it easy to follow the others' parts. They finish after six o'clock and Tolkien goes home to his family, while the brothers heartily enjoy fried fish and a savoury omelette, with beer, at the nearby Eastgate Hotel.

Sunday 3 June 1934: Warren records that two of Lewis's friends are up in Oxford: Barfield taking his BCL law examination and Dyson examining in the university English School.

1935: Lewis begins writing his volume of the *Oxford History of English Literature*, after completing of *The Allegory of Love*, at the suggestion of Professor F.P. Wilson, one of the series editors. In the early part of the year, Lewis's GP, Dr "Humphrey" Havard, attends him for influenza (as he recalled many years later), and they discuss Aquinas. Soon afterwards he is invited to join the Inklings circle, because of his evident interest in "religio-philosophical discussion". The Inklings are described to Havard as a group who meet on Thursday evenings, read papers they have written, and discuss them. The group is made up of friends of Lewis's, and it is only later he learns their names.

A SELECT INKLINGS CHRONOLOGY

Wednesday 11 March 1936: Lewis first writes to Charles Williams, in appreciation of his novel *The Place of the Lion*. The letter carries the first known use of "the Inklings", to which Williams is invited.

Spring 1936: Lewis and Tolkien discuss writing time and space stories. Tolkien recalled in a letter[1] that Lewis had one day remarked to him that since "there is too little of what we really like in stories", they ought to write some themselves.

Thursday 21 May 1936: Publication of Lewis's *The Allegory of Love*. It wins the Hawthornden Prize.

Sunday 28 June 1936: Lewis writes to Owen Barfield about his children's story: "I lent *The Silver Trumpet* to Tolkien and hear that it is the greatest success among his children that they have ever known." He signs the letter "The Alligator of Love".

Wednesday 25 November 1936: Tolkien gives the Sir Isaac Gollancz Memorial Lecture to the British Academy on "Beowulf: The Monsters and the Critics", early drafts of which have been read by Lewis.

1937: Lewis is pressing ahead with his story of space travel, *Out of the Silent Planet*, reading it chapter by chapter to the Inklings as it is written.

Thursday 9 September 1937: Lewis refers to Charles Williams's novel *Descent into Hell*, in a letter to him, as "a thundering good book and a real purgation to read".

Tuesday 21 September 1937: The Hobbit is published, complete with Tolkien's own illustrations. W.H. Auden writes in a review that *The Hobbit* "in my opinion, is one of the best children's stories of this century".

Mid-December 1937: Tolkien begins writing the "new Hobbit" (*The Lord of the Rings*).

Friday 18 February 1938: Tolkien writes to his publisher, Stanley Unwin, concerning Lewis's science-fiction story, *Out of the Silent Planet*. It had been, he says, read aloud to the Inklings ("our local club"). He records that it proved to be exciting as a serial, and was highly approved by all of them. Tolkien reveals that he and Lewis each planned to write an excursionary thriller into space or time, each encountering myth. *Out of the Silent Planet* was the space story. His own, on time, was only a fragment (this was *The Lost Road*). Later he was to explore the same theme in the also unfinished *The Notion Club Papers*, loosely based on Inklings gatherings.

4 July 1938: Lewis meets Charles Williams in London. Later, in *Essays Presented to Charles Williams* (1947), Lewis remembers the meeting as "a certain immortal lunch", which was followed by an "almost Platonic discussion" in St Paul's churchyard, which lasted for about two hours.

Saturday 2 September 1939: Evacuee children arrive at The Kilns. Around this time Lewis begins a story about some evacuees who stay with an old professor, which he soon abandoned. After the war he will pick up the story again, and it becomes, after Aslan the lion bounds into it, *The Lion, the Witch and the Wardrobe.*

4 September 1939: Warren Lewis is recalled to active service the day after Britain declares war on Germany, and is initially posted to Catterick, Yorkshire.

7 September 1939: Charles Williams and the London branch of Oxford University Press move to Oxford for safety.

October 1939: Warren is assigned to serve with No. 3 Base Supply Depot, Le Havre, France.

Thursday 2 November 1939: At an Inklings gathering attended by Lewis, Williams, Tolkien, and Charles Wrenn, the discussion turns to the issue of God's goodness and the damned.

Thursday 9 November 1939: After dining at Oxford's Eastgate Hotel, the Inklings listen to Tolkien reading an early part of *The Lord of the Rings*, Charles Williams reading a Nativity play, and Lewis reading a chapter from *The Problem of Pain.*

Thursday 30 November 1939: There is no Inklings meeting, as Charles Williams and Gerard Hopkins (of the Oxford University Press) are both away. Lewis goes around to Tolkien's house in Northmoor Road, where they read to each other chapters from *The Problem of Pain* and *The Lord of the Rings.*

1940: Lewis begins lecturing on Christianity for the Royal Air Force, which he continues to do until 1941.

27 January 1940: Warren is granted the temporary rank of major (later made permanent).

Thursday 1 February 1940: Dr Humphrey Havard reads a short paper on the clinical experience of pain, prepared as an appendix for Lewis's book *The Problem of Pain.*

5 February 1940: Charles Williams celebrates the theme of chastity in Milton's *Comus* in a lecture.

Wednesday 7 February 1940: Dr James Welch, the Director of the British Broadcasting Corporation's religious programming department, writes to Lewis, saying how impressed he is by the "depth of his conviction" and the "quality of his thinking". He presses him to give a series of radio talks on the BBC.

Wednesday 14 February 1940: T.S. Eliot writes to Charles Williams, commenting that "one of your most important functions in life (which I tried to emulate in *The Family Reunion*) is to instil sound doctrine into people (tinged sometimes with heresy, of course, but the very best heresy) without their knowing it… ".

Thursday 15 February 1940: Up from London, Owen Barfield attends an Inklings meeting.

Thursday 29 February 1940: Hugo Dyson visits the Inklings meeting from Reading, so all are present except for Warnie Lewis and Owen Barfield. Adam Fox reads a poem about Blenheim Park in winter.

Friday 5 to Monday 8 April 1940: With his friends Cecil Harwood, Walter Field, and Owen Barfield, Lewis has a walking tour on Exmoor, starting and finishing at Minehead.

Thursday 25 April 1940: The first weekly Thursday-evening Inklings of the term takes place, in Lewis's college rooms as usual. Charles Williams, Tolkien, and Dr Humphrey Havard are among those in attendance. Havard reads a vivid account he has written of mountain climbing, in direct, straight-talking language. Writing to his absent brother, Lewis describes it as making their hair stand on end. Tolkien makes reference to his son John, at college in Rome as part of his training for the Roman Catholic priesthood.

Thursday 2 May 1940: Writing to Warnie, Lewis recounts an unusually good Inklings at which Charles Williams "read us a Whitsun play, a mixture of very good stuff and some deplorable errors in taste".

Thursday 16 May 1940: Lewis, writing to the absent Warnie, recalls sitting in the north room in Magdalen College, looking out on the hawthorn in the grove, as he awaits the arrival of the Inklings. He much regrets the fact that his brother is not there.

Thursday 30 May 1940: The first troops arrive in England in an unprecedented mass evacuation from Dunkirk, employing naval vessels and

volunteer civilian boats of all shapes and sizes. Warnie Lewis has shortly
before been evacuated, with his unit, from France to Wenvoe Camp, Cardiff,
in South Wales.

Sunday 21 July 1940: During morning service at his local church, Holy Trinity,
Headington, Lewis suddenly has the idea of writing a series of letters from
a senior to a junior devil. It will employ the inverse perspective of hell on
a young man who "unfortunately" comes to believe in Christianity. This
becomes *The Screwtape Letters.*

Monday 14 October 1940: Lewis's *The Problem of Pain* is published. It is
dedicated to the Inklings

Tuesday 7 January 1941: Dr Havard drives Tolkien and the Lewis brothers
to a pub at Appleton, some miles west of Oxford. It is a snowy night, and
the roads are slippery. Tolkien's offer of snuff, a recent gift, is taken up by
several locals, and Major Lewis recounts an amusing story about visiting
Blackwell's Bookshop in Oxford with the irrepressible "Hugo" Dyson.

Friday 2 May 1941: The first instalment of what becomes *The Screwtape Letters*
appears in a weekly religious paper, *The Guardian.*

Sunday 8 June 1941: Lewis preaches a momentous sermon, "The Weight of
Glory", at the church of St Mary the Virgin in Oxford. The church is packed
with students.

Tuesday 23 June 1941: "Lord David [Cecil] was very agreeable last night; sorry
he missed you; looks forward to meeting you; has ordered the *Dove*; didn't
know of the novels"(letter from Charles Williams to Michal Williams).

6 August 1941: Lewis gives the first of a series of five fifteen-minute talks
on BBC radio on the subject of *Right and Wrong: A Clue to the Meaning of the
Universe.* It is entitled "The Law of Human Nature". The series is broadcast
weekly, with the last being on 6 September. This answers listeners' questions
and is entitled "Some Objections". Other series follow, leading to twenty-five
talks in all. They are eventually edited and published as *Mere Christianity.*

Thursday 7 August 1941: Charles Williams refers in a letter to his wife, Michal,
to Lewis as the person out of all in Oxford who understands his thinking.

Mid-December 1941: Stella Aldwinckle sets up a club at Oxford University
to follow up on questions about Christian faith raised by doubters and
unbelievers, and those who have lost their once-held faith. Lewis helps her to
found the Socratic Club, and serves as president. Its committee will scour the
pages of *Who's Who* to find leading and articulate atheists or others critical
of Christian belief who might come and present their creeds in a spirit of

intellectual enquiry. Several of the Inklings, and future Inklings, attend, and some participate.

Sunday 21 December 1941: In a letter to Dom Bede Griffiths, Lewis describes Charles Williams and lists the members of the Inklings: "He is an ugly man with rather a cockney voice. But no one ever thinks of this for five minutes after he has begun speaking. His face becomes almost angelic.... Charles Williams, Dyson of Reading, & my brother (Anglicans) and Tolkien and my doctor, Havard (your church) are the 'Inklings' to whom my *Problem of Pain* was dedicated."

1942: Warren writes his first book, *The Splendid Century: Some Aspects of French Life in the Reign of Louis XIV* (not published until 1953).

1942: Charles Williams's *The Forgiveness of Sins* is published, dedicated to the Inklings.

Monday 26 January 1942: The first meeting of the "Socratic Club" is held in Oxford. R.E. Havard speaks on "Won't Mankind Outgrow Christianity in the Face of the Advance of Science and of Modern Ideologies?"

Monday 9 February 1942: The Screwtape Letters is published by Geoffrey Bles and is dedicated to J.R.R. Tolkien, much to his bemusement.

Monday 2 March 1942: Charles Williams addresses the Oxford University Socratic Club on "Are There Any Valid Objections to Free Love?", to a full house.

Wednesday 22 April 1942: Lewis goes by train to London to give the Annual Shakespeare Lecture to the British Academy on "Hamlet: The Prince or the Poem?"

April 1942: Lewis gives his first travelling talks to the RAF. His visit on this occasion is to the base at Abingdon, near Oxford. Some weeks later he writes to Sister Penelope: "As far as I can judge, they were a complete failure.... One must take comfort in remembering that God used an ass to convert the prophet." His responsibilities to the RAF mean much travelling throughout Britain, with most weekends taken up.

Thursday 8 October 1942: Publication of Lewis's scholarly work *A Preface to Paradise Lost*, a book of literary criticism partly inspired by Charles Williams's view on one of Lewis's long-loved authors, John Milton. Its index contains the entry "Rabbit, Peter".

Monday 16 November 1942: C.S. Lewis speaks to the Socratic Club on "Christianity and Aesthetics, or 'The Company Accepts No Liabilities'".

8 February 1943: C.S. Lewis addresses the Socratic Club, his subject: "If We Have Christ's Ethics, Does the Rest of the Christian Faith Matter?"

Wednesday 17 February 1943: Lewis gives a dinner party at Magdalen College for the writer E.R. Eddison, author of a fantasy approved by the Inklings, *The Worm Ouroboros.* Afterwards he takes him across to his college rooms for a meeting of the Inklings, attended by Tolkien, Warnie, and Charles Williams.

18 February 1943: Sheldonian Theatre, Oxford. An honorary MA is awarded to Charles Williams, with many of the Inklings in attendance.

Monday 22 to Friday 26 February 1943: Warnie accompanies Lewis to Durham by train, where his brother gives the Riddell Memorial Lectures (later to be published as *The Abolition of Man*).

Wednesday 5 May 1943: Charles Williams, in letter to his wife, Michal, mentions Havard turning up in a naval lieutenant's uniform. Havard, Tolkien, the Lewis brothers, and Charles Williams have lunch at the George Hotel.

Friday 15 October 1943: Charles Williams writes in a letter to Michal: "To-night Gervase Mathew is to take me to meet a clergyman called Austin Farrer, a philosopher and theologian – whose books are far too learned for me. But Beatrice has allured him, I am told." Williams is referring to his book *The Figure of Beatrice*, on Dante and romantic love.

Monday 15 November 1943: C.S. Lewis speaks that night to the Socratic Club, on the topic of "Science and Miracles".

Thursday 9 December 1943: Lewis hears Charles Williams read more of his novel in progress, *All Hallows' Eve*, probably at an Inklings meeting at Magdalen College.

Tuesday 14 December 1943: Lewis makes a point of inviting Charles Williams to Magdalen in order to meet "Hugo" Dyson, who is over from Reading, where he teaches at that time.

Friday 24 December 1943: Lewis has finished *That Hideous Strength,* the third volume of his science-fiction trilogy, and writes the short preface.

1944: Charles Williams continues reading *All Hallows' Eve* to the Inklings as it is being written.

Wednesday 5 January 1944: Charles Williams writes to Michal about a *Time* magazine journalist writing on Lewis. Having interviewed Lewis, he wants the view of Charles Williams, as a friend. The cover feature eventually appears in 1947 and helps to ensure Lewis's popularity in the United States.

Saturday 5 February 1944: Charles Williams writes to Michal: "I have found myself thinking how admirable it would be if I could get a Readership here when I retire. I know it may only be a dream; on the other hand, Lewis and Tolkien are only human, and are likely to take more trouble over a project which would enable them to see a good deal more of me than over anything which didn't." Lewis and Tolkien had evidently discussed this aspiration with Williams; a Readership is a senior university appointment.

Tuesday 22 February 1944: In the evening Lewis broadcasts on the BBC. On seven consecutive Tuesdays, from 22 February to 4 April between 10:15 and 10:30 p.m., he gives the talks known as "Beyond Personality".

Monday 7 February 1944: Lewis speaks to the Socratic Club on what he calls "Bulverism; or The Foundation of Twentieth-Century Thought".

Wednesday 1 March 1944: In a letter, Tolkien comments on the *Daily Telegraph*'s description of the "ascetic Mr Lewis": "I ask you! He put away three pints in a very short session we had this morning, and said he was 'going short for Lent'."

Tuesday 11 April 1944: Tolkien spends two hours with Lewis and Charles Williams, during which he reads a recently composed chapter from *The Lord of the Rings* – to the pleasure of the others.

Thursday 13 April 1944: In a letter to his son Christopher, in South Africa, Tolkien writes that he is going to Magdalen College that night for an Inklings meeting. He anticipates that those attending will be the Lewis brothers, Charles Williams, David Cecil, and probably Dr Havard ("the Useless Quack", who was "still bearded and uniformed"). In the event all turn up except David Cecil, and they stay until midnight.

Wednesday 19 April 1944: Tolkien reads his chapter on the passage of the Dead Marshes from the unfolding *The Lord of the Rings* to an approving Lewis and Charles Williams that morning.

Spring or summer vacation, 1944: Charles Williams reads the first two chapters of a work never completed, *The Figure of Arthur*, to Lewis and Tolkien.

Monday 8 May 1944: Tolkien reads a fresh chapter of *The Lord of the Rings*, in which Faramir, a new character, comes on the scene. It receives "fullest approbation" from the listeners, Lewis and Charles Williams.

Monday 22 May 1944: After an exhausting day writing a new chapter of *The Lord of the Rings*, Tolkien is rewarded by its warm reception by Lewis and Charles Williams.

Thursday 25 May 1944: Tolkien records, in a letter to his son Christopher, a long, very enjoyable Inklings. "Hugo" Dyson attends from Reading. Tolkien thinks him tired-looking, but still "reasonably noisy". Warnie Lewis reads another chapter from his book on the times of Louis XIV, and his younger brother reads extracts from *The Great Divorce* (then going by the title of "Who Goes Home?" – which Tolkien quips should rather be called "Hugo's Home").

Monday 29 May 1944: Tolkien reads the latest two chapters from *The Lord of the Rings* to Lewis in the morning, "Shelob's Lair" and "The Choices of Master Samwise". Lewis approves of them with unusual fervour, according to Tolkien, and is moved to tears by the second chapter.

Monday 5 June 1944: Lewis speaks to the Socratic Club on the subject "Is Institutional Christianity Necessary?"

Thursday 8 June 1944: The Inklings assemble in Lewis's rooms at Magdalen College, those present being Tolkien, the Lewis brothers, Charles Williams, and E.R. Eddison (on his second visit). There are three and a half hours of reading, including a long chapter from Warnie Lewis's book on Louis XIV, a new extract from *The Lord of the Rings*, an unrecorded piece from Lewis, and a new chapter from Eddison of a work in progress, *The Mezentian Gate* (which remained incomplete at his death in 1945).

Wednesday 12 July 1944: Charles Williams records going with Tolkien to visit Lewis in a nursing home. Lewis has had a minor operation on his arm. He finds the nurses "strong-minded" in not giving him enough to eat and washing him as if he couldn't wash himself.

Monday 14 August 1944: In a letter to Michal, Charles Williams refers to an ideal life, which includes "a Tuesday drink with the Magdalen set [the Inklings] and a sometimes Thursday evening".

Thursday 31 August 1944: An Inklings evening is attended by Lewis, Charles Williams, and others. Lewis reads a long paper on Kipling, and Williams reads his essay on that author from his book *Poetry at Present*.

Thursday 21 September 1944: An Inklings at Magdalen College is attended by the Lewis brothers, Tolkien, and Charles Williams. Warnie Lewis reads the final chapter of his book on Louis XIV, and they hear from Lewis an unnamed article and a long extract from his translation of Virgil's *Aeneid*. Tolkien walks part of the way home afterwards with Charles Williams, discussing the concept of freedom, and its misuses. The Inklings agree that if they are spared to have one, their victory celebration will consist of hiring a country inn for at least a week and spending the time entirely in beer and talk, totally ignoring any clock.

Tuesday 3 October 1944: At noon Tolkien and Charles Williams look in at the Bird and Baby (Eagle and Child) pub. Surprisingly, the Lewis brothers are already there (records Tolkien in a letter to Christopher). The conversation becomes lively. Tolkien notices a "strange gaunt man" rather like Strider at the inn in Bree. He doesn't have the usual "pained astonishment of the British (and American) public" on encountering the Lewises and Tolkien in a pub, but rather shows an attentive interest in the conversation. Eventually he interjects a comment on Wordsworth. The stranger turns out to be the right-wing poet and soldier Roy Campbell, recently lampooned by Lewis in *The Oxford Magazine*. He is promptly invited to the next Inklings on Thursday.

Saturday 14 October 1944: Writing to Michal, Charles Williams refers to the Inklings as the "Tolkien-Lewis group".

Monday 6 November 1944: Lewis gives a talk to the Socratic Club: "Is Theology Poetry?"

Thursday 23 November 1944: Tolkien, Charles Williams, and Dr Havard dine at The Mitre before joining Lewis and Barfield, who have dined at Magdalen College. Tolkien considers Barfield the only person who can tackle Lewis when in full flood of argument, "interrupting his most dogmatic pronouncements with subtle *distinguo's*". Writing about the evening to his son Christopher, Tolkien describes it as "most amusing and highly contentious". Items they hear include a short play by Barfield concerning Jason and Medea, and two sonnets that have been sent to Lewis. They discuss ghosts, the special nature of hymns (following Lewis's involvement with the revision of *Hymns Ancient and Modern* for the Church of England), and other subjects.

24 December 1944: In a letter to Christopher, Tolkien relates Charles Williams's comment on the unfolding chapters of *The Lord of the Rings*: "Charles Williams who is reading it all says the great thing is that its *centre* is not in strife and war and heroism (though they are understood and depicted) but in freedom, peace, ordinary life and good living."[2]

1945: Tolkien takes up the Merton Chair of English Language and Literature.

Monday 14 May 1945: The day before his friend and fellow Inkling Charles Williams unexpectedly dies, Lewis gives a talk at the Socratic Club on the subject of "Resurrection".

THE OXFORD INKLINGS

Tuesday 15 May 1945: Warnie Lewis records in his diary the death of Charles Williams: "And so vanishes one of the best and nicest men it has ever been my good fortune to meet. May God receive him into His everlasting happiness."

Monday 4 June 1945: Inklings member Gervase Mathew addresses the Socratic Club on the topic of "Christian and Non-Christian Mysticism".

Tuesday 11 to Friday 14 December 1945: The Inklings celebrate the war's end at The Bull, Fairford. The group includes the Lewis brothers and Tolkien, with Dr Humphrey Havard present for some of the time.

Thursday 28 March 1946: Warnie Lewis records that an Inklings gathering included himself, Lewis, Christopher Tolkien, Humphrey Havard, Colin Hardie, and Gervase Matthew. Among other things they discussed the possibility of dogs having souls.

Thursday 8 August 1946: In his diary, Warnie notes an Inklings meeting attended by himself, his brother, Hugo Dyson, Dr Havard, Tolkien, Gervase Matthew, and a visitor, Stanley Bennett of Cambridge. It is not, he writes, the sort of evening he enjoys: "mere noise and buffoonery".

Thursday 22 August 1946: There is an Inklings meeting attended by Tolkien, his son Christopher, and the Lewis brothers. Warnie Lewis records his brother reading a poem on Paracelsus's view of gnomes, and Tolkien reading from his "Papers of the Notions Club" – on the downfall of Númenor.

Tuesday 10 September 1946: Dr Humphrey Havard picks up the Lewis brothers and Christopher Tolkien from Magdalen College and drives them out to The Trout, a favoured inn at Godstow, near Oxford. They sit in the garden, records Warnie, and discuss the views Dr Johnston would probably have had on contemporary literature. They also talk about the nature of women.

8 September 1947: A *Time* magazine cover feature on Lewis, "Don v. Devil", describes his growing influence, Oxford life, and conversion from atheism, where he "found himself part of a small circle of Christian Oxonians who met informally each week or so to drink and talk". *Time* described "his handsome, white-panelled college room overlooking the deer park" and "his tiny, book-crammed inner study".

Thursday 13 November 1947: Warnie Lewis, in his diary, records an Inklings meeting at Merton (Tolkien's college). There "Tollers" [Tolkien] read "a rich melancholy poem on autumn, which J[ack] very aptly described as 'Matthew Arnold strayed into the world of Hobbit'".

A SELECT INKLINGS CHRONOLOGY

Thursday 27 November 1947: Warnie's diary notes the topics aired at an Inklings meeting that night, attended by Tolkien, Lewis, Stevens, Havard, and himself: "We talked of B[isho]p. Barnes, of the extraordinary difficulty of interesting the uneducated indifferent in religion: savage and primitive man and the common confusion between them: how far pagan mythology was a substitute for theology: bravery and panache."

Septuagesima (Sunday 25 January) 1948: Tolkien writes to Lewis about often wanting noise, despite appearances: "I know no more pleasant sound than arriving at the B.[ird] and B.[aby] and hearing a roar, and knowing that one can plunge in." [3]

Thursday 20 October 1949: This is the last Thursday-night Inklings meeting that is explicitly recorded in Warnie's diary. "No one turned up" the following week. This seems to mark the end of the Inklings as a writing group meeting regularly, though the friends continue to meet mainly for conversation on Tuesdays and later Mondays in the Eagle and Child and other pubs (such as the King's Arms) until Lewis's death in 1963.

1954: Publication of the first two volumes of *The Lord of the Rings*. This first edition Tolkien dedicates to the Inklings.

Tuesday 9 November 1954: Roger Lancelyn Green notes in his diary an Inklings meeting that included Tolkien, indicating that he was normally in attendance at the group at this time.

1955: At the beginning of this year, the regular Inklings pub meetings moved from Tuesday to Monday mornings, to accommodate Lewis, now that he spent part of the week in term time at Cambridge University.

1955: Publication of the final volume of *The Lord of the Rings*.

1959: Tolkien retires from teaching at Oxford.

Monday 17 June 1963: In his diary Roger Lancelyn Green notes one of the last records of an Inklings meeting, now held at the Lamb and Flag in St Giles.

Friday 22 November 1963: Lewis dies at home.

Monday 9 April 1973: Warren Lewis dies, still mourning his beloved brother.

Sunday 2 September 1973: Tolkien dies.

Friday 6 June 1975: Death of H.V.D. ("Hugo") Dyson.

Wednesday 17 July 1985: Death of Dr Robert Emlyn ("Humphrey") Havard.

Sunday 14 December 1997: Owen Barfield dies, just short of his century.

Bibliography

(1) Notes on other books on the Inklings

The Inklings, **Humphrey Carpenter (1978)**

Though this book is beautifully written, much more is now known about the Inklings than when it was written. It makes two controversial points: (1) It denies that Lewis and Tolkien had any real influence on each other; (2) The Inklings are defined simply as a group of Lewis's friends. No common purpose or project shaped them, according to Carpenter.

The Magical World of the Inklings, **Gareth Knight (1990)**

This focuses on key books by the four main Inklings, Tolkien, Lewis, Williams, and Barfield, and brings out their main themes. The author's interest in paganism particularly illuminates esoteric and magical elements in the books.

The Company They Keep: C.S. Lewis and J.R.R. Tolkien as Writers in Community, **Diana Pavlac Glyer (2007)**

This ground-breaking book focuses on the Inklings as a writers' group, and analyses their influence on each other's writings. It is at an academic level, though clearly and engagingly written.

The Inklings of Oxford: C.S. Lewis, J.R.R. Tolkien and Their Friends, **Harry Lee Poe (writer) and James Ray Veneman (photographer) (2009)**

This is a full-colour, large-format, coffee-table book, lavishly illustrated, the text of which briefly but effectively tells the story of the Inklings. The photographs focus on the Oxford places associated with the group and there are useful Inklings walking-tour guides at the end.

(2) Select bibliography

Adey, Lionel, *C.S. Lewis's "Great War" with Owen Barfield*, Victoria, BC: University of Victoria Press, 1978.

Aldwinckle, Stella, *Christ's Shadow in Plato's Cave: A Meditation on the Substance of Love*, Oxford: The Amate Press, 1990.

Anscombe, G.E.M., *Collected Philosophical Papers Vol. II: Metaphysics and the Philosophy of Mind*, Oxford: Blackwell, 1981.

Armstrong, Helen (ed.), *Digging Potatoes, Growing Trees: 25 Years of Speeches at the Tolkien Society's Annual Dinners*, Telford: The Tolkien Society, 1998.

Barfield, Owen, *Romanticism Comes of Age*, London: Anthroposophical Publishing Co., 1944.

Barfield, Owen, *This Ever Diverse Pair*, London: Gollancz, 1950.

Barfield, Owen, *Worlds Apart*, London: Faber and Faber, 1963.

Barfield, Owen (Jocelyn Gibb, ed.), *Light on C.S. Lewis*, London: Geoffrey Bles, 1965.

Barfield, Owen, *Saving the Appearances: A Study in Idolatry*, New York: Harcourt, Brace and World, 1965.

Barfield, Owen, *Poetic Diction*, London: Faber and Gwyer, 1928; new edition by Barfield Press, Oxford, 2010.

Barkman, Adam, *The Philosophical Christianity of C.S. Lewis*, doctoral thesis at the Vrije Universiteit Amsterdam, 2009.

Blamires, Harry, "Against the Stream: C.S. Lewis and the Literary Scene", in *Journal of the Irish Christian Study Centre Vol. 1*, 1983.

Carey, John, *William Golding: The Man Who Wrote Lord of the Flies,* London: Faber and Faber, 2010.

Carpenter, Humphrey, *J.R.R. Tolkien: A Biography*, London: George Allen & Unwin, 1977; Boston: Houghton Mifflin, 1977.

Carpenter, Humphrey, *The Inklings: C.S. Lewis, J.R.R. Tolkien, Charles Williams and Their Friends*, London: George Allen & Unwin, 1978; Boston; Houghton Mifflin, 1979.

Carpenter, Humphrey (ed.), *Letters of J.R.R. Tolkien*, London: George Allen & Unwin, 1981.

Cecil, Lord David, *The Stricken Deer, or The Life of Cowper*, London: Constable, new edition, 1943.

Cecil, Lord David, "Oxford's Magic Circle", *Books and Bookmen*, 24, No. 4, January 1979.

Como, James T. (ed.), *C.S. Lewis at the Breakfast Table and Other Reminiscences*, New York: Macmillan, 1979.

Cunningham, Valentine, *British Writers of the Thirties*, Oxford: Oxford University Press, 1989.

Dorsett, Lyle, *Joy and C.S. Lewis*, London: HarperCollins, 1988 and 1994.

Dorsett, Lyle W. and Mead, Majorie Lamp (eds.), *Letters to Children*, New York: Collins; London: Collier Macmillan, 1985.

Downing, David C., *The Most Reluctant Convert: C.S. Lewis's Journey to Faith*, Downers Grove, IL: IVP Books, 2004.

Drout, Michael D.C. (ed.), *J.R.R. Tolkien Encyclopedia: Scholarship and Critical Assessment*, New York and London: Routledge, 2007.

Duriez, Colin, "Tolkien and the Other Inklings", in Patricia Reynolds and Glen H. GoodKnight, *Proceedings of the J.R.R. Tolkien Centenary Conference: Keble College, Oxford, 1992*, Milton Keynes: The Tolkien Society and Altadena, CA: Mythopoeic Press, 1995.

Duriez, Colin, "The Theology of Fantasy in C.S. Lewis and J.R.R. Tolkien", in *Themelios*, Vol. 23, No. 2, February 1998.

Duriez, Colin, *Tolkien and the Lord of the Rings: A Guide to Middle-earth*, London: SPCK, 2001; Mahwah, NJ: The Paulist Press, 2001.

Duriez, Colin, and David Porter, *The Inklings Handbook: The Lives, Thought and Writings of C.S. Lewis, J.R.R. Tolkien, Charles Williams, Owen Barfield and Their Friends*, London: SPCK, 2001.

Duriez, Colin, *J.R.R. Tolkien and C.S. Lewis: The Story of Their Friendship*, Mahwah, NJ: The Paulist Press, 2003; Stroud, Gloucestershire: Sutton Publishing, 2005 [as *J.R.R. Tolkien and C.S. Lewis: The Story of a Friendship*].

Duriez, Colin, *J.R.R. Tolkien: The Making of a Legend*, Oxford: Lion Hudson, 2012.

Duriez, Colin, *C.S. Lewis: A Biography of Friendship*, Oxford: Lion Hudson, 2013.

Duriez, Colin, *Bedeviled: Lewis, Tolkien, and the Shadow of Evil*, forthcoming, Downers Grove, IL: IVP.

Bibliography

Edwards, Bruce L. (ed.), *C.S. Lewis: Life, Works and Legacy*, 4 Vols, Westport, CT: Praeger Publishers, 2007.

Flieger, Verlyn, *Splintered Light: Logos and Language in Tolkien's World*, Grand Rapids, MI: Eerdmans, 1983.

Gardner, Helen, "Clive Staples Lewis 1898–1963", in *Proceedings of the British Academy 51*, 1965, pages 417–428.

Glyer, Diana Pavlac, *The Company They Keep: C.S. Lewis and J.R.R. Tolkien as Writers in Community*, Kent, OH: Kent State University Press, 2007.

Golding, William, *The Inheritors*, London: Faber and Faber, 2011.

Graham, David (ed.), *We Remember C.S. Lewis: Essays and Memoirs*, Nashville, TN: Broadman & Holman, 2001.

Green, Robert Lancelyn, and Hooper, Walter, *C.S. Lewis: A Biography*, first edition, London: William Collins, 1974; revised edition, London: HarperCollins, 2002.

Gresham, Douglas, *Lenten Lands: My Childhood with Joy Davidman and C.S. Lewis*, London: Collins, 1989.

Hadfield, Alice Mary, *An Introduction to Charles Williams*, London: Robert Hale, 1959.

Hadfield, Alice Mary, *Charles Williams: An Exploration of his Life and Work*, Oxford: Oxford University Press, 1983.

Harwood, Laurence, *C.S. Lewis, My Godfather: Letters, Photos and Recollections*, Downers Grove, IL: IVP, 2007.

Havard, R. E., "Professor J.R.R. Tolkien: A Personal Memoir", *Mythlore*, Issue 64, Winter 1990.

Heck, Joel D. (ed.), *Socratic Digest* (Austin, TX: Concordia University Press, 2012). Reprinted from five issues originally published separately between the years 1943 and 1952.

Hooper, Walter (ed.), *C.S. Lewis; Narrative Poems*, London: Geoffrey Bles, 1969.

Hooper, Walter (ed.), *C.S. Lewis: Selected Literary Essays*, Cambridge: Cambridge University Press, 1969.

Hooper, Walter, (ed.), *All My Road Before Me: The Diary of C.S. Lewis, 1922–27*, London: HarperCollins, 1991.

Hooper, Walter, *C.S. Lewis: A Companion and Guide*, London: HarperCollins,

1996.

Hooper, Walter (ed.), *C.S. Lewis: Collected Letters Vol. One: Family Letters 1905–1931*, London: HarperCollins, 2004.

Hooper, Walter (ed.), *C.S. Lewis: Collected Letters Vol. Two: Books, Broadcasts and War 1931–1949*, London: HarperCollins, 2004.

Hooper, Walter (ed.), *C.S. Lewis: Collected Letters Vol. Three: Narnia, Cambridge and Joy 1950–1963*, London: Harper Collins, 2006.

Horne, Brian (ed.), *Charles Williams: A Celebration*, Leominster: Gracewing, 1995.

Jacobs, Alan, *The Narnian: The Life and Imagination of C.S. Lewis*, New York: HarperOne, 2010.

Keefe, Carolyn (ed.), *C.S. Lewis: Speaker and Teacher*, London: Hodder, 1974.

Kilby, Clyde S., *Tolkien and The Silmarillion*, Wheaton, IL: Harold Shaw, 1976; Berkhamstead: Lion Publishing, 1977.

Kilby, Clyde S. and Douglas R. Gilbert, *C.S. Lewis: Images of His World*, Grand Rapids, MI: Eerdmans, 1973.

Kilby, Clyde S. and Mead, Majorie Lamp (eds.), *Brothers and Friends: The Diaries of Major Warren Hamilton Lewis*, San Francisco: Harper and Row, 1982; New York: Ballantine Books, 1988.

King, Don W. (ed.), *Out of My Bone: The Letters of Joy Davidman*, Grand Rapids, MI: Eerdmans, 2009.

Knight, Gareth, *The Magical World of the Inklings*, Longmead, Dorset: Element Books, 1990.

Kuhl, Rand, "Owen Barfield in Southern California", *Mythlore*, Issue 4, October 1969.

Lawlor, John, *C.S. Lewis Memories and Reflections*, Dallas: Spence Publishing Company, 1998.

Lang-Sims, Lois, *Letters to Lalage*, Kent, OH, and London: The Kent State University Press, 1989.

Lange, Simon Blaxland-de, *Owen Barfield: Romanticism Comes of Age – A Biography*, Forest Row: Temple Lodge, 2006.

Lewis, C.S., *God in the Dock: Essays on Theology and Ethics*, (edited by Walter Hooper), Grand Rapids, MI: Eerdmans, 1970.

BIBLIOGRAPHY

Lewis, C.S., *Rehabilitations and Other Essays*, London: Oxford University Press, 1939.

Lewis, C.S., *The Problem of Pain*, London: Geoffrey Bles, 1940.

Lewis, C.S., *Miracles*, London: Geoffrey Bles, 1947; new edition: Collins, 2012.

Lewis, C.S. (ed.), *Essays Presented to Charles Williams*, London: Oxford University Press, 1947.

Lewis, C.S., *Arthurian Torso: Containing the Posthumous Fragment of the Figure of Arthur by Charles Williams and A Commentary on the Arthurian Poems of Charles Williams by C.S. Lewis*, London: Oxford University Press, 1948.

Lewis, C.S., *Dymer*, new edition, London: J.M. Dent, 1950.

Lewis, C.S., *Surprised by Joy: The Shape of My Early Life*, London: Geoffrey Bles, 1955.

Lewis, C.S., *The Allegory of Love*, New York: Oxford University Press, 1958.

Lewis, C.S., *The Four Loves*, London: Geoffrey Bles, 1960.

Lewis, C.S., *A Grief Observed*, London: Faber and Faber, 1961; new edition, 2013.

Lewis, C.S., *The Abolition of Man*, New York: HarperCollins, 2001.

Lewis, W.H. (ed.), *Letters of C.S. Lewis*, London: Geoffrey Bles, 1966.

Manlove, C.N., *Modern Fantasy*, Cambridge: Cambridge University Press, 1975.

Manlove, C.N., *Christian Fantasy: From 1200 to the Present*, Basingstoke and London: Macmillan, 1992.

Martin, Thomas L. (ed.), *Reading the Classics with C.S. Lewis*, Grand Rapids, MI: Baker Academic; Carlisle, UK: Paternoster, 2000.

McGrath, Alister, *C.S. Lewis, A Life: Eccentric Genius, Reluctant Prophet*, London: Hodder & Stoughton, 2013.

Moorman, Charles, *The Precincts of Felicity: The Augustinian City of the Oxford Christians*, Gainesville: University of Florida Press, 1966.

Newman, Barbara, "Eliot's Affirmative Way", *Modern Philology*, Vol. 108, No. 3, February 2011, pages 427–461.

Phillips, Justin, *C.S. Lewis at the BBC*, London: HarperCollins, 2002.

Poe, Harry Lee and James Ray Veneman (photographer), *The Inklings of Oxford: C.S. Lewis, J.R.R. Tolkien and Their Friends*, Grand Rapids, MI: Zondervan, 2009.

Rateliff, John D., *The History of the Hobbit*, one-volume edition, London: HarperCollins, 2011.

Ready, William, *Understanding Tolkien and The Lord of the Rings*, New York: Warner Books, 1978.

Reilly, Robert J., *Romantic Religion: A Study of Barfield, Lewis, Williams and Tolkien*, Athens: University of Georgia Press, 1971.

Reynolds, Patricia and Glen H. GoodKnight, *Proceedings of the J.R.R. Tolkien Centenary Conference: Keble College, Oxford, 1992*, Milton Keynes: The Tolkien Society; Altadena, CA: Mythopoeic Press, 1995.

Reynolds, Barbara (ed.), *The Letters of Dorothy L. Sayers, Vol. 4, 1951–1957: In the Midst of Life*, Cambridge: The Dorothy L. Sayers Society, 2000.

Richards, I.A., *Principles of Literary Criticism*, Abingdon: Psychology Press, 2001.

Ridler, Anne (ed.), Charles Williams, *The Image of the City and Other Essays*, London: Oxford University Press, 1958.

Russell, Bertrand, *History of Western Philosophy*, London: George Allen & Unwin, new edition, 1961.

Sayer, George, *Jack: C.S. Lewis and His Times*, London: Macmillan, 1988.

Schofield, Stephen (ed.), *In Search of C.S. Lewis*, NJ: Bridge, 1984.

Scull, Christina, and Wayne G. Hammond, *The J.R.R. Tolkien Companion and Guide: Chronology*, London: HarperCollins, 2006.

Scull, Christina, and Wayne G. Hammond, *The J.R.R. Tolkien Companion and Guide: Reader's Guide*, London: HarperCollins, 2006.

Segura, Eduardo, and Thomas Honegger (eds.), *Myth and Magic: Art According to the Inklings*, Zollikofen, Switzerland: Walking Tree Publishers, 2007.

Shideler, Mary McDermott, *The Theology of Romantic Love: A Study in the Writings of Charles Williams*, Grand Rapids, MI: W.B. Eerdmans, 1962.

Shippey, Tom, *J.R.R. Tolkien: Author of the Century*, London: HarperCollins, 2000.

Sibley, Brian, *Shadowlands*, London: Hodder, 1985.

Stewart, J.I.M., *The Young Pattullo*, New York: W.W. Norton & Company, 1975.

Tennyson, G.B. (ed.), *Owen Barfield on C.S. Lewis*, Middletown, CT: Wesleyan University Press, 1989.

Tolkien, J.R.R., *The Silmarillion*, London: George Allen & Unwin, 1977.

Tolkien, J.R.R., *The Letters of J.R.R. Tolkien* (edited by Humphrey Carpenter with the assistance of Christopher Tolkien), London: George Allen & Unwin; Boston: Houghton Mifflin, 1981.

Tolkien, J.R.R., *The Monsters and the Critics and Other Essays* (edited by Christopher Tolkien), London: George Allen & Unwin, 1983.

Tolkien, J.R.R., *The Book of Lost Tales, Part Two*, Vol. 2 of The History of Middle-earth (edited by Christopher Tolkien), London: George Allen & Unwin, 1984.

Tolkien, J.R.R., *The Lays of Beleriand*, Vol. 3 of The History of Middle-earth (edited by Christopher Tolkien), London: George Allen & Unwin, 1985.

Tolkien, J.R.R., *Sauron Defeated*, a volume of *The History of The Lord of the Rings* (edited by Christopher Tolkien), London: HarperCollins, 2002.

Tolkien, J.R.R., *The Legend of Sigurd and Gudrún* (edited by Christopher Tolkien), London: HarperCollins, 2009.

Tolkien, John and Priscilla, *The Tolkien Family Album*, Boston: Houghton Mifflin; London: Unwin/Hymen, 1992.

Tolley, Trevor (ed.), *John Heath-Stubbs: The Literary Essays*, Manchester: Carcanet Press Ltd, 1998.

Wain, John, *Sprightly Running: Part of an Autobiography*, London: Macmillan, 1962.

Walker, Andrew and James Patrick (eds), *A Christian for All Christians: Essays in Honour of C.S. Lewis*, London: Hodder & Stoughton, 1990.

Walsh, Chad, *C.S. Lewis: Apostle to the Skeptics*, New York: Macmillan, 1949.

Walsh, Chad, *The Literary Legacy of C.S. Lewis*, New York: Harcourt Brace Jovanovich, 1979.

Ward, Michael, *Planet Narnia: The Seven Heavens in the Imagaination of C.S. Lewis*, New York and Oxford: Oxford University Press, 2008.

Wilson, A.N., *C.S. Lewis: A Biography*, London: Collins, 1990.

Notes

Publication details can be found in the Bibliography unless otherwise stated.

Introduction

1 Letter of 7 December, 1954; in Barbara Reynolds (ed.), *The Letters of Dorothy L. Sayers, Vol. 4, 1951–1957: In the Midst of Life*, page 186.

2 C.S. Lewis, *De Descriptione Temporum,* in Walter Hooper (ed.), *C.S. Lewis: Selected Literary Essays*, pages 5, 10.

3 *ibid.*, pages 13–14.

4 Letter 13 December 1954, in Don W. King (ed.), *Out of My Bone: The Letters of Joy Davidman*, page 228.

5 Letter to C.S. Lewis from Dorothy L. Sayers, 4 April 1955, in Barbara Reynolds (ed.), *The Letters of Dorothy L. Sayers, Vol. 4, 1951–1957: In the Midst of Life*, page 223.

6 In Oxford, Magdalen College is on the River Cherwell.

7 Walter Hooper (ed.), *C.S. Lewis: Collected Letters Vol. Three*, page 578.

8 Tom Shippey, "C.S. Lewis", in Michael D.C. Drout (ed.) *J.R.R. Tolkien Encyclopedia: Scholarship and Critical Assessment*.

9 Letter 24 June 1936, in Walter Hooper (ed.), *C.S. Lewis: Collected Letters Vol. Two*.

10 Letter 26 February 1936, in Walter Hooper (ed.), *C.S. Lewis: Collected Letters Vol. One*.

11 Letter to Charles Williams from C.S. Lewis, 11 March 1936, in Walter Hooper (ed.), *C.S. Lewis: Collected Letters Vol. Two*.

12 Jocelyn Gibb (ed.), *Light on C.S. Lewis*, page 62.

1 Through love and beyond: Charles Williams, the enigmatic Inkling

1 John Wain, *Sprightly Running*, page 147.

2 John Wain, *Sprightly Running*, page 182.

3 Its full name was New Connection Publications Office & Bookroom.

4 Alice Mary Hadfield, *Charles Williams: An Exploration of his Life and Work*, page 12. Quoted from MS by Edith Williams, "Memories of Early Days at Home".

5 Alice Mary Hadfield, *An Introduction to Charles Williams*, page 157.

6 Overheard by the poet Anne Ridler. Anne Ridler, "Introduction", in Anne Ridler (ed.), Charles Williams, *The Image of the City and Other Essays*, page xx.

7 John Wain, *Sprightly Running*, page 149.

8 Lois Lang-Sims, *Letters to Lalage*, page 21.

9 He was deeply influenced by Waite's 1909 publication, *The Hidden Church of the Holy Graal*. See Roma A. King Jr., "The Occult as Rhetoric in the Poetry of Charles Williams", in *The Rhetoric of Vision: Essays on Charles Williams* (edited by C.A. Huttar and P.J. Schakel), Lewisburg, PA: Bucknell University Press, 1996.

10 In later life, Evelyn Underhill corresponded with C.S. Lewis, and one letter on the wildness of animals may have influenced the creation of Aslan in the Narnia stories. See Colin Duriez, *J.R.R. Tolkien and C.S. Lewis: The Story of Friendship*, Stroud, Gloucestershire: Sutton Publishing, 2005, pages 138–139.

11 David Porter, "Co-inherence", in Colin Duriez and David Porter, *The Inklings Handbook*, pages 82–83.

12 Alice Mary Hadfield, *An Introduction to Charles Williams*, page 157.

13 Towards the end of his life, Lewis seems to have moved somewhat towards a more "catholic" kind of Anglicanism, perhaps influenced by the Oxford theologian Austin Farrer, but continued to portray "mere Christianity" in his books and essays, and in his personal correspondence. He also had some evangelical traits, which he never abandoned.

14 Barbara Newman, "Eliot's Affirmative Way", *Modern Philosophy*, Vol. 108, No. 3, February 2011, page 431.

15 John Heath-Stubbs, "Charles Williams", in Trevor Tolley (ed.), *John Heath-Stubbs: The Literary Essays*, page 155.

16 See David Porter, "Women and Charles Williams", in Colin Duriez and David Porter, *The Inklings Handbook*, pages 227–228.

2 Roots and shoots: Friends who will become Inklings

1 Nevill Coghill, "The approach to English", in Jocelyn Gibb (ed.), *Light on C.S. Lewis*, pages 52–53. Note the golden chessman found in the ruins of Cair Paravel in the Narnian tale *Prince Caspian*.

2 See http://www.snsbi.org.uk/Nomina_pdf/Nomina_v5_p63_McClure. pdf, which explores the use of nicknames in closed systems such as English public schools. Accessed 29 October 2014.

3 Simon Blaxland-de Lange, *Owen Barfield: Romanticism Comes of Age – A Biography*, page 15.

4 *ibid.*, page 15.

5 *ibid.*, page 16.

6 *New York Times* obituary, 19 December 1997.

7 *ibid.*

8 C.S. Lewis, *Surprised by Joy: The Shape of My Early Life*, chapter 1.

9 *ibid.*

10 *ibid.*

3 The 1920s: Oxford, wistful dreams, and a war with Owen Barfield

1 I owe this insight to Lauren Jones, President of the Newman Carnegie Library, Newnan, GA, USA.

2 C.S. Lewis, *Dymer*, page xi.

3 I.A. Richards, *Principles of Literary Criticism*, chapter one.

4 For more on the impact of Richards on literary study, see http://www. english.cam.ac.uk/classroom/pracrit.htm. Accessed 29 October 2014

5 C.S. Lewis, *Surprised by Joy*, chapter 13.

6 John Carey, *William Golding: The Man Who Wrote Lord of the Flies*, page 48.

7 C.S. Lewis, *Surprised by Joy*, chapter 13.

Notes

8 For an important study of Barfield's influence on Tolkien, see Verlyn Flieger, *Splintered Light: Logos and Language in Tolkien's World*.

9 Lewis explains this idea for the general reader in his chapter "Horrid Red Things" in *Miracles* (1960), and more technically in his chapter "Bluspels and Flalansferes" in Walter Hooper (ed.), *C.S. Lewis: Selected Literary Essays*.

10 Owen Barfield, *Saving the Appearances*, 1957, page 42. Barfield defined original participation as the belief that "there stands behind the phenomena, and on the other side of them from me, a represented which is of the same nature as me... of the same nature as the perceiving self, inasmuch as it is not mechanical or accidental, but psychic and voluntary".

11 Owen Barfield, *Romanticism Comes of Age*, page 230.

12 Owen Barfield, *Poetic Diction*, 1952 edition.

13 William Golding, *The Inheritors*, chapter 1.

14 William Golding's son, David, studied for a year at Michael Hall, before doing his A levels elsewhere.

15 The published *The Silmarillion* (1977) is a distillation, edited by Tolkien's son Christopher, of a vast body of unfinished material written between 1917 and his death in 1973.

16 His daughter, Priscilla, was born in Oxford in 1929.

17 See C.S. Lewis's letter to Owen Barfield, probably 1929, and 21 October 1929 in Walter Hooper (ed.), *C.S. Lewis: Collected Letters Vol. Three*.

18 Oral history interview with Owen Barfield, The Marion E. Wade Center, Wheaton College, IL.

19 See his account of the origin of *Poetic Diction* quoted in Simon Blaxland-de Lange, *Owen Barfield: Romanticism Comes of Age – A Biography*, page 28.

20 W.H. Lewis, "Memoir of C.S. Lewis", in W.H. Lewis (ed.), *Letters of C.S. Lewis*, page 20.

21 Quoted by Don W. King in *C.S. Lewis, Poet: The Legacy of His Poetic Impulse*, Kent, OH: The Kent State University Press, 2001, page 109.

22 G.B. Tennyson (ed.), *Owen Barfield on C.S. Lewis*, page 6.

23 C.S. Lewis, "Preface by the Author to the 1950 Edition [of *Dymer*]", in Walter Hooper (ed.), *C.S. Lewis; Narrative Poems*, page 3.

24 C.S. Lewis, "Is Theology Poetry?"

4 J.R.R. Tolkien returns to Oxford and C.S. Lewis meets God

1   It is included in J.R.R. Tolkien, *The Lays of Beleriand*, Vol. 3 of The History of Middle-earth.

2   This is included in J.R.R. Tolkien, *The Book of Lost Tales, Part Two*, Vol. 2 of The History of Middle-earth.

3   A.N. Wilson, *C.S. Lewis: A Biography*, page 117.

4   Cited in William Ready, *Understanding Tolkien and The Lord of the Rings*, page 17.

5   See, for example, J.I.M. Stewart, *The Young Pattullo*, pages 106–108.

6   Discerning students of Tolkien's picked up on his fervent and inspiring love of language and medieval literature.

7   Oxford did, however, grant John Betjeman an honorary doctorate of letters in 1974, nearly fifty years later.

8   J.R.R. Tolkien, *The Legend of Sigurd and Gudrún*.

9   Walter Hooper (ed.), *C.S. Lewis: Collected Letters Vol. One*, letter to Arthur Greeves, 17 October 1929.

10 Italics mine. Lord David Cecil, *The Stricken Deer, or The Life of Cowper*. Lord David was referring to the poets Thompson and Crabbe as representative of the mainstream. "The light that never was, on land and sea" is a quotation from Wordsworth's poem *Lines Suggested by a Picture of Peele Castle in a Storm* (1807).

11 For a fuller account of their friendship, see Colin Duriez, *J.R.R. Tolkien and C.S. Lewis: The Gift of Friendship*.

12 Helen Gardner, "Clive Staples Lewis 1898–1963", in *Proceedings of the British Academy* 51, 1965, pages 417–428.

13 There would remain an option to study Victorian literature, but this option was not encouraged, it seems.

14 In one place, Lewis wonders whether the radical divide goes back even further in its earliest seeds to ideas of the great medieval philosopher St Thomas Aquinas. He writes in *The Allegory of Love*: "Aristotle is, before all, the philosopher of divisions. His effect on his greatest disciple [Aquinas], as M. Gilson has traced it, was to dig new chasms... The danger of Pantheism grew less: the danger of mechanical Deism came a step nearer. It is almost as if the first, faint shadow of Descartes, or even of 'our present discontents' had fallen across the scene", page 88.

15 Christopher Ricks's review of Humphrey Carpenter's *The Inklings* in *New York Times*, http://www.nytimes.com/books/01/02/11/specials/tolkien-carpenter.html (accessed 29 October 2014). The familiar title of Tolkien's *The Lord of the Rings* was created many years later. Another friend, Cecil Harwood, in this early period was called by his friends "the lord of the walks", as he arranged walking excursions for them.

16 Jared Lobdell, "The Cave", in Michael D.C. Drout (ed.), *J.R.R. Tolkien Encyclopedia: Scholarship and Critical Assessment*.

17 David C. Downing's excellent *The Most Reluctant Convert* does just that.

18 W.H. Lewis (ed.), *Letters of C.S. Lewis*, page 141.

19 *ibid.*, chapter 3.

20 In an early, unfinished account of his conversion to theism, he declared: "I am an empirical Theist. I have arrived at God by induction."

5   The birth of the Inklings

1 Clyde S. Kilby and Marjorie Lamp Mead (eds.), *Brothers and Friends*, page 26.

2 C.S. Lewis, "Introductory", in *The Problem of Pain*.

3 The full title is *The Lewis Papers: Memoirs of the Lewis Family 1850–1930*, which would eventually run to eleven volumes, and be completed by 1935.

4 Valentine Cunningham, *British Writers of the Thirties*, page 226.

5 Clyde S. Kilby and Marjorie Lamp Mead (eds.), *Brothers and Friends*, pages 92–93.

6 Robert Lancelyn Green and Walter Hooper, *C.S. Lewis: A Biography*, London: William Collins, 1974, page 102.

7 To Arthur Greeves, letter 27 December 1929, Walter Hooper (ed.), *C.S. Lewis: Collected Letters Vol. One*.

8 Assuming this is the same conversation recorded in *Surprised by Joy*, which is likely.

9 Lewis and Warnie took another trip to Whipsnade, on their own, a week later, and Lewis made a further trip the following spring in a car with a very talkative colleague, Revd Edward Foord-Kelsey, and Arthur Greeves, which doesn't appear conducive to the decisive conversion experience as described by Lewis. Warnie was clear in his mind which day was the momentous one marking his brother's return to Christianity; his

record would have been based on conversations and other knowledge, not simply on surviving letters from his brother. In Lewis's much later *Surprised by Joy* there is a paragraph describing Whipsnade at that period, in contrast to its loss of glory in the 1950s. Alister McGrath argues that mainly because bluebells, which are spring flowers, are mentioned in the description (which he takes as a description only of the day of conversion, rather than of that period), Lewis's conversion might have occurred during the spring visit of 1932. In view of the documentation of the time in letters, Warnie's diary, details in his unpublished biography of his brother, and other pointers, it seems to me that Warnie is the best authority we have for identifying Lewis's acceptance of Christian belief with the Whipsnade visit of September 1931.

10 Published in C.S. Lewis, *God in the Dock: Essays on Theology and Ethics,* (edited by Walter Hooper).

11 Owen Barfield could talk about myth becoming fact in Jesus Christ as a belief already there in Steiner's thought. However, Steiner had a very different view of fact from Lewis and Tolkien. Steiner interpreted the Gospel records according to hidden knowledge.

12 C.S. Lewis, *Surprised by Joy*, chapter 15.

13 Humphrey Carpenter, *J.R.R. Tolkien: A Biography*, page 152.

14 Maria Kuteeva, "Myth", in Thomas L. Martin (ed.), *Reading the Classics with C.S. Lewis*, page 269.

15 *They Stand Together: The Letters of C.S. Lewis to Arthur Greeves,* London: Collins, 1979. 5 September 1931.

16 Letter 4 February 1933 in Walter Hooper (ed.), *C.S. Lewis: Collected Letters Vol. Two*, London: HarperCollins, 2004.

17 Letter 25 March 1933.

18 Clyde S. Kilby and Marjorie Lamp Mead (eds.), *Brothers and Friends,* page 102.

19 The book was given by Bede Griffiths; letter to W.H. Lewis, 24 October 1931, Walter Hooper (ed.), *C.S. Lewis: Collected Letters Vol. One*

20 Entry 19 January 1932, in *Brothers and Friends*, 1988 edition, page 107.

21 C.S. Lewis, *The Four Loves*, page 83.

22 John Rateliff, note 8 in "Introduction", *The History of the Hobbit* (one-volume edition), Kindle location 20468.

23 See Warren Lewis's diary, 21 Dec 1933, in Clyde S. Kilby and Marjorie Lamp Mead (eds.), *Brothers and Friends*.

24 Nevill Coghill married in 1927, and had one daughter.

25 See Warren Lewis's diary, 19 July 1934, cited in Christina Scull and Wayne G. Hammond, *The J.R.R. Tolkien Companion and Guide: Chronology*, page 174.

26 By Hugo Dyson, after forgetting his name.

27 B.G. Charlton, "Reflections on a scientific paper of 1926 by the medical 'Inkling' Robert Emlyn Havard (1901–1985)" in *Medical Hypotheses*, 2009, Vol. 72, pages 619–620.

28 He recalled the date to John Rateliff, in "Introduction", *The History of the Hobbit*, Kindle location 20469; see also Robert E. Havard, "Philia", in James T. Como (ed.), *C.S. Lewis at the Breakfast Table and Other Reminiscences*, page 215, and in oral history interview with Havard by The Marion E. Wade Center, Wheaton, IL, 1984.

29 R.E. Havard, "Professor J.R.R. Tolkien: A Personal Memoir", *Mythlore*, Issue 64, Winter 1990, page 61.

30 John Rateliff, "Introduction", *The History of the Hobbit*, Kindle location 20469.

31 C.S. Lewis, *The Four Loves*, chapter 4.

6 The 1930s: Writing books they liked to read

1 From a computer printout in the Bodleian Library, Barfield Collection, Dep. C. 1156. The article appeared in *The World and I*, January or February 1990.

2 J.R.R. Tolkien, "On Fairy Stories," in C.S. Lewis (ed.), *Essays Presented to Charles Williams*, page 47.

3 The lecture is available in a collection of essays by Tolkien, edited by his son Christopher Tolkien: J.R.R. Tolkien, *The Monsters and the Critics and Other Essays*.

4 Preface in C.S. Lewis (ed.), *Essays Presented to Charles Williams*, page vi.

5 David L. Russell, "C.S. Lewis", in *British Children's Writers, Vol. 160 of Dictionary of Literary Biography, Vol. 160*, Detroit, MI: Bruccoli Clark Layman, 1996, pages 134–149.

6 C.S. Lewis, *The Allegory of Love*, page 44. At this point Lewis in a footnote simply refers the reader to Owen Barfield's *Poetic Diction* (1928). Barfield in that book argues that an original unified consciousness in humans has become fractured.

7 The unfinished poetic version is found in J.R.R. Tolkien, *The Lays of Beleriand Vol. 3 of The Histoy of Middle-earth*, 1985.

8 C.S. Lewis, *Rehabilitations and Other Essays*, page 157.

9 Lewis was trying to show that the virtues and values resided in something even larger than the entire "Old West" – that is, our essential humanity, carrying the image of God. It was an ambitious natural theology by a layperson.

10 C.S. Lewis, *The Abolition of Man*.

11 Harry Blamires, "Against the Stream: C.S. Lewis and the Literary Scene", in *Journal of the Irish Christian Study Centre* 1, 1983, page 15.

7 The war years and the Golden Age of the Inklings

1 Barfield's knowledgeable biographer, Simon Blaxford-de Lange, writes of "the art of conversation" as being "the essential hallmark of the Inklings circle" (*Owen Barfield: Romanticism Come of Age – A Biography*, page 45).

2 There was no absolute distinction between the two types of meeting. There was much conversation in the evening meetings, and in a documented meeting in a pub (the White Horse) Tolkien read a new chapter of *The Lord of the Rings* to C.S. Lewis and Charles Williams (on Wednesday 12 April 1944), indicating (given the scarcity of documentation on get-togethers of the Inklings) that there may have been rare readings from time to time in pubs.

3 Lord David Cecil, who joined the Inklings during the war, explicitly states that Inklings meetings took place weekly during the university terms. See Cecil, "Oxford's Magic Circle", *Books and Bookmen*, 24, No. 4, January 1979, page 10.

4 Victory in Europe.

5 Roger Lancelyn Green and Walter Hooper, *C.S. Lewis: A Biography*, page 157. The "best of all public-houses" was the Eagle and Child, in St Giles.

6 The last record I can find of Adam Fox's attendance at an Inklings meeting is on 29 February 1940. See Lewis's letter to his brother, Warren, in Walter Hooper (ed.), *C.S. Lewis: Collected Letters Vol. Two*, pages 359–60.

7 Quoted in Clyde S. Kilby and Douglas R. Gilbert, *C.S. Lewis: Images of His World*, page 12.

8 John Wain, *Sprightly Running,* pages 147–152.

9 Letter of Charles Williams to Florence Williams, 9 November 1943. Archived at The Marion E. Wade Center, Wheaton College, IL.

10 Chad Walsh, *C.S. Lewis: Apostle to the Skeptics*, pages 16–17.

11 Letter 11 January, 1939, in Walter Hooper (ed.), *C.S. Lewis: Collected Letters Vol. Two*.

12 Letter to Warren Lewis, 11 April 1940.

13 See Laurence Harwood, *C.S. Lewis, My Godfather: Letters, Photos and Recollections*.

14 For even more glimpses, gleaned from the sparse documentation we have, see Appendix 2: A select Inklings chronology.

15 *The Lord of the Rings* is divided into six books. It was initially published in three volumes, each consisting of two books. With the publishing technology that existed in the 1950s, it seems that a one-volume edition of the work was not possible, even if it had been financially suitable.

16 Letter from C.S. Lewis to W.H. Lewis, 11 November 1939, in Walter Hooper (ed.), *C.S. Lewis: Collected Letters Vol. Two*, pages 288–289. The theme of devilry in the writings of the Inklings, and the related issue of the conflict between good and evil, is explored in Coin Duriez, *Bedeviled: Lewis, Tolkien, and the Shadow of Evil*, forthcoming.

17 Lewis notes in a letter to Warnie that a couple of nights before, the cold had woken him despite his wearing a pullover and having a great number of blankets on his bed. He couldn't take a sip of water from the tumbler beside his bed as the water had frozen.

18 Lewis tended to refer to the Inklings in the singular, perhaps implying it was an entity with a definite character, rather than merely a higgledy-piggledy circle of his friends (see chapter 11).

19 That is, classes or orders in the British body politic.

20 Letter from C.S. Lewis to W.H. Lewis, 3 March 1940.

21 Major Lewis was not, it seems, evacuated from Dunkirk (at the end of May 1940), as stated in *Brothers and Friends*, page 201.

22 The student, Karl Leyser, later left his studies to fight with the Black Watch (an elite Scottish infantry regiment). After the war he was a history don at Magdalen College, and later a Professor of Medieval History at Oxford University. A high proportion of the Jewish population of Holland were sent to no-return Concentration Camps such as Auschwitz.

23 Robert E. Havard, "Philia: Jack at Ease", in James T. Como (ed.), *C.S. Lewis at the Breakfast Table and Other Reminiscences*, page 217.

24 Letter to Anne Barrett, 7 August 1964, in Humphrey Carpenter (ed.), *Letters of J.R.R. Tolkien*.

25 C.S. Lewis, "Introductory", in *Arthurian Torso: Containing the Posthumous Fragment of the Figure of Arthur by Charles Williams and A Commentary on the Arthurian Poems of Charles Williams by C.S. Lewis*, page 2.

26 John Wain, *Sprightly Running*, page 184.

27 The Acland Nursing Home was on Banbury Road, near the Radcliffe Infirmary.

28 Clyde S. Kilby and Marjorie Lamp Mead (eds.), *Brothers and Friends,* pages 184–85.

8 The close of the Golden Age

1 Clyde S. Kilby and Marjorie Lamp Mead (eds.), *Brothers and Friends*, pages 218–19.

2 *ibid.*, page 200.

3 John Wain, *Sprightly Running: Part of an Autobiography*, London: Macmillan, 1962, page 182.

4 His letter to the editor was published in *Encounter,* XX, No. 1 (January 1963), page 81, with the title "Wain's Oxford".

5 19 September.

6 Clyde S. Kilby and Marjorie Lamp Mead (eds.), *Brothers and Friends*, 1988 edition, page 264.

7 *ibid.*, page 226.

8 See Lewis's preface in C.S. Lewis (ed.), *Essays Presented to Charles Williams*.

9 See Colin Duriez, *J.R.R. Tolkien: The Making of a Legend*, pages 78–79.

10 Published with the Notion Club Papers after Tolkien's death in *Sauron Defeated*, a volume of *The History of The Lord of the Rings*, edited by Christopher Tolkien.

11 "Memoir of C.S. Lewis" in W.H. Lewis (ed.), *Letters of C.S. Lewis*, pages 13–14.

12 For more on Tolkien's work on the earlier ages of Middle-earth, and *The Silmarillion*, see Colin Duriez, *Tolkien and the Lord of the Rings: A Guide to Middle-earth*.

13 Specifically, Parts One and Two.

14 Barfield was of the opposite opinion about Carpenter's reconstruction. David C. Downing also reconstructs an Inklings conversation, this time in the Eagle and Child pub, in his novel *Looking for the King*.

Notes

15 See Ford Maddox Brown's reproduction of Ruskin's conversation with Carlyle at Cheyne Row; http://art.yodelout.com/the-pre-raphaelite-brotherhood-especially-dante-gabriel-rossetti-with-reminiscences/ Accessed 29 October 2014.

16 For a full account of the friendship, see Colin Duriez, *Tolkien and C.S. Lewis: The Gift of Friendship* – published as *J.R.R. Tolkien and C.S. Lewis: The Story of Their Friendship* in the UK.

17 C.S. Lewis (ed.), *Essays Presented to Charles Williams*, London: Oxford University Press, 1947.

18 Published by Geoffrey Bles.

19 The BBC was forced to abandon pioneering work on developing television broadcasting as a result of the onset of war and the initial fear of invasion by the enemy, so its wartime output was solely on radio. (See Justin Phillips, *C.S. Lewis at the BBC*.

20 Joel D. Heck (ed.), *Socratic Digest*, page 8. Reprinted from five issues originally published separately between the years 1943 and 1952.

21 Iris Murdoch, "Foreword", in Stella Aldwinckle, *Christ's Shadow in Plato's Cave: A Meditation on the Substance of Love*, page 7. Iris Murdoch spoke to the Socratic Club after the war on the subject of "The Existentialist Political Myth", when she was a fellow of St Anne's College, Oxford. Joel D. Heck (ed.), *Socratic Digest*, pages 232–240.

22 David Graham (ed.), *We Remember C.S. Lewis*, page 51.

23 Joel D. Heck (ed.), *Socratic Digest*, page 25.

24 Derek Brewer, "The Tutor: A Portrait", in James T. Como, *C.S. Lewis at the Breakfast Table and Other Reminiscences*, page 57.

25 I owe this insight to David Porter, co-author with me of *The Inklings Handbook*, in conversation.

26 Joel D. Heck (ed.), *Socratic Digest*, page 96.

27 There is a parallel shift of emphasis in Tolkien's writing, as his exploration of mythologies carried in language shifted in emphasis from his scholarly to his fictional output. See Colin Duriez, *J.R.R. Tolkien: The Making of a Legend*.

28 Owen Barfield wrote powerfully against a logical positivist approach to language in his introduction to the third edition of his *Poetic Diction* (1984).

29 See her "Introduction" in *Collected Philosophical Papers, Vol. II: Metaphysics and the Philosophy of Mind*, pages vii–x.

30 Interview with Basil Mitchell, in Andrew Walker and James Patrick (eds.), *A Christian for All Christians*.

31 Letter to Stella Aldwinckle, 12 June 1950, in Walter Hooper (ed.), *C.S. Lewis: Collected Letters of C.S. Lewis Vol. Three.*

9 The Inklings: The final years

1 Barfield tells the story in a humorous fiction about the conflicts of creativity and humdrum duty based on his experiences in the family law firm. It is called *This Ever Diverse Pair*, and was admired by Walter de la Mare.

2 The founder was actually Stella Aldwinckle – see the previous chapter.

3 Helen Gardner, "Clive Staples Lewis 1898 –1963", in *Proceedings of the British Academy*, 1965, pages 424–425. 4   Some of Lewis's replies were published in *Letters to Children*. See also Walter Hooper (ed.), *C.S. Lewis: Collected Letters Vol. Three.*

5 Roger Lancelyn Green would write a significant booklet on Lewis in the Bodley Head series, and write much of the first edition of *C.S. Lewis: A Biography*, co-authored with Walter Hooper.

6 For more on Joy Davidman, see Colin Duriez, *C.S. Lewis: A Biography of Friendship.*

7 C.S. Lewis, *A Grief Observed*, page 8.

8 James Dundas-Grant, "From an 'Outsider'", in James T. Como (ed.), *C.S. Lewis at the Breakfast Table and Other Reminiscences*, page 231.

9 *ibid.*, page 231.

10 C.S. Lewis, "The Weight of Glory", in C.S. Lewis, *Transposition and Other Addresses*, London: Geoffrey Bles, 1949.

11 Quoted in Robert Lancelyn Green and Walter Hooper, *C.S. Lewis: A Biography*, 2002, page 307.

12 Green and Hooper, *C.S. Lewis: A Biography* (first edn), London: Collins, 1974, page 158.

13 *ibid.*, pages 158–159.

14 See *ibid.*, page 158.

15 Quoted in Bertrand Russell, *History of Western Philosophy*, page 63.

16 Letter to Nathan Comfort Starr, 22 April 1959, in Walter Hooper (ed.), *C.S. Lewis: Collected Letters, Vol. Three.* There is no documentation of when Tolkien completely stopped attending the morning meetings of the Inklings. It may have been partly due to his house move in 1953 to 76 Sandfield Road, which took him further from the town centre and out to

Headington. It may also reflect the cooling of his friendship with Lewis, and his growing lack of interest now there was no longer reading of work in the group.

17 *ibid.*, page 159.

18 Letter to Mrs Jones, 16 November 1963, in Walter Hooper (ed.), *C.S. Lewis: Collected Letters, Vol. Three.*

19 Letter 251, letter to Priscilla Tolkien, 26 November 1963, in *The Letters of J.R.R. Tolkien.*

20 This is more fully explored in Colin Duriez, *Tolkien and C.S. Lewis: The Gift of Friendship*, published in the UK as *J.R.R. Tolkien and C.S. Lewis: The Story of Their Friendship.*

21 See, for instance, Christina Scull and Wayne G. Hammond, *The J.R.R. Tolkien Companion and Guide: Chronology*, pages 367–368, 372–373, 382, 396, 399, etc.

22 Letter from C.S. Lewis to Owen Barfield, 29 March 1962, in Walter Hooper (ed.), *C.S. Lewis: The Collected Letters Vol. Three. Worlds Apart* was published by Faber in 1963.

23 Joanna Tolkien is the daughter of his son Michael Tolkien.

24 Helen Armstrong (ed.), *Digging Potatoes, Growing Trees: 25 Years of Speeches at the Tolkien Society's Annual Dinners*, page 34.

25 For more on Joy Davidman's involvement with *Till We Have Faces*, and possibly further collaboration in Lewis's writings, see Colin Duriez, *C.S. Lewis: A Biography of Friendship.*

10 After the Inklings

1 The talk, simply entitled "C.S. Lewis", was given on 16 October 1964, but not published until twenty-five years later, in Owen Barfield (edited by G. B. Tennyson), *Owen Barfield on C.S. Lewis.*

2 *ibid.*, page 3.

3 On 1 January 1966 he wrote: "Oh if only I could have known in time that he was to die first, how I would have Boswellised him!" James Boswell, companion of Dr Johnson, wrote his friend's biography, using his journalistic experience to reproduce his wise and witty conversation.

4 Clyde S. Kilby and Marjorie Lamp Mead (eds.), *Brothers and Friends*, page 326.

11 The Inklings: Just a group of friends?

1 Clyde S. Kilby and Marjorie Lamp Mead (eds.), *Brothers and Friends*, page 268. The book is Charles Moorman, *The Precincts of Felicity: The Augustinian City of the Oxford Christians*.

2 Barfield is reported and quoted in Rand Kuhl, "Owen Barfield in Southern California", *Mythlore*, Issue 4, October 1969.

3 C.S. Lewis, preface, in *Essays Presented to Charles Williams*, page vi.

4 See the Introduction to this book.

5 See Colin Duriez, "The Theology of Fantasy in Lewis and Tolkien" in *Themelios*, February 1998, Vol. 23, No. 2, pages 35–51; also Colin Duriez, "Myth, Fact and Incarnation", in Eduardo Segura and Thomas Honegger, *Myth and Magic: Art According to the Inklings*, pages 71–98. See also Michael Ward on the medieval astrological underpinning of the Narnian Chronicles in *Planet Narnia*. A similar schema of the seven astrological planets is to be found in Edmund Spenser's *The Faerie Queene*, according to Alistair Fowler in his book *Spenser and the Numbers of Time*, London: Routledge and Kegan Paul, 1964.

6 Lord David Cecil, "Oxford's Magic Circle", *Books and Bookmen*, 24, No. 4, January 1979.

7 C.S. Lewis, *The Four Loves*, chapter 4.

8 Diana Pavlac Glyer, *The Company They Keep: C.S. Lewis and J.R.R. Tolkien as Writers in Community*. An adaptation by Diana Glyer of the book is in preparation with the title, *Bandersnatch: The Creative Genius of C.S. Lewis, J.R.R. Tolkien, and the Inklings*, to be published by Black Squirrel Books.

9 *ibid.*, page 42.

10 Karen Burke LeFevre, *Invention as a Social Act*, Carbondale, IL: Southern Illinois University Press, 1987, page 34.

Appendix 2   A select Inklings chronology

1 Letter 294, *The Letters of J.R.R. Tolkien*.

2 Letter 93, *The Letters of J.R.R. Tolkien*.

3 Letter 113, *The Letters of J.R.R. Tolkien*.

Index

Fictional characters and places are indicated by an asterisk

275

INDEX

INDEX

279

INDEX

INDEX

Acknowledgments

pp. 9, 130–131, 228: Extracts from *The Four Loves* by C.S. Lewis, copyright © C.S. Lewis Pte Ltd. 1960; pp. 57, 60, 69, 72, 104, 107: Extracts from *Surprised by Joy* by C.S. Lewis, copyright © C.S. Lewis Pte Ltd. 1955; pp. 75, 76: Extracts from *That Hideous Strength* by C.S. Lewis, copyright © C.S. Lewis Pte Ltd. 1945; pp. 134, 220: Extracts from *Essays Presented to Charles Williams* by C.S. Lewis, copyright © C.S. Lewis Pte Ltd. 1947; pp. 144, 145: Extracts from *The Allegory of Love* by C.S. Lewis, copyright © C.S. Lewis Pte Ltd. 1936; p. 89: Extract from *Narrative Poems* by C.S. Lewis, copyright © C.S. Lewis Pte Ltd. 1969; pp. 61–62, 87, 177–78: Extracts from *Letters of C.S. Lewis* by W.H. Lewis, copyright © C.S. Lewis Pte Ltd. 1966; pp. 23, 24, 99, 116, 123: Extracts from *C.S. Lewis: Collected Letters Vol. One: Family Letters 1905–1931* by C.S. Lewis, copyright © C.S. Lewis Pte Ltd.; pp. 25, 122: Extracts from *C.S. Lewis: Collected Letters Vol. Two: Books, Broadcasts and War 1931–1949* by C.S. Lewis, copyright © C.S. Lewis Pte Ltd.; pp. 191, 202, 203: Extracts from *C.S. Lewis: Collected Letters Vol. Three: Narnia, Cambridge and Joy 1950–1963* by C.S. Lewis, copyright © C.S. Lewis Pte Ltd. Reprinted by permission of the C. S. Lewis company.

p. 47: Extract from *Light on C.S. Lewis* edited by Jocelyn Gibb, copyright © Owen Barfield, 1965. Originally published by Geoffrey Bles; pp. 88, 213, 214: Extracts from *Owen Barfield on C.S. Lewis* edited by G.B. Tennyson, copyright © Owen Barfield, 2006. Originally published by The Barfield Press; p. 133: Extract from "The Inklings Remembered" by Owen Barfield in *The World and I*, copyright © Owen Barfield. Reprinted by permission of Owen A. Barfield.

pp. 50, 127: Extracts from *The J.R.R. Tolkien Companion and Guide: Chronology* by Christina Scull and Wayne G. Hammond, copyright © Christina Scull and Wayne G. Hammond, 2006. Reprinted by permission of HarperCollins Publishers Ltd.

pp. 52–53, 74: Extracts from *Owen Barfield: Romanticism Comes of Age – A Biography* by Simon Blaxland-de-Lange, copyright © Simon Blaxland-de-Lange, 2006. Reprinted by permission of Temple Lodge Publishing.

p. 76: Extract from *The Inheritors* by William Golding, copyright © William Golding, 2011. Reprinted by permission of Faber & Faber.

pp. 100–101, 194: Extracts from "Clive Staples Lewis 1898–1963" by Helen Gardner, in *Proceedings of the British Academy* 51, copyright © Helen Gardner, 1965. Reprinted by permission of The British Academy.

pp. 110, 114–15, 123–24, 171, 174, 216: Extracts from *Brothers and Friends: The Diaries of Major Warren Hamilton Lewis* edited by Clyde S. Kilby and Marjorie Lamp Mead, copyright © The Marion E. Wade Center, Wheaton College, Wheaton Illinois. Reprinted by permission.

p. 128: Extract from "Professor J.R.R. Tolkien: A Personal Memoir" by R.E. Havard, in *Mythlore*, copyright © R.E. Havard, 1990. Reprinted by permission.

pp. 166, 200: Extracts from *C.S. Lewis at the Breakfast Table and Other Reminiscences* edited by James T. Como, copyright © James T. Como, 1980. Originally published by Simon and Schuster, reprinted by permission of James T. Como.